468
BE

CliffsAP™

Spanish Language

_by_

By Gisela Bencomo

WILEY

Wiley Publishing, Inc.

About the Author

Gisela Bencomo, A.B.D., has taught AP Spanish Language and Literature at Miami Southridge Senior High School in Miami, Florida since 1989. In addition to teaching, she is a reader for the AP Spanish Exams and a consultant for the College Board. She served as a member of the AP Spanish Development Committee for five years, and also is a presenter of workshops for AP teachers.

Publisher's Acknowledgments

Editorial

Project Editor: Ben Nussbaum

Acquisitions Editor: Greg Tubach

Copy Editor: Suzanna R. Thompson

Technical Editor: Dr. Gilda Nissenberg

Production

Proofreaders: Amy Adrian, Enrica Ardemagni, PhD

Wiley Publishing Indianapolis Composition Services

CliffsAP™ Spanish Language

Published by:
Wiley Publishing, Inc.
909 Third Avenue
New York, NY 10022
www.wiley.com

Copyright © 2003 Wiley Publishing, Inc. New York, New York

Published by Wiley Publishing, Inc., New York, NY
Published simultaneously in Canada

Library of Congress Cataloging-in-Publication Data available from publisher

ISBN: 0-7645-8688-2

Printed in the United States of America

10 9 8 7 6 5 4 3 2 1

1B/RQ/RS/QS/IN

Wiley Publishing, Inc. is a trademark of Wiley Publishing, Inc.

Author's Acknowledgments

This book is dedicated to my parents, Mercedes y Luis, whose support and understanding made this book possible. I would also like to acknowledge the invaluable help and advice of my friend, colleague, and technical editor, Dr. Gilda Nissenberg, and the help and support of friend and colleague Eyleen de la Guardia. Finally, I would like to thank all of my AP students at Miami Southridge SHS, who through the years have inspired me to continue teaching this course.

Table of Contents

PART IV: THREE FULL-LENGTH PRACTICE TESTS

PART V: APPENDICES

Credits

Augusto Monterroso, "El búho que quería salvar a la humanidad," *Cuentos, fábulas y lo demás es silencio*, Aguilar, Altea, Taurus, Alfaguara S.A. de C.V., 1996.

Augusto Monterroso, "Tú dile a Sarabia que digo yo . . . , " *Cuentos, fábulas y lo demás es silencio*, Aguilar, Altea, Taurus, Alfaguara S.A. de C.V., 1996.

Augusto Monterroso, "Recuerdos de mi vida con un gran hombre," *Cuentos, fábulas y lo demás es silencio*, Aguilar, Altea, Taurus, Alfaguara S.A. de C.V., 1996.

Augusto Monterroso, "Diógenes también," *Cuentos, fábulas y lo demás es silencio*, Aguilar, Altea, Taurus, Alfaguara S.A. de C.V., 1996.

Augusto Monterroso, "La Honda de David," *Cuentos, fábulas y lo demás es silencio*, Aguilar, Altea, Taurus, Alfaguara S.A. de C.V., 1996.

Isaac Hernández, "Isabel Allende," Nexos, American Airlines Publishing, April-June 2002.

Guillermo de la Corte, "El arte de Priscilla Bianchi," Nexos, American Airlines Publishing, April-June 2002.

Guillermo de la Corte, "Aceite de oliva: manantial de salud," Nexos, American Airlines Publishing, April-June 2002.

Carmen Laforet, *Nada*, Ediciones Destino, 1989.

Ruben Benitez and Paul C. Smith, "La extinción de especies animals," *Hablando seriamente: Textos y pretextos para conversar y escribir*, Prentice Hall, December 1988.

Ruben Benitez and Paul C. Smith, "La riqueza étnica de los Estados Unidos," *Hablando seriamente: Textos y pretextos para conversar y escribir*, Prentice Hall, December 1988.

Ruben Benitez and Paul C. Smith, "La desigualdad social entre los sexos," *Hablando seriamente: Textos y pretextos para conversar y escribir*, Prentice Hall, December 1988.

Ruben Benitez and Paul C. Smith, "Costumbres alimenticias del hombre contemporáneo," *Hablando seriamente: Textos y pretextos para conversar y escribir*, Prentice Hall, December 1988.

"El organismo nacional de loterías y apuestas del astado," *Anuario El País*, Ediciones El País, 1995.

"El filólogo mexicano Ilan Stavans reescribe 'El Quijote' en 'spanglish,'" Ediciones El País, July 6, 2002.

Rafael Abella, "Griselda," *Mitos y leyendas de España*, Ediciones Martínez Roca, S.A., 2000.

"A la caza de los vampiros," *Geomundo,* August 1990.

"La ciudad colonial más Antigua de la Florida: San Agustín," *Geomundo,* May 1997.

"El euro: Una moneda común para la Unión Europa," *Geomundo*, November 1997.

"Insecticidas de la era ecológica," *Geomundo,* February 1998.

"La sobrepoblación: Un síntoma de nuestra civilización," *Geomundo,* February 1998.

"La alegría del fuego," *Geomundo,* June 1998.

"Las cuentas: Monedas del pasado," *Geomundo,* June 1998.

"La Tomatina," *Geomundo,* August 1998.

"Museo Interactivo," *Geomundo,* August 1998.

"Lodo Verde para comer," *Geomundo,* September 1998.

"Las esponjas," *Geomundo,* December 1998.

"Peligro latente," *Geomundo,* December 1998.

"Trilobites," *Geomundo,* December 1998.

"Castilla: tierra de castillos," *Geomundo,* February 1999.

"Origen de la escritura," *Geomundo,* March 1999.

"La feria de Sevilla," *Geomundo,* April 1999.

"Colágeno," *Geomundo,* April 1999.

"Maine Coon el más grande de los gatos," *Geomundo,* September 1999

"Veracruz: La belleza de lo desconocido," *Geomundo,* July 2001.

Ramón del Valle Inclán, "Beatriz," *Antología del cuento español 1900-1939*, Editorial Castalia, S.A., 1994.

Azorín, "La ecuación," *Antología del cuento español 1900-1939*, Editorial Castalia, S.A., 1994.

Eduardo Zamacois, "Noche," *Antología del cuento español 1900-1939*, Editorial Castalia, S.A., 1994.

"Manuel Benítez," *La Revista El Mundo,* February 27, 2000.

"Trujillo, el dictador novelado," *La Revista El Mundo,* March 5, 2000.

"Cristina Hoyos," *La Revista El Mundo,* June 13, 1999.

"Laura Esquivel," *La Revista El Mundo,* November 1, 1998.

Andreé Bertino and Fredo Valla, "Las cigüeñas en África," *366 . . . y más historias de animals*, Plaza & Janés Editores, S.A., 1988.

José Calvo Poyato, *La biblia negra,* Plaza & Janés S.A., 2000.

Study Guide Checklist

❏ 1. Become familiar with the test format, page 3.

❏ 2. Read the Questions and Answers on pages 5 to 8 to find out more about the AP Spanish Language exam.

❏ 3. Flip to the very back of the book to find out about the CDs.

❏ 4. Take the Diagnostic Test to get a feel for your strengths and weaknesses, beginning on page 111. An answer key, score converter, and explanations are included.

❏ 5. Carefully read through the review sections, pages 11–108. Use these sections to become extremely familiar with the exam content. Use the practice problems to work on incorporating the suggested strategies.

❏ 6. Take the first practice exam, page 133. Try to simulate an actual test environment.

❏ 7. After you've graded the exam, go back and reread some of the review sections. Make sure that you're using the suggested strategies.

❏ 8. Continue taking the practice exams. Use the explanations to help you understand the problems you missed AND the problems you got correct.

You can also go to www.cliffsnotes.com/extras on the Web in order to find additional information, including lists of classified vocabulary and lists of idioms, that will help you on the AP Spanish Exam.

PART I

INTRODUCTION TO THE AP SPANISH LANGUAGE EXAM

In this section, you will find general information about the AP Spanish Language Exam, including:

- The format of the exam
- How the exam is scored
- A general description of the exam
- Frequently asked questions about the AP Spanish Language Exam
- Some successful test-taking strategies

Introduction

Format of the AP Spanish Language Exam

Section I	Multiple Choice	90 questions	90 minutes
Part A	Listening Questions	30 questions	30 minutes
Part B	Cloze Passages	20 questions	60 minutes
Part C	Error Recognition Sentences	15 questions	
Part D	Reading Comprehension Passages	25 questions	
Section II	**Free Response**		**80 minutes**
Part A (writing)	Paragraph Fill-Ins	10 questions	60 minutes
	Discrete Sentence Fill-Ins	10 questions	
	Essay	1 topic	
Part B (speaking)	Picture Sequence	1 sequence	20 minutes
	Directed Response Questions	5 questions	

Scoring of the AP Spanish Language Exam

How the Multiple Choice score is calculated. In this part of the exam, you earn one point for each correct answer. One-third of a point is deducted from the total for each wrong answer, to adjust for any random guessing. Unanswered questions count neither for nor against your score. The score of this section is 50% of your total score.

How the Paragraph and Discrete Sentence Fill-Ins are scored. These two exercises are scored according to a given scoring guide. You receive one point for each correct answer. This score is then calculated to be equivalent to 7.5% of your total score.

How the Essay is scored. The essay is scored holistically, and the score ranges from 0 to 9. This score is calculated to be equivalent to 22.5% of your total score. In Part II of this book, you will find a set of guidelines similar to those used to evaluate the AP Spanish Language Exam Essay.

How the Picture Sequence is scored. The Picture Sequence is scored holistically, and the score ranges from 0 to 9. This score is calculated to be equivalent to 10% of your total score. In Part II of this book, you will find a set of guidelines similar to those used to evaluate the AP Spanish Language Exam Picture Sequence.

How the Directed Response questions are scored. These responses are graded individually. You may earn 0 to 4 points for each response. The total score is then calculated to be equivalent to 10% of your total score. In Part II of this book, you will find a set of guidelines similar to those used to evaluate the AP Spanish Language Exam Directed Response questions.

How the weighted scores are calculated. Since each section consists of more than two parts, those parts need to be weighted according to the value established by the Developing Committee. At the end of each full-length exam in Part IV of this book, you will find a chart to help you calculate the weighted scores of both sections.

How the composite score is calculated. The composite score is obtained by adding both weighted scores. This score is then converted to a five-point scale, which is the grade you will receive in July.

General Description

The objective of the AP Spanish Language Exam is to evaluate test takers' level of performance in the use of the language. Some of the sections attempt to measure performance in understanding both the written and the spoken language, while others are specifically designed to evaluate the productive skills of speaking and writing with ease in correct and idiomatic Spanish.

If you have not completed three years of high school Spanish, you probably feel that you lack the vocabulary and the grammar structures necessary to earn a high score on the exam. In Part V of this book, you will find valuable information to help you achieve a higher level of performance in accordance with the standards of the exam. You may earn college credit by scoring 3 or higher on the AP Spanish Language Exam. In some colleges and universities, the AP Spanish Language Exam will allow you to eliminate the basic Spanish courses, which can be worth four or five credit hours each.

This is a timed exam, and its total duration is 2 hours and 50 minutes. It consists of two main sections: the Multiple Choice section and the Free Response section. Each section contains different types of exercises specially designed to measure your level of performance in each of four skills: listening, speaking, reading, and writing.

The Multiple Choice section consists of 90 questions, and it accounts for 50% of your total score. It contains four different types of exercises, which attempt to evaluate your level of performance in understanding written and spoken Spanish. In Part II of this book, you will find a more detailed explanation of each type of question, strategies as to how to approach each one, and sample questions with answers and explanations.

The Free Response section consists of two main parts: writing and speaking. It accounts for the other 50% of your total score. In the writing part, you will be working with two sets of Fill-Ins (paragraph and discrete sentence) and an Essay. Part II provides explanations, strategies, sample questions with answers and explanations, and scoring guidelines for these types of exercises. In the speaking part, there are two tasks designed to evaluate your speaking skills: one Picture Sequence and a set of five Directed Response questions. Both types of exercises are explained in detail in Part II of this book. You will also find sample questions and strategies, as well as the scoring guidelines for these exercises.

The Multiple Choice section is scored by computer. The Free Response section is scored at the AP Reading (which takes place around the second week of June) by a group of readers, called consultants. These consultants are high school teachers and college professors from across the United States and around the world. The consultants are carefully trained to evaluate the questions following a set of pre-established guidelines. Each consultant is trained to evaluate only one specific question. Consultants evaluating the Directed Response questions score all five of them. In 2002, nearly 600 readers gathered during a seven-day period to read approximately 80,000 AP Spanish Language exams.

Questions Commonly Asked about the AP Spanish Language Exam

Q. What is the Advanced Placement Program?

A. The Advanced Placement Program is a program administered by the College Board since 1955. It provides standard achievement examinations that provide high school students with the opportunity to pursue college-level preparation and credits while still in high school.

Q. Who writes the AP Spanish Language Exam?

A. The exam is written every year by the Developing Committee. The committee consists of seven college Spanish professors and high school Spanish instructors.

Q. When are exams given?

A. Exams are generally given during the month of May. Check the College Board Web site (http://www.collegeboard.com/ap/students/index.html) for specific dates and times.

Q. Who receives my AP score?

A. When taking the exam, you're given the opportunity to select one university to receive your AP score. After the AP Reading in June, this institution will receive your score, then your school, and then yourself. If you want additional colleges and universities to receive your score, you have to fill out a Transcript Request Form. There is a charge of $13.00 for each transcript. You can also request a transcript by phone:1-888-308-0013; there is an extra charge of $7.00 for this.

Q. Would I pass the exam without taking an AP course?

A. It is not necessary to take an AP course to take the exam and pass it. You should have a level of Spanish equivalent to three years of high school Spanish classes, but with this book, you may prepare yourself to achieve that level without taking the course.

Q. How do I register for the exam if I am not taking an AP course?

A. To register for an AP exam without taking an AP course, you should contact your school's AP coordinator and tell him or her about your intention to take the exam. Contact the AP coordinator as early as February of the year you plan to take the exam.

Q. How can I get my score earlier than the established date?

A. To get your score earlier, call 888-308-0013 after July 1. There is a fee of $13.00 per call. You will need a valid major credit card when you call.

Q. If I don't pass the test or I don't like my score, how do I cancel it?

A. It is your decision whether a college or university receives your score. You should be cautious when canceling a score, however, because once it is canceled, it is deleted from the College Board records. There will be no evidence in the transcripts sent to the colleges and universities that you ever took the exam. There is no fee for this service, but you must send your documents to request cancellation of scores before June 15. If you are not sure you want to cancel a score, you may choose to merely withhold it. There is a $5.00 fee for withholding a score, and you must make your request before June 15 to prevent that score going to the college or university you specified when you took the exam. A withheld score may be released at any time in the future, free of charge, should you decide to do so.

Q. Besides taking an AP course, how can I prepare for the exam?

A. It is very important that you be familiar with the format of the exam, the number and types of questions, the instructions, strategies to approach each task, and how to use your time. Using this book will help you not only improve your abilities in using and understanding Spanish, but also with the technical aspects of the exam.

Q. How are the AP Spanish Language and AP Spanish Literature exams different?

A. The two exams are different in nature. The AP Spanish Language Exam is a performance exam in which you demonstrate your ability to understand and use Spanish in different contexts and situations. The AP Spanish Literature Exam is a content exam in which test takers have to be able to do close readings of Spanish literary texts of all genres and carry on literary analysis and interpretation using the appropiate Spanish terminology.

Q. Approximately how many students take the AP Spanish Language Exam each year?

A. The number of students taking the AP Spanish Language Exam increases every year. In 2002, approximately 80,000 students took it.

Q. Are all Multiple Choice questions counted in the final score?

A. Only the questions you have answered are counted toward your final score.

Q. Am I penalized for guessing in the Multiple Choice questions?

A. Yes, one-third of a point is deducted for each wrong answer to account for any random guessing. You should guess only if you are able to eliminate at least two choices.

Q. What are the prerequisites to take the AP Spanish Language Exam?

A. You may take the AP Spanish Language Exam at any time you consider that you are ready, but if you want to earn a passing score, it is important to first achieve a level of proficiency in the four skills (listening, speaking, reading, and writing) equivalent to three years of high school instruction.

Q. What happens if I don't finish the Multiple Choice section?

A. Not finishing the Multiple Choice section of the exam does not mean that you will not pass the exam. To compensate for any unanswered questions in the Multiple Choice section, you must show accuracy on the questions you did anwer, as well as get a good score on the Free Response section. Do not rush or fill in the ovals at random in order to answer every single question in the Multiple Choice section because you may get many of them incorrect and, thus, be penalized for random guessing.

Q. Do accents and spelling count in the writing parts?

A. Yes. To receive credit on the sentence completions, your answer must not only be grammatically correct within the context, but it should also exhibit perfect spelling and accentuation. In the Essay, points are not deducted for individual spelling or accentuation errors, but these errors are taken into consideration in the holistic evaluation. Committing too many spelling and accentuation mistakes may result in the lowering of your Essay score by one category.

Q. If I am a native speaker of Spanish, why should I take the exam?

A. Taking the AP Spanish Language Exam is a way to document your knowledge of Spanish while perhaps earning college credits.

Q. Being a native speaker of Spanish, should I take the exam without preparing myself?

A. Not all native speakers of the language possess the same level of proficiency in the four skills (listening, speaking, reading, and writing). Also, remember that having a Hispanic last name does not mean that you are ready for the test. As any other individual, you may take the exam without taking an AP course, but it is recommended that you become familiar with the format of the exam and the different types of questions involved.

Q. Is there any way to get old AP exams for practice?

A. Complete, previously administered exams are released every four or five years, and they are made available to teachers and students. You may contact the College Board online for information on how to order this material.

Q. Who proctors the AP exams?

A. Most of the time, school counselors are in charge of proctoring the AP exams at each testing site.

Q. What is the fee for taking an AP exam?

A. Each exam costs $78.00. There is a $22.00 fee reduction available for individuals with financial needs. Some school districts and states pay the fee for all students taking the exam, regardless of their financial situations.

Q. If I am a disabled individual, can special arrangements be made for me to take the exam?

A. Yes, there are special arrangements for individuals with disabilities. You must first, however, be approved by the department of the College Board. For more information, call 609-771-7137 (voice), 609-882-4148 (TTY), and 609-771-7944 (fax).

Q. How many times may I take the same exam?

A. You may take any specific exam at any time it is offered.

Q. What materials do I need to bring to the exam?

A. You need to bring several No. 2 pencils with erasers, and a black or blue ballpoint pen. You should also bring a watch so that you can administer your time well.

Q. May I use a dictionary or an electronic translator during the exam?

A. You may not use either of these aids.

Q. What happens if I don't finish the Essay?

A. If you do not finish the Essay, your Essay score will probably be lowered, depending on how much and how well you wrote. Your final score may not be greatly affected.

Q. What happens if I don't cover all pictures in the Picture Sequence?

A. Although it is recommended that you refer to all frames, points are not deducted specifically for not finishing. This exercise is graded holistically, and, as you may see in the guidelines given in Part II of this book, many different elements of your speech sample are taken into consideration when determining the total score.

Q. In the Directed Response questions, do I have to speak for the entire 20 seconds?

A. Your response should be elaborate enough to take up the entire time allotted, but, once again, these responses are evaluated using different aspects, and the length of your response may not greatly affect your final score.

Some Successful Testing Strategies

Become familiar with the format of the exam. Before taking the exam, you should know how many questions and what types of questions are on the exam. You should also know what basic skills you need in order to respond correctly to each type of question, as well as how much time you have to complete each section of the exam. All this information is provided in Part II of this book.

Be aware of what is expected by the test makers. To be successful when taking the AP Spanish Language Exam, it is important to know the purpose behind each type of question. Knowing what kinds of answers are expected will help you make educated guesses when a particular answer is not obvious to you.

Know the directions beforehand. The AP Spanish Language Exam is structured in such a way that, by knowing what you are supposed to do in each section beforehand, you can save yourself some time, which you can use to work on your answers. Being familiar with the instructions will also avoid any type of confusion as to how to arrive at the correct answer.

Make sure that your answers are clear and legible. If you skip a question in the Multiple Choice section, make sure that you enter the answer to the next question in the corresponding oval. For the Essay and the two types of Fill-Ins, make sure that you write legibly so that the reader who evaluates your test is able to understand what you are saying. Make sure that accent marks are visible and distinguishable from mere dots. In the speaking part, make sure that you speak clearly and at an average speed. Don't rush your answers.

Practice! Given the nature of this exam, practice is of the essence. You should practice in settings as similar to testing conditions (in regard to time and place) as possible. Also, practice recording your voice so that you can achieve the best possible outcome on the speaking parts of the exam. Finally, practice the four skills (listening, speaking, reading, and writing) in informal practice exercises, such as listening to the radio or watching television shows in Spanish to improve your listening skills, or speaking Spanish in as many situations as possible to get used to hearing yourself speaking the language.

PART II

ANALYSIS OF EXAM AREAS

All the parts of the AP Spanish Language exam are covered in the sections that follow. For your reference, the table from the Introduction showing how the exam is broken up is reprinted here.

Section I	Multiple Choice	90 questions	90 minutes
Part A	Listening Questions	30 questions	30 minutes
Part B	Cloze Passages	20 questions	
Part C	Error Recognition Sentences	15 questions	60 minutes
Part D	Reading Comprehension Passages	25 questions	
Section II	Free Response		80 minutes
Part A (writing)	Paragraph Fill-Ins	10 questions	
	Discrete Sentence Fill-Ins	10 questions	60 minutes
	Essay	1 topic	
Part B (speaking)	Picture Sequence	1 sequence	20 minutes
	Directed Response Questions	5 questions	

Explaining Dialogues and Narratives

Dialogues and Narratives are the first part of the Multiple Choice section of the exam. The multiple choice section has 90 questions, and accounts for 50% of your overall score on the AP Spanish Language exam. The Multiple Choice section is comprised of the following sections:

- Dialogues and Narratives (the listening section)
- Cloze Passages
- Error Recognition
- Reading Comprehension

Dialogues and Narratives

In this part of the exam, you will hear different types of speech, in the following order:

- **Three short dialogues.** Each dialogue is followed by a few questions, which are not printed on the exam booklet. (The answers, however, are.)
- **Two short narratives.** These resemble short television or radio news reports. Like the dialogues, each short narrative is followed by a few questions (not printed in the exam booklet).
- **Two longer narratives.** Each of these is approximately five minutes in length and is accompanied by several questions. You are allowed to take notes while listening to the long narratives. The long narrative takes various forms, including interviews, journalistic articles, or lectures about any cultural aspect of Hispanic countries.

These speech selections are all on a master tape; once the exam has started, the tape will not be stopped or rewound.

There are around 30 questions of this type on any given version of the AP Spanish Language Exam. There are 3 dialogues, 2 short narratives, and 2 longer narratives. You should spend about 30 minutes on these question, but remember the time in this part is paced by a master tape.

Ability Tested

This section tests your ability to understand oral Spanish as spoken by native speakers of various origins, in different contexts and situations.

Basic Skills Necessary

You need to be able to:

- Follow conversations between native speakers of Spanish. These conversations may include idiomatic and colloquial expressions that are used in different regions where the language is spoken.

- Obtain information from oral reports, lectures, and news-like contexts.

- Identify voice inflections, tones, and intonations of the speakers to improve your aural comprehension.

To understand the Spanish language as spoken by a native speaker, you need to master a series of linguistic elements in addition to utilizing nonlinguistic resources. Vocabulary and language mechanics are essential to successfully understanding the spoken language. Your vocabulary must be within the range expected for a third-level student of Spanish as a second language. When you have command of an ample vocabulary—even if you do not clearly understand the pronunciation of the words on the tape—you will be able to figure out what the selection is about.

You should also be able to identify important word types, such as nouns, adjectives, and verbs. Recognizing these types of words will give you a general idea of what the selection is about. Also, your knowledge of Spanish grammar must be deep enough to be able to discriminate past tense from present or future, or to be able to figure out the subject of a sentence.

Your familiarity with Hispanic culture, as well as your own life experiences, will be of great help in achieving a good command of Spanish listening skills. The strategies you use to follow a conversation in your native language can also be useful in understanding a spoken second language. For example, your ability to use guessing strategies to compensate for a lack of vocabulary can help you with listening comprehension. Try to identify words that are cognates, that is, words that may sound a bit different in another language but have the same meaning (such as *león* and *lion, navegar* and *navigate,* and so on). Recognizing cognates will facilitate your understanding of the selection as a whole, as well as provide you with some specific details.

Finally, to be successful in this section you need a lot of practice; listening to many stimuli is important to developing an ear for any given language.

One technique that is of great help to second-language learners trying to develop listening skills is "shadowing." When you shadow, you listen to selections in the target language, repeating exactly what you hear, as you hear it. Try to keep up with the speed of the speaker. When practicing, you can always play the selection once and just listen to it, then play it a second time while shadowing as well as you can. The practice selection should not exceed two minutes in length, and you may pause the recording whenever you need to. (Remember, though, that you will not be able to stop the tape during the actual exam.) If you have a script for your selection, identify the parts that you were not able to shadow. Repeat the process without reading the script as many times as necessary. By practicing this technique before the exam, you can improve your score on the listening section of the AP Spanish Language Exam.

Directions

In Part A of the multiple-choice section, you will be working with three different types of questions: dialogues, short narratives, and longer narratives. For each set of questions, you will be given specific directions. The directions are given to you both orally and in writing, in English and Spanish. Concentrate on the directions in the language you feel most comfortable with.

The following directions resemble what you will read and hear during Part A of the multiple-choice section of the AP Spanish Language Exam. It is important to be familiar with the directions for each section *before* you take the test so that you can concentrate on listening during the test.

Dialogues

You will hear a few dialogues. At the end of each, you will hear several questions about what you have just listened to. From the choices printed in your test booklet, select the one that best responds to each question.

Ahora vas a oír algunos diálogos. Al final de cada uno, escucharás unas preguntas sobre lo que has escuchado. De entre las opciones que aparecen en el cuadernillo de examen, escoge la que mejor responda a cada una de las preguntas.

Short Narratives

You will hear a few short narratives. At the end of each, you will hear several questions about what you have just listened to. From the choices printed in your test booklet, select the one that best responds to each question.

Ahora vas a oír algunas narraciones cortas. Al final de cada una, escucharás unas preguntas sobre lo que has escuchado. De entre las opciones que aparecen en el cuadernillo de examen, escoge la que mejor responda a cada una de las preguntas.

Longer Narratives

You will hear a longer selection. It is about five minutes in length. You may take notes in the space provided, although you will not receive a grade for these notes. At the end of the selection, you will answer several questions about what you have just listened to. Select the best answer for each question from the choices printed in your test booklet. Base your selections on the information you have just heard.

Ahora vas a oír una selección más extensa. Su duración es de aproximadamente cinco minutos. Debes tomar apuntes en el espacio disponible en esta página, aunque los mismos no serán calificados. Al final de la selección, tendrás que contestar varias preguntas sobre lo que acabas de escuchar. De entre las opciones que aparecen en el cuadernillo de examen, escoge la que mejor responda a cada una de las preguntas, teniendo en cuenta la información que has escuchado.

Suggested Strategies for Dialogue and Narrative Questions

Be aware that you are dealing with three types of exercises: dialogues, short narratives, and longer narratives. It is important to be familiar with the three types because, even though they are all listening-comprehension exercises that test your ability to understand spoken Spanish, they are different in nature.

For the entire listening section:

- **Remember that the time in which you must answer the questions is very brief.** The time is paced by the master tape that the proctor uses to administer the exam. At the end of the selection, you will be informed about the amount of time you have left to answer the questions.

  First, answer the questions you know the answers to, either because you remember the information or because you jotted it down in your notes. Then, go for the ones you may have to think about a little more; use logical thinking to come up with the most appropriate answer.

- **Notice the title of the selection or any other initial indication as to where the dialogue occurs.** If you understand the title of the selection or any other initial clue, your mind is already prepared to hear words that belong in a specific context. For example, if you hear "En la cafetería de la escuela," and you can identify the two main words (*cafetería* and *escuela*), your mind will most likely pick up on words that correspond with that specific setting. Recognizing key words will also help you decide between two words that are very close in pronunciation but belong in different contexts. For example, if you know the selection occurs at the beach, you will realize that *ola* refers to the condition of the sea, not to the greeting *hola*. By ruling out possibilities that would not fit in a specific setting, you can decide which word you think you heard.

- **Concentrate on listening.** This is one of the most important strategies for listening tasks. It may sound simple, but sometimes you get distracted, and when you lose your concentration, you do not listen anymore—even in your native language.

  Many of these selections are brief, and if you are able to keep your concentration to a maximum for the amount of time each selection lasts, you will obtain better results. Remember that the master tape will not be rewound for any reason, so losing your concentration during one or more selections may mean that you won't able to answer several questions.

- **Do not expect to understand or hear every single word.** Try to listen for main points and concentrate on picking up on words that you are familiar with. Do not get distracted by unknown words. If, at the beginning of the selection, you are able to identify the setting and the general context, you will immediately have an idea of the words you may hear. Remember that, when you listen to a conversation or a news segment in your native language, you do not need to hear and/or understand every single word in order to answer general questions about what you heard.

For the dialogues:

- **Notice the non-verbal clues.** These help you understand the conversation, where it takes place, and so on. Background sounds help you identify the setting and/or situation. For example:

  - Bells would suggest that the conversation takes place in a school.

  - Car horns or other street sounds may signal that someone's asking for directions.

  - Clinking of glass or silverware could indicate that the conversation takes place in a restaurant and may center on food.

- **Pay attention to the speakers' voice inflections and intonation.** These help you determine important information such as the speaker's attitude and/or intentions. Sometimes you may be asked about one character's feelings or emotions; being able to identify emotions such as happiness, anger, admiration, surprise, doubt, and so on, based on the inflections and intonations of the characters, as well as by the words you may hear that express such emotions, can be useful.

For the narratives:

- **Pay attention to specific vocabulary that may relate to the topic.** Doing so will help you answer "who, what, where, when, why, and how" questions, the most common types of questions asked in this section.

- **For the longer narratives, be sure to take notes.** Your notes may be of great help when answering the questions at the end of the selections. You are not allowed to take notes while listening to the dialogues and short narratives.

Sample Dialogues and Narratives: Questions, Answers, and Explanations

Below are two sets of sample dialogues and narratives. Locate these selections on the audio CD that accompanies this book and listen to them, following both the directions that you hear and the directions on the next few pages. After you finish Set 1, see "Answers and Explanations for Set 1" (below) to check your answers. Repeat the process with the Set 2 selections.

Set 1

Dialogue

PLAY TRACK 1 ON CD 1

1. A. Colecciones de poemas.
   B. Biografías de españoles famosos.
   C. Novelas interesantes.
   D. Libros de escritores desconocidos.

2. A. Porque reside fuera.
   B. Porque solamente lee novelas policíacas.
   C. Porque está de vacaciones.
   D. Porque solamente lee a Arturo Pérez Reverte.

3. A. Ninguno, porque ya conoce a Pérez Reverte.
   B. Solamente un ejemplar.
   C. Todos los más vendidos.
   D. Un ejemplar de las tres más famosas

Short Narrative

PLAY TRACK 2 ON CD 1

1. A. Es una moneda de uso común.
   B. Es una moneda antigua.
   C. Es una moneda de transición.
   D. Es una moneda temporal.

2. A. Acreditar el buen estado de su economía.
   B. Pasar por la etapa de transición.
   C. Cumplir todos sus contratos.
   D. Pagar todas sus deudas.

3. A. Solamente una.
   B. Solamente dos.
   C. Más de dos.
   D. Tantas como sean necesarias.

4. A. En la primavera de 1998.
   B. En enero de 1999.
   C. En enero de 2002.
   D. En julio de 2002.

Longer Narrative

PLAY TRACK 3 ON CD 1

1. ¿Por qué fue importante históricamente la ciudad de Sevilla?

   A. Porque facilitó las relaciones comerciales con América.

   B. Porque es la capital de Andalucía.

   C. Porque es una ciudad de mucho tráfico.

   D. Porque celebra ferias ganaderas.

2. ¿Con qué otra festividad se relaciona la Feria de Sevilla?

   A. Con el día de Navidad.

   B. Con el día de San Alfonso.

   C. Con la Semana Santa.

   D. Con el Descubrimiento de América.

3. ¿Por qué no era adecuado el Prado de San Sebastián para celebrar la Feria?

   A. Porque no estaba cerca del Guadalquivir.

   B. Porque estaba al lado del Ayuntamiento.

   C. Porque estaba cerca de unos cementerios.

   D. Porque tenían que cerrar los comercios por la noche.

4. ¿Qué carácter tiene hoy en día la Feria de Abril?

   A. Mercantil.

   B. Ganadero.

   C. Folclórico.

   D. Histórico.

5. ¿Cómo es el vestido típico que usan las sevillanas en la Feria?

   A. Humilde y sin volantes.

   B. Vistoso y de gran colorido.

   C. Muy antiguo y con un delantal.

   D. Ceñido a la cintura con una flor.

Answers and Explanations for Set 1

Dialogue

1. B. At the beginning of the conversation, the lady asks for the section where the novels are located. The rest of the dialogue deals with different types of novels and their authors.

2. A. When the clerk asks if she is looking for a particular title, the lady responds that she is not familiar with contemporary Spanish novelists because she has been living outside Spain for some time (*Hace tiempo que resido fuera*).

3. D. The clerk suggests that she buy some (*algunos*), and the lady seems to agree by using an expression (*Perfecto*) that hints that she is going to by more than one. In the end, she decides to buy three (*tres*).

Short Narrative

1. A. At the very beginning of the lecture, this fact is stated, and the idea that several nations are going to use the euro is present throughout the narrative.

2. A. The next statement says that the euro will be used only in European countries that are able to prove that their economies are in good condition (*acrediten el buen estado de sus economías*).

3. B. The answer is clearly stated in the lecture: It will take place in two stages (*Se llevará a cabo en dos etapas*).

4. D. This is the final date to start using the euro. Even though January 1, 2002 looks very attractive, this is just the day when the second phase will start.

Longer Narrative

1. A. In reality, the importance of Seville is that the Guadalquivir River is excellent for navigation; in fact, it facilitated maritime activities during the colonization of America.

2. C. Near the beginning of the narrative, you learn that the *Feria* is celebrated two weeks after Easter. At the end, you are told that the exact date of the fair depends on Holy Week. Here, both vocabulary and cultural knowledge are important. The word *Pascua* is used in Spanish to refer to two different holidays: Christmas and Easter. For Christmas, the plural (*las Pascuas*) is more commonly used; for Easter, *Pascua Florida* is widely used.

3. C. Besides the fact that *el Prado de San Sebastián* was a place where many people were burned during the Inquisition, the narrative also states that two cemeteries were near it (*además se encontraba próximo a dos cementerios*).

The word *cementerio* is a cognate of the English *cemetery*. You can easily deduce that people would not like to have any type of celebration near this place.

4. **C.** Towards the middle of the selection, the actual character of the fair is addressed. You learn that it lost its original character to become more a folkloric and popular festivity (*para convertirse en muestra folclórica, festiva y popular*).

These words are cognates of the English terms. Even if you do not know the exact meaning of the term in Spanish, you can deduce it.

5. **B.** Even though the typical *sevillana* dress has its origins in the humble and simple outfit worn by women on the farm, it is now a very colorful and attractive costume (*vistosos coloridos trajes de volantes*). An apron is mentioned, but it is not part of the actual dress, and the flower is not used to tighten the dress but is worn on the head.

Set 2

Dialogue

PLAY TRACK 4 ON CD 1

1. **A.** De patinar.
   B. De una cita con Laura.
   C. De una fiesta familiar.
   D. De un compromiso con los amigos.

2. **A.** Tomás se quedó dormido.
   B. Tomás se desmayó.
   C. Era de madrugada.
   D. Había mucha nieve.

3. **A.** Porque se rompió muchos huesos.
   B. Porque el coche era de Laura.
   C. Porque se destruyó su coche nuevo.
   D. Porque sufrió un desmayo.

Short Narrative

PLAY TRACK 5 ON CD 1

1. **A.** Un alimento verde de los aztecas.
   B. El lago de Texcoco.
   C. Unas aves típicas de México.
   D. El lodo que había en México.

2. **A.** Un tipo de vitamina.
   B. Un tipo de proteína.
   C. Un alga muy alimenticia.
   D. Un tipo de ave mexicana.

3. **A.** Está muy extendido por México.
   B. Solamente lo consumen los españoles.
   C. Solamente se encuentra en tiendas naturistas.
   D. No se puede comprar porque no es legal.

Longer Narrative (Interview)

PLAY TRACK 6 ON CD 1

1. Según Cristina Hoyos, ¿a qué se debe el hecho de que la gente tenga prisa por triunfar?

   A. A la competencia.

   B. A la falta de medios de comunicación.

   C. A la vida agitada.

   D. Al riesgo de enfermarse.

2. ¿Por qué es muy conocida Sara Baras?

   A. Porque baila muy bien.

   B. Porque vende lencería.

   C. Porque sale mucho en televisión.

   D. Porque es amiga de Antonio Gades.

3. ¿Qué hecho de la vida de Cristina Hoyos puede deducirse de la entrevista?

   A. Sufrió una operación.

   B. Se retiró del flamenco.

   C. Miente a la prensa.

   D. Está cansada de trabajar.

4. ¿Por qué decide Saura no usar a Cristina para ser la protagonista de Carmen?

   A. Porque quería a una persona más joven.

   B. Porque estaba enamorado de Laura Sol.

   C. Porque Cristina Hoyos no tenía buena técnica.

   D. Porque Antonio Gades se lo pidió.

Answers and Explanations for Set 2

Dialogue

1. **C.** Tomás suffered the accident late Saturday night when he was coming back from his cousin Laura's engagement party (*regresaba de la fiesta de compromiso de mi prima Laura*).

2. **D.** When Cecilia asks about the cause of the accident, without waiting for the answer, she suggests that Tomás probably fell asleep. He denies it and explains that it had snowed a lot (*había nevado mucho*) during the afternoon and the car slid. Choice **B** is attractive because, in fact, Tomás fainted, but this was as a result of the accident and not the cause of it.

3. **C.** Tomás did not suffer any injuries as the result of the accident, but the car was totally destroyed (*mi pobre coche nuevo está totalmente destrozado*). In this same statement, we learn that it was not Laura's car, but his own (*mi*).

Short Narrative

1. **A.** The selection begins talking about how repugnant a type of greenish food (*sustancia verdosa*) eaten by the natives of the Valley of Mexico was to the Spanish conquerors.

2. **C.** The "greenish mud" the Aztecs used to eat is a type of algae, called spiruline, which according to the selection is very nutritious (*con más proteínas, ocho aminoácidos . . .*).

3. **C.** The passage emphasizes the fact that the ignorance shown by the Spaniards many years ago is still present in Mexico because *espirulina* is practically unknown, and only people who are curious about it buy it in health-food stores (*tiendas naturistas*).

Longer Narrative

1. **A.** At the beginning of the interview, she makes a statement comparing art to business and says that it is necessary to obtain success and money before others step on you (*tienes que alcanzar el éxito y el dinero antes de que otro te lo pise*); therefore, competition is the reason to rush to get success and money.

2. **C.** Sara Baras apparently dances well, but most people know her because of her frequent appearances on TV (*sale mucho en la tele*), not because they have seen her dancing in theaters.

3. **A.** A health problem is mentioned in the interview, and then Cristina relates an anecdote about when she got out of the operating room (*quirófano*); therefore, you may conclude that she had some type of surgery. The other answers are attractive, but they contradict the information given in the interview. Choice **B** is incorrect because the fact that Cristina has a dance company (*una compañía*) is stated in the interview. Choice **C** is incorrect because, in a couple instances, Cristina mentions that she is a sincere person, so the listener has no indication that she may be lying to the interviewer.

4. **A.** Cristina does not get the role of the main character because Saura wants somebody younger than she. Choice **B** may be attractive because Cristina mentions that Saura was *encantado* with Laura del Sol, but the word *encantado* is not equivalent to being in love (*enamorado*). Choice **C** is also incorrect because, at the time of the production of Carmen, Cristina had many years of experience dancing with Gades and her technique was not a problem.

> **If you had any trouble following the CD, go to www.cliffsnotes.com/extras and check out the CD script. This Web site also has other great content that will help you on the test.**

This part of the exam, in addition to Part D, Reading Comprehension, deals with reading. The section consists of two reading selections that contain numbered blanks indicating that words or phrases have been omitted. You are given four options for each blank, but only one is correct. The purpose of this exercise is to test your vocabulary and your knowledge of Spanish grammar.

There are approximately 2 Cloze Passages and 20 questions about the passages on any given version of the AP Spanish Language Exam. You should spend about 10 minutes on these questions.

Ability Tested

This part of the exam deals with reading, and it tests your ability to understand specific words and/or idiomatic expressions and grammar patterns.

Basic Skills Necessary

You need to be able to:

- Demonstrate control of an ample range of Spanish vocabulary, including idiomatic expressions.
- Determine the correct grammatical form of a word according to the context of the passage.

To understand the written Spanish language within the context of journalistic or literary texts, you need two things:

- Your vocabulary must be within the range expected for a third-level student of Spanish as a second language. You can greatly increase your command of Spanish vocabulary and grammar by reading the different types of selections found in newspapers, magazines, or the Internet, or by reading literary passages from short stories or novels. Although Part V of this book provides you with different lists of classified vocabulary and a glossary, you should also have your own bilingual dictionary.
- Your knowledge of Spanish grammar must be advanced enough to be able to discriminate past tense from present or future, to recognize the use of different modes of speaking (such as indicative and subjunctive), and to figure out the subject of a sentence.

Vocabulary and language mechanics are of the essence if you want to be successful in this part of the exam.

Your familiarity with Hispanic culture, as well as your own life experiences, will be of great help in achieving a good command of Spanish reading skills. For example, your ability to use guessing strategies to compensate for a lack of vocabulary can help you with reading comprehension. Try to identify words that are cognates, that is, words that may look a bit different in another language but have the same meaning (such as *león* and *lion, navegar* and *navigate,* and so on). Recognizing cognates will facilitate your understanding of the selection as a whole, as well as provide you with some specific details. Part V of this book contains a section that will help you identify cognates.

It is also important to think in Spanish. Translating word for word could lead you to arrive at the wrong meaning because some words have different meanings in different contexts. For example, the word *grado* is a cognate of the word *grade* when speaking of the school year (such as 7th grade), but it also has other meanings, such as *degree* when speaking about temperature and *rank* when speaking about the military. Translating word for word will lead you to make these kinds of mistakes; reading the passage as a whole will help you avoid these kinds of mistakes.

You must also remember that there are idiomatic expressions that, when you try to translate them word for word, lose their meaning or do not make any sense. For example, in English, when someone is playing a joke on you, you may say, "You're pulling my leg." This is an idiomatic expression and, of course, should not be taken literally. If you decide that you want to express the same idea in Spanish, the correct expression is "*Me estás tomando el pelo*" (which translates literally to "You are taking my hair"). As you see, the Spanish expression, once translated word for word into English, completely loses its meaning.

For questions dealing with grammar, you must be able to work with the Spanish grammatical patterns that are most commonly used in this type of exercise, such as the correct usage of verb tenses, prepositions, and pronouns. In Part V, you can find a summary of grammatical topics that you must master in order to be successful in this part of the exam.

Directions

In Part B of the Multiple Choice section, you will be working with Cloze Passages. These are reading passages in which some words (usually 10) have been substituted by numbered blanks; you must select from the four choices given the word or words that make sense or are grammatically correct. The directions are given to you in writing, in English and Spanish. Concentrate on the directions in the language you feel most comfortable with.

The following directions resemble what you will read during Part B of the Multiple Choice section of the AP Spanish Language Exam. It is important to be familiar with the directions for each section *before* you take the test so that you can use your time more efficiently during the test.

Each of the following passages contains numbered blanks, which indicate that words or groups of words are missing. There are four options to fill in each blank, but only one is correct.

In order to determine the general meaning of the passage, read quickly through it first. Then read it again and select the option that best fills each blank according to the context of the complete passage.

Cada uno de los siguientes pasajes contiene espacios en blanco numerados para indicar que faltan palabras o grupos de palabras. Hay cuatro opciones para llenar cada espacio, pero solamente una es correcta.

Para poder determinar el sentido general del pasaje, léelo rápidamente; luego léelo de nuevo y selecciona la opción que mejor complete cada espacio de acuerdo con el contexto total del pasaje.

Suggested Strategies for Cloze Passages

The Cloze Passage exercises are modified reading exercises; therefore, some of the strategies necessary to be successful in this portion of the exam are reading strategies. On the other hand, since your answers are based on your knowledge of grammar and vocabulary, there are other strategies that are directly related to how to manipulate the information you can glean from these two areas.

- **Read the complete selection first.** It is important to perform a first reading without attempting to answer any of the questions. Reading the entire passage will give you an idea of what the passage is about, what tense predominates throughout the narration, and what type of vocabulary you will encounter. For example, once you discover that the passage deals with someone's summer vacation in Acapulco, you can expect to see words like *playa* (beach) and *arena* (sand) later in the text. At the same time, if you encounter several verbal forms in the preterit or the imperfect, you can determine the time frame of the selection.

- **Use your existing knowledge of the world.** Once you have read the passage once, think about what you know about the topic or the experiences presented in the passage. For example, if you recognize that the selection is about somebody who has traveled to Spain, you can use any travel experience you've had, as well as any cultural knowledge you have about Spain. Use your knowledge about the subject to help you read for meaning and to predict what information the text will present.

- **Look at each group of options individually to determine whether the item is vocabulary or grammar related.** This step is extremely important because, depending on whether the item relates to grammar or vocabulary, you will apply different procedures to select the correct option. For example, if you observe that the four choices are verbs in the infinitive form (*cantar, leer,* and so on), you can deduce that, since all the options have the same grammatical value, only the meaning will determine the correctness of the option. On the other hand, if you notice that all the options are different forms of the same verb (*canto, canté, cantaba,* and so on), you will know that you must look for clues about what tense is required according to the time sequence of the passage.

- **Recognize cognates.** You know that there are many Spanish words that resemble and have the same meaning as English words. These words are called *cognates.* When you are able to recognize cognates, it is easier to grasp the general meaning of the passage and to select the correct choice, either because the choice may be a cognate itself, or because some of the incorrect options are cognates.

- **Identify words by examining word formation.** In Spanish, words are grouped into *families of words*. This means that, out of one simple word, other words can be formed by adding prefixes and suffixes. For example, the word *decente* (a cognate of the English *decent*) is an adjective that can be used to form other words such as *indecente* (English *indecent*), *decencia* (English *decency*), and so on. By recognizing words that belong to the same family and relating them to words you do know, you can figure out the meaning of unfamiliar words.

- **Use the context of the passage to figure out the meaning of unfamiliar words.** When you read a text, the word *context* refers to the words that surround an unfamiliar word. The context is very useful because it limits the meaning of a word. By using the context, you can eliminate some of your options.

  For example, you can determine the meaning of the word *comodidad* by taking note of its context in the following sentence: "*La mujer de hoy busca la comodidad y compra ropa que tenga esa característica, ropa que pueda usar en muchas ocasiones y sentirse bien, a gusto, pero también elegante.*" Once you conclude that the sentence deals with what today's woman (*la mujer de hoy*) looks for in clothing (*ropa*), you will realize that the last words (*pero también elegante*) signal a contrast. From this clue, you can deduce that *comodidad* is a false cognate: It does not mean *commodity;* rather, it means something the opposite of *elegant.*

- **Try to eliminate as many options as possible based on the knowledge you have of each.** In every group of options related to vocabulary, there are words whose meaning you should be able to determine by using any of the previous strategies. Once you are certain of the meaning of a word, place it in the corresponding blank to see if it makes any sense in the context. If it doesn't, you can eliminate it.

- **Identify the time sequence.** This strategy is important in order to appropriately identify the correct answer in items that deal with verbal forms in different tenses. If you identify when one event took place, and whether it took place before or after another event, you will be able to make the correct choice. One good way of identifying the time sequence is by looking at the adverbial phrases of time (such as *la semana pasada, al año siguiente,* and so on).

- **Identify the subject of a sentence.** If an item lists as its options four forms of the same verb, you need to figure out the subject of the sentence. The correct choice is based on the agreement between subject and verb. For example, if your choices are forms of the same verb in the same tense (such as *canté, cantaste, cantó, cantaron*), you must look for the subject of the sentence because all the choices are equivalent except in person and number.

Remember that selecting and using these cues and strategies will help you avoid decoding the text word by word, understand the meaning of the passage, and successfully select the correct answer.

An Example of How to Read a Passage and Work Through Questions

Here is an example of a Cloze Passage that you may find on the exam. Below the passage is a suggestion for how you may be able to tackle the passage and arrive at the correct answers in a reasonable amount of time. The first few questions are also given.

En los (1) tiempos, parece ser que beber agua embotellada se ha puesto de moda. (2) fuentes periodísticas, en los últimos años la industria del agua embotellada (3) de forma inusual. Por ejemplo, (4) España se ha producido un crecimiento de un 5% de esta industria. Este incremento (5) debe a las nuevas tendencias aparecidas en la década de los 90 de que beber mucha agua es una manera de mantenerse sano.

Hoy en día, por donde (6) que uno mira se encuentra con una "botellita de agua." Hasta las bolsas deportivas tienen un compartimento especial para (7).

Sin embargo, los verdaderos precursores del (8) de agua como fuente de salud fueron los romanos. Cuando uno visita Roma, enseguida (9) algo curioso: A cada paso, en cada plaza, de la parte antigua de la ciudad, se encuentra (10) fuente de agua mineral para que los ciudadanos puedan beber. Ahora, claro está, los turistas que visitan la bella ciudad, rellenan su botellita.

1. A. primeros
   B. tantos
   C. últimos
   D. muchos

2. A. Sin embargo
   B. Por consiguiente
   C. A pesar de
   D. Según

3. A. ha crecido
   B. crecerá
   C. crezca
   D. crecería

If you encounter this passage, you could go through a process similar to the one given below:

1. **Read the entire passage.**

   Many students are tempted to skim the passage and then read the questions, or read the questions and then read the passage, or read just the first few sentences of the passage and then read the questions. However, reading the *entire* passage is always a good idea. In this case, you would realize that this passage is about the new trend of drinking bottled water. It also provides some facts about how this habit has affected other aspects of life.

2. **Think about what you know about the topic.**

   If you have a lot of outside knowledge about the topic, this will help you on the exam. Observe that there are many words that are frequently used in Spanish (including *ser, beber, agua, años, nuevas*) that you should know by now. Use your knowledge of the topic to help you with the many cognates that you may easily recognize, such as *industria* (industry), *forma* (form), *producido* (produced), and *tendencias* (tendencies). Be cautious, though: *Sano* is a false cognate that means *healthy* in English.

3. **Move on to the questions.**

   For the first question, determine whether it is testing your knowledge of grammar or your vocabulary. Notice that all four choices are adjectives in the masculine and plural form. Because they have the same grammatical value, it is apparent that this is a vocabulary item. All the choices are frequently used words in Spanish, and, from the context and your previous knowledge on the subject, you will be able to pick *últimos* (last) as the correct answer because the entire passage deals with the trend that has developed lately of drinking bottled water.

4. **Go on to the next question, and repeat the process.**

   Once again, this is a vocabulary item. Notice that the choices are expressions that have a very specific meaning and whose function is to keep the logic of the text. From your experience, you know that when someone is giving data, she is probably using another source of information to back up what she is saying. The correct answer here is Choice **D** because *según* means *according to*. Of the four choices given, this is the only one that helps keep the logic of the text. The expressions given in Choice **A** and Choice **C** normally introduce a contradiction, and the expression in Choice **B** is generally used after a cause to introduce the effect.

5. **As you continue to fill in the blanks, the text will make more sense to you.**

   Move to the next question. As soon as you see that the four choices given are different forms of the same verb, you will know that this is a grammar item.

   You already know that this passage deals with facts; therefore, the subjunctive and conditional forms can be eliminated. This leaves you with two choices: Choice **A** and Choice **B**. Choice **B** is the in future form, however, and you know that the passage relates what has been happening in the last few years. If you recollect what you know about verbal tenses, you will remember that the present perfect (used in Choice **A**) may be used as equivalent of the preterit, or to indicate an action that began in the past and that may or may not continue into the future.

One good technique to decide whether any given tense of a verb is correct is to go to the text and locate other verbal forms used in it. The logic of the language will help you here: If the preterit predominates in the passage, you may want to select the preterit form as your answer. In this specific passage, two verbal forms located near the omitted word are in the present perfect tense: *ha puesto* and *ha producido*. If you are trying to make an educated guess, you will select Choice **A**, which is in the present perfect form.

Sample Cloze Passages: Questions, Answers, and Explanations

Below are two sample Cloze Passages. Follow the directions, and, after you finish with the first sample, see "Answers and Explanations for Sample 1" (below). Make sure that you understand the reason for each correct answer. Repeat the process with Sample 2.

Sample 1

Si todo el hielo existente en el planeta (1) a derretirse, el proceso (2) miles de años y el aumento del peso del agua probablemente causaría el hundimiento de las hoyas oceánicas y la elevación de las masas continentales. (3) otra parte, el nivel del mar podría (4) en todas las costas hasta 170 o 200 metros. Solamente la capa (5) hielo antártica cubre (6) seis millones de millas cuadradas y, en caso de (7), produciría unos 6.5 millones de millas cúbicas de agua, cantidad suficiente para abastecer al Río Mississippi durante más de 50 mil años. Un aumento del nivel del mar de sólo 35 metros (8) casi toda la costa atlántica de los Estados Unidos y afectaría a las principales ciudades de este litoral. (9), podemos mantener la calma, ya que, desde siempre, los científicos (10) este suceso como una posibilidad sumamente remota.

1. A. llegara
    B. llegará
    C. llegó
    D. llegue

2. A. evitaría
    B. causaría
    C. tendría
    D. tardaría

3. A. Con
    B. En
    C. Para
    D. Por

4. A. salir
    B. seguir
    C. sentir
    D. subir

5. A. a
    B. con
    C. de
    D. en

6. A. aproximadamente
    B. rápidamente
    C. típicamente
    D. simplemente

7. A. derretirse
    B. derritiendo
    C. se derrita
    D. derretido

8. A. inunda
    B. inunde
    C. inundará
    D. inundaría

9. A. a pesar de
    B. al contrario
    C. sin embargo
    D. en cambio

10. A. considerarán
    B. considerarían
    C. han considerado
    D. hubieran considerado

Answers and Explanations for Sample 1

Remember that, although this is not a reading comprehension exercise, you must understand the text in order to select the correct option to fill in the blank. Some of the questions test your vocabulary; therefore, understanding the context is extremely important. Here are some tips to help you with this task:

- Use the content knowledge that you have acquired about environmental science in your science class, in other classes, or from your own experience to determine the theme of the passage and to anticipate the information the passage may include.

- Identify the cognates to determine that the purpose of the passage is to give information about natural phenomena: *planeta, proceso, probablemente, elevación, masas, continentales,* and so on.

- Pick out words that are used frequently in Spanish and that you are familiar with, such as *hielo, años, agua,* and so on.

- Focus on the time frame. Notice the absence of the present and past tenses in the passage. Scan the reading and identify the verb forms that appear, such as *causaría* and *produciría.* You can also identify the infinitives *causar* and *producir* and the endings attached to them to determine that these are conditional forms and that this passage presents a hypothesis. These clues will help you predict that you may encounter a subjunctive form, as is the case in the first question.

Below are the answers and explanations for each question in Sample 1.

1. **A.** This a grammar item. You immediately see that the four choices are forms of the same verb. The word *si* (if) is your clue that this is not a fact that has happened already; therefore, you can eliminate Choice **C**, which is in the preterit form. The subjunctive is the tense used to speak about speculations, and there are two forms of the subjunctive given, one in Choice **A** and another in Choice **C**. The use of the subjunctive in this if clause indicates that the event is not likely to occur, and the use of the conditional form *causaría* is a key element for selecting Choice **A**. The pattern here is "if *x*, then *y*," where *x = llegara* and *y = causaría*.

2. **D.** This is a vocabulary item. The four choices are all verbs in the conditional form, so all of them would be grammatically correct. Once you determine that this passage presents a hypothesis, you can concentrate on the meaning of each choice and how it would or would not fit in the passage. *Causaría* is a cognate (to cause); *tendría* is a form of *tener.* You are left with two choices: If you relate *tardaría* or *tardar* to the word *tarde,* you will recognize this family of words and be able to select the correct answer.

3. **D.** This is a grammar item that tests your knowledge of the use of prepositions. Of the four choices, *por* and *para* are the ones that are most easily confused; therefore, you can eliminate Choice **A** and Choice **B**. Now you can look for a reason to select Choice **C** or Choice **D**. The preposition *por* is used in common expressions. In this case, it's used in the expression *on the other hand.* For more on the uses of *por* and *para,* see Objective 19 in the Grammar Review appendix.

4. **D.** This is a vocabulary item. The choices *salir* and *sentir* are frequently used in Spanish and you probably know they mean *to leave or go out* and *to feel,* respectively. The verb that would follow the noun phrase *el nivel del mar* must be *subir* because it is the one that indicates the rising of the water level.

5. **C.** This is a vocabulary item. All four choices are prepositions. The preposition *de* is used to form noun phrases that are equivalent to noun + noun in English: in this case, *la capa de hielo = the ice cap.*

6. **A.** The adverb *aproximadamente* (approximately) is used before a quantity.

7. **A.** This is a grammar item. *Derritiendo* is a distracter that appeals to English speakers; in Spanish, however, the infinitive (not the gerund) is used following a preposition. For more details on the use of the infinitive and the gerund, see Objective 17 in the Grammar Review appendix.

8. **D.** This is a grammar item, in which the four choices given are forms of the verb *inundar.* Use the conditional to maintain the hypothetical nature of the passage.

9. **C.** This is a vocabulary item. A vocabulary review will be useful in order to be able to choose the word according to the meaning you make of the passage. *Sin embargo* (however) is used to show the contrast between the previous statement and the next. *A pesar de* (in spite of), *al contrario* (on the contrary), and *en cambio* (on the other hand) are not appropriate answers. (Notice that *al contrario* includes a cognate.)

10. **C.** The use of present perfect indicates that the action was initiated in the past and continues in the present. This is the only sentence in the passage that includes a verb in a tense other than the conditional or the subjunctive. The clue to the correct answer is the phrase *desde siempre:* Because both *desde* (from) and *siempre* (always) are common words in Spanish, you can pick out the correct answer based on your prior knowledge of the language.

Sample 2

Investigaciones recientes (1) que los cambios climáticos que se registran a nivel mundial (2) las condiciones ecológicas favorables (3) que el nacimiento y desarrollo de insectos (4) día con día. Las noticias acerca de desastres ocasionados por plagas en cultivos y ganado, principalmente, se (5) en los últimos años. La Universidad de la Florida, en su departamento de entomología y hematología, trabaja en un proyecto, en el que se desarrollan nuevos controles que (6) el nacimiento y crecimiento de estos animales. Los insecticidas (7) aquí no llevan los pesticidas químicos que (8) incluyen estos productos y que dañan la capa de ozono. (9) otro lado, en el mismo proyecto, la bióloga Marie Knox (10) un silbato de tres pulgadas que se utiliza para localizar cucarachas, consideradas la peor plaga doméstica.

1. **A.** datan
   B. entregan
   C. rebelan
   D. revelan

2. **A.** crean
   B. crearán
   C. crearían
   D. han creado

3. A. de
   B. en
   C. para
   D. por

4. A. aumenta
   B. aumente
   C. aumentó
   D. aumentaría

5. A. incrementan
   B. incrementarán
   C. han incrementado
   D. incrementen

6. A. conducen
   B. producen
   C. reducen
   D. traducen

7. A. elaborados
   B. elaboraron
   C. elaborando
   D. elaborar

8. A. al revés
   B. al tanto
   C. por el contrario
   D. por lo general

9. A. Desde
   B. En
   C. Por
   D. Para

10. A. analizó
    B. inventó
    C. ocurrió
    D. sustituyó

Answers and Explanations for Sample 2

To help you answer these questions correctly, you may:

- Use the content knowledge you have acquired about insects in your science class, in other classes, or from your own experience to determine the theme of the passage and to anticipate the information the passage may include.

- Identify the cognates to determine that the purpose of the passage is to give information about natural phenomena: *climático, condiciones, favorables, insectos, universidad, entomología, hematología, animales,* and so on.

- Focus on words that are used frequently in Spanish and that you are familiar with, such as *día, noticias, años, trabaja,* and so on.

- Focus on the time frame. Notice the abundance of verbs in the present tense, such as *registran, trabaja, desarrollan,* and so on. This passage addresses an ongoing process: therefore, your choices need to be consistent with this time frame. Besides the present and the present subjunctive, the other tense that fits in this sequence is the present perfect, especially in reference to an action that began in the past but may be still happening.

Below are the answers and explanations for each question in Sample 2.

1. **D.** This is a vocabulary item. Because your four choices are verbs in the same form, they are grammatically equivalent. You may be able to eliminate Choice **A** because you can relate it to the word *date*. Choice **C** is a good distracter because of its spelling; in fact, a native speaker of Spanish may select it due to a lack of spelling knowledge. Choice **D** is a cognate, and, if you try to fit it within the context, you will see that it is the correct answer: To give the appropriate meaning to the sentence, it needs to state that recent research reveals a fact.

2. **D.** This is a grammar item. The choices given are four verbal forms of *crear.* The use of the present perfect indicates that the action was initiated in the past and continues in the present.

3. **C.** This item requires the knowledge of the usage of prepositions, especially *por* and *para. Por* followed by *que* is used to introduce a cause. *Para que* introduces a clause that demonstrates an action that is a result of another. This type of clause requires the subjunctive.

4. **B.** This is a grammar item. Because the verb is part of a clause with *para que,* the subjunctive mode is required. The use of the subjunctive in the second part of the clause indicates the goal of an action, whether it is accomplished or not. For a more detailed explanation on the uses of the subjunctive, refer to Objective 14 in the Grammar Review appendix.

5. **C.** The use of the present perfect indicates that the action was initiated in the past and continues in the present. Look for a clue that will help you choose the appropriate tense: *En los últimos años* refers to a point in time in the past and helps you eliminate the other choices because they include the present tense (Choice **A**), the future tense (Choice **B**), and the present subjunctive (Choice **D**).

6. **C.** This is a vocabulary item, where three out of the four choices are cognates, including the correct answer. Apply your previous knowledge about the subject to choose the appropriate answer to this item. Choice **C** (*reducen*) is the correct choice because the sentence needs to state that the project's goal is to reduce the number of insects.

7. **A.** This is a grammar item that tests your knowledge of impersonal forms of verbs. The past participle is the only one that may be used as an adjective. When used as an adjective, it must agree in gender and number with the noun. For a more detailed explanation of the impersonal forms of verbs, see Objective 17 in the Grammar Review appendix.

8. **D.** *Por lo general* is an idiomatic expression equivalent to *in general.* Studying a list of phrases such as this one will be useful because they are used rather frequently in Spanish. For a list of phrases such as this one, see the list of idiomatic expressions in Part V.

9. **C.** The preposition *por* is used in common expressions such as *por otro lado.* For a more detailed explanation on the uses of *por* and *para,* see Objective 19 in the Grammar Review appendix.

10. **B.** This is a vocabulary item, for which it is useful to rely on your knowledge of cognates. For example, *inventó* is a form of *inventar* (to invent): Thus, you know that, as a result of the research, the biologist invented a whistle.

Explaining Error Recognition Exercises

This part of the exam addresses your knowledge of grammatical structures. In error recognition exercises, you must identify the word or phrase that is grammatically incorrect within the context of a sentence. Each sentence contains four underlined parts, but only one of those parts is grammatically incorrect. The purpose of this exercise is to test your knowledge of Spanish grammar.

There are around 15 questions of this type on any given version of the AP Spanish Language Exam. You should spend about 10 minutes on these questions.

Ability Tested

This part of the exam is related to language structure and syntax, and it tests your knowledge of grammar patterns, such as the use of different verb tenses and modes, the maintenance of agreement between a noun and its determinants (articles, adjectives, and so on) and between a subject and a verb, and the use of prepositions.

Basic Skills Necessary

You need to be able to:

- Demonstrate control of complex Spanish structures.

- Know how to use prepositions, verbal tenses, and idiomatic expressions that require a given grammatical structure.

- Recognize the gender and number of nouns.

In this type of exercise, you are most likely to encounter the types of errors commonly made by learners of Spanish as a second language who have not mastered some specific rules. Among the most common errors:

- Incorrect verb conjugation within the context of a sentence. For example:

  • *Ayer los alumnos van a la escuela.*

    In this sentence, the error is in the use of the present tense of *ir* (*van*). The word *ayer* (yesterday) requires the use of the preterit tense: *fueron*.

  • *Mis padres no quieren que yo voy al cine sola.*

    In this sentence, the error is in the use of the present tense of the indicative (*voy*). This is an example of a dependent clause preceded by an independent clause that expresses a desire. In this case, the subjunctive mode (*vaya*) is required.

- Lack of agreement between noun and article, noun and adjective, and subject and verb. For example:

  - *No comprendí muy bien la tema de biología de esta mañana.*

    In this sentence, the error is in the use of *la* as the article that accompanies the noun *tema*. Although the noun ends in *-a*, this word is an exception to the rule of genders in Spanish: A series of words of Greek origin that end in *-ma*, *-pa*, and *-ta* are masculine in gender. *Tema* is one of them; other examples are *problema*, *mapa*, and *planeta*. For more detailed information about the genders of Spanish nouns, see Objective 5 in the Grammar Review.

  - *Al tener coche nueva, Pedro solamente quiere salir con chicas bonitas.*

    This sentence contains an error that exemplifies a lack of agreement in gender between the noun and the adjective. *Coche* is masculine, so the adjective should be *nuevo.*

- Lack of agreement between pronouns and the nouns they substitute for. For example:

  - *Yo le dije a mis padres que me dieran dinero para el almuerzo.*

    This is one of the most common mistakes found in Spanish when dealing with pronouns. The pronoun in this sentence stands in for *padres,* which is plural; therefore, you must use *les* rather than *le.*

  - *A Juan no les gustan las fresas.*

    In this case, with the verb *gustar,* the pronoun must agree with the subject (*Juan*). The correct form of the pronoun used in this example is *le.*

- Failure to follow the correct pattern for comparison structures. For example:

  - *María es más alta como Rosario.*

    The error here is in the comparison pattern. This is a comparison of inequality, that is, someone or something possesses a characteristic or a quality in a larger or smaller quantity than someone or something else. To express this type of comparison in Spanish, you must follow the following patterns: *más* + adjective + *que* (for superiority) and *menos* + adjective + *que* (for inferiority). Therefore, in this example, the word *que* rather than *como* would make the sentence correct.

  - *Creo que Roberto es tan inteligente que Manuela.*

    This sentence contains another type of comparison structure, a comparison of equality. The correct pattern for this structure is *tan* + adjective + *como*. Substituting *como* for *que* would make the sentence correct.

- Failure to use conjunctions and adverbs in an appropriate way. For example:

  - *María y Isabel vendrán a casa esta tarde.*

    The problem with this sentence is with the conjunction *y*. In Spanish, when you have two words separated by *y* and the second one starts with an "i" sound, *e* is used rather than *y* to avoid the repetition of the sound. To be correct, this sentence should read: *María e Isabel vendrán a casa esta tarde.* Similarly, when the conjunction used is *o* and the next word starts with an "o" sound, *u* is used instead.

- *No me metí en el agua porque estaba demasiada fría.*

  What you have in this sentence is a case of confusing an adjective with an adverb. The word *demasiado* may be used to modify nouns, adjectives, and verbs. When it modifies a noun, it is functioning as an adjective and, therefore, must maintain the agreement with the noun it modifies (for example, *Tienes demasiadas cosas en tu bolsa*). In the sentence above, *demasiado* is functioning as a modifier of the adjective *fría;* thus, it is an adverb, and adverbs in Spanish are invariable, that is, they do not undergo any gender or number change. The corrected sentence reads: *No me metí en el agua porque estaba demasiado fría.*

■ Inappropriate selection of prepositions. For example:

- *Tengo que terminar el trabajo por mañana a las cinco.*

  One of the most common errors among students of Spanish is in the use of the prepositions *por* and *para.* The reason for this is that both prepositions may be used as an equivalent for the English word *for.* But although both may mean *for,* they are not interchangeable. In the sentence above, *para* is the correct preposition because the idea expressed is that the work has to be completed tomorrow, not in the morning. For more details on the correct use of *por* and *para,* see Objective 19 in the Grammar Review.

- *Yo sueño de llegar a ser un gran médico.*

  The sentence above contains an error in the use of the preposition *de.* This error is due to English language interference, because the preposition *of (de)* is used in English with the verb *to dream.* In Spanish, the correct preposition is *con.*

■ Incorrect use of definite and indefinite articles. For example:

- *Javier es un arquitecto.*

  In this sentence, the indefinite article *un* must be omitted. With professions and occupations, the indefinite article is used only if the noun is modified by an adjective (for example, *Tu hermana es una excelente profesora de español*). For more details on the use of indefinite articles, see Objective 4 in the Grammar Review in Part V.

■ Incorrect use of negative words. For example:

- *No tengo algún dinero.*

  In Spanish, there are negative patterns that require a double negative. This sentence is an example of this phenomenon. The sentence should read: *No tengo ningún dinero.*

- *Nadie no vino a la fiesta.*

  When the negative word is placed before the verb, the word *no* is omitted: *Nadie vino a la fiesta.* The same idea may be expressed as: *No vino nadie a la fiesta.*

■ Incorrect use of the impersonal forms of the verbs. For example:

- *Los libros fueron impreso en Argentina.*

  In this sentence, the past participle of a verb (*impreso*) is being used in a passive voice pattern. In this case, it must agree in gender and number with the subject of the sentence (*libros*); therefore, *impresos* is required to make the sentence grammatically correct.

In the Grammar Review appendix, you can find a summary of grammatical topics that you need to master in order to be successful on this part of the exam.

Directions

In Part C of the Multiple Choice section, you will be working with sentences that contain four underlined parts. One of these parts is grammatically incorrect in the context of the sentence. You are to select from the four underlined parts the one that makes the sentence grammatically incorrect. The directions are given to you in writing, in English and Spanish. Concentrate on the directions in the language you feel most comfortable with.

The following directions resemble what you will read during Part C of the Multiple Choice section of the AP Spanish Language Exam. It is important to be familiar with the directions for each section *before* you take the test so that you can use your time more efficiently during the test.

In the following sentences, select the underlined part of the sentence that needs to be changed in order to make the sentence grammatically correct.

En las oraciones que aparecen a continuación, escoge la parte subrayada que habría que cambiar para que la oración sea gramaticalmente correcta.

Suggested Strategies for Error Recognition Exercises

In this part of the exam, your success depends on your knowledge of Spanish grammar; therefore, it is essential to study the rules of the language and practice a lot.

- **Read each sentence completely.** In your first reading, you may be able to determine what is wrong with the sentence.

- **Look at each underlined part separately.** Some errors are easier to detect than others. If you clearly recognize that an underlined part is correct, you can eliminate it immediately.

- **Identify the subject and the verb of the sentence.** This will help you recognize any error that deals with agreement between subject and verb, as well as any error that deals with gender and number agreement between a noun and/or pronoun and its modifiers.

- **Try to recognize a time sequence.** Most of the time, a verb that is not underlined can help you decide whether a verb that is underlined is incorrect. If you identify when one event took place and whether it took place before or after another, you will be able to make the correct selection. One good way to identify the time sequence is to look for adverbial phrases of time, such as *la semana pasada* (last week), *al año siguiente* (next year), and so on.

- **Identify any existing relation between nouns and pronouns.** Figuring out what noun a pronoun is replacing can be difficult because the positioning of pronouns in Spanish can be quite different than in English. For example, note the placement of *me* in relation to the verbs in the following sentences: *Juan* **me** *ayuda a terminar mi tarea* and *Juan helps* **me** *finish my assignment.*

- **Determine whether prepositions and conjunctions are used correctly.** Prepositions are difficult to master because many of them are used with verbs and with idiomatic expressions that have a concrete meaning. Among the prepositions that are commonly confused are *por* and *para.* Observe the difference in meaning that results from the use of *por* and *para* in the following sentences: *Viaja por la ciudad* (travel through the city) and *Viaja para la ciudad* (travel toward the city).

- **Determine the type of sentence you are dealing with.** This is important because different types of sentences require different grammatical patterns. For example, in a negative sentence, make sure that the negative words (such as *nada* or *nadie*) are accompanied by a double negative. A sentence that expresses commands or desires will most likely require the use of the subjunctive mode.

- **Be aware of the position of any adjectives.** This could help you in two ways: First, some adjectives are shortened before masculine and singular nouns (for example, *Yo vivo en el tercer piso*). Second, some adjectives change their meaning when they are located in front of the noun they modify (for example, *Es un hombre grande* and *Es un gran hombre* mean, respectively, *He is a big man* and *He is a great man*).

- **Check for any type of comparison.** Comparisons require the use of different patterns, depending on whether they express equality, superiority, or inferiority. Also, look for the incorrect use of superlatives.

A Guide to the Grammar Review Appendix

A detailed review of Spanish grammar is included in the Grammar Review appendix. To succeed on the Error Recognition portion of the AP Spanish Language Exam, you must completely understand some key points of grammar. Below, you can find a summary of those grammar points, as they are presented in the Grammar Review appendix. The topics in the Grammar Review are listed as objectives, so the list below also follows this structure.

This list is included here because a good understanding of the rules of grammar is essential to performing well on Error Recognition problems.

Syllabication

Objective 1: To learn how to divide Spanish words into syllables.

In this part, you will find the rules that you must know in order to divide Spanish words into syllables correctly. Although you are not tested directly for this skill on the AP Spanish Language Exam, you must have this knowledge in order to accent words correctly. Accentuation is an important element in the writing portions of the exam.

Rules for Word Stress in Spanish

Objective 2: To master the rules of accentuation in Spanish.

Here, you are presented with the rules used to accent words correctly. Examples of special cases of accentuation are also included. In the written portion of the exam, writing accents correctly affects your total score.

Articles

Objective 3: To use definite articles correctly.

This is an introduction to the four definite articles in Spanish. There are detailed explanations on the use and omission of the definitive articles, both of which are illustrated with various examples. This is evaluated in the Error Recognition part of the exam as well as in the writing parts.

Objective 4: To use indefinite articles correctly.

In this section, the indefinite articles are listed, and an explanation on when to use or not to use them is presented. Various examples illustrate the rules discussed. Knowing how to use indefinite articles will help you succeed in the Error Recognition portion of the test as well as in the writing parts.

Nouns

Objective 5: To identify the gender of nouns.

In this part, the general rules to help you identify the gender of Spanish nouns are explained and illustrated with some examples. Being able to identify noun gender is especially useful in the Error Recognition part of the exam.

Objective 6: To correctly form the plural of nouns.

Plural formation rules are discussed in this section, and each rule is illustrated with some examples. This is important to master because the writing part of the exam tests plural formation. Knowing how to correctly form the plural of nouns will especially be of help in the Paragraph Fill-Ins portion of the exam.

Adjectives

Objective 7: To correctly use adjectives in order to maintain gender and/or number agreement with the noun.

This section addresses the changes undergone by an adjective to maintain gender and/or number agreement with the noun it modifies. Knowing how to maintain gender and/or number agreement between adjectives and nouns will be of help in the Paragraph Fill-Ins portion of the exam.

ctives correctly within a sentence.

anish presents some level of difficulty for students. Because this is
grammar of the language, this part is dedicated to explaining the
and their correct placement within a sentence. Adjectives that
on their position in a sentence are also discussed.

rect form of a personal pronoun in order to maintain agree-
s to.

ns in Spanish is not an easy task. In this part of the Grammar
sonal pronouns listed by the function they perform in a sentence.
is also discussed and illustrated with numerous examples. Using
al pronoun is of great importance to successfully complete the
raph Fill-Ins portions of the exam.

regular verbs correctly in all tenses in order to maintain
of the sentence.

re than anything to the mechanical part of the language.
in all tenses requires a lot of practice.

conjugate stem-changing verbs.

planation of the different types of Spanish verbs that undergo a
tate the learning process, the verbs are grouped by the type of
ost commonly used verbs are included.

Objective 12. To correctly conjugate the most common irregular verbs.

The section consists mainly of charts in which the most common irregular Spanish verbs are completely conjugated in the irregular forms. Regular forms have been omitted.

Objective 13: To correctly use the preterit versus the imperfect tense, according to the context.

One of the most difficult tasks for the Spanish learner is to master the usage of the preterit and the imperfect. In this section, you will find the rules for using them correctly, along with examples to illustrate each point.

Objective 14: To correctly use the subjunctive mode.

This is one of the most important objectives of the Grammar Review. The subjunctive is very much used in Spanish to express numerous situations, but it is difficult for students to master the many structures in which the subjunctive is required. This part is a summary of the uses of the subjunctive. Each use is discussed and illustrated with examples.

Objective 15: To use commands correctly.

Giving commands is a very common function of the language. In this section of the Grammar Review, all forms of Spanish commands and their uses are discussed.

Objective 16: To use the future and the conditional tenses.

The uses of both tenses are discussed and illustrated with examples.

Objective 17: To correctly form and use the impersonal forms of verbs.

Impersonal forms of verbs play an important role in different language patterns. In this section, the formation and the usage of the three impersonal forms of verbs—infinitive, gerund, and past participle—are discussed and illustrated with examples.

Objective 18: To correctly use the verbs ser and estar.

The correct selection of the verbs *ser* or *estar* within a given context is a difficult task for learners of Spanish because both verbs are equivalent to the English verb *to be*. This part is a summary of the uses of both verbs, and it includes examples to illustrate each of these uses.

Prepositions

Objective 19: To correctly use the prepositions por and para.

In Spanish, there are 19 simple prepositions and numerous prepositional groups or combinations. One of the most difficult tasks is to correctly use the prepositions *por* and *para*. As you probably know, although in many instances they are both equivalent to the English preposition *for,* they are not interchangeable in Spanish. In fact, using one rather than the other changes the meaning of the sentence in which they are used. In this part, you will find a detailed list of when these two prepositions are used. The explanations are illustrated with examples.

Examples of How to Work through Problems

As you tackle Error Recognition exercises on the AP Spanish Language Exam, it's important to work methodically and not get flustered when you encounter a difficult problem. The following examples illustrate some ways that you could think through challenging Error Recognition exercises.

Here is one example:

> Yo <u>haré</u> todo lo que <u>esté</u> a mi alcance para <u>logrando</u> mi propósito, aunque tenga que
>   [A]   [B]   [C]
>
> <u>trabajar</u> sin descanso.
>   [D]

Your thought process could follow these steps:

1. You read the entire sentence carefully. The mistake doesn't jump out at you, so you look carefully at each underlined word.

2. You know that Choice **A** is grammatically correct because the verb agrees with the subject; in addition, the context of the sentence allows for a future tense. So you're now picking from three possible choices.

3. Choice **B** is also a verb. It is in the subjunctive mode, and you realize that it is correct because the speaker is talking about undefined things. The subject of this verb is the neutral *lo,* which is replacing something (whatever may be within my reach). You have two choices left.

4. You focus now on Choice **C**. It is a verb following the preposition *para.* You have learned that after *para,* you need to use the infinitive form of the verb, not the gerund. Thus, you have found the correct answer.

5. If you think you have found the correct answer, you may ignore the rest of the choices. If you want to verify that you are selecting the correct option, however, look at the remaining option(s). In this case, it is Choice **D**. This option is a verb in the infinitive following the expression *tener que,* which you have learned is indeed the correct structure.

Now, take a look at this one.

> Cuando <u>tienes</u> más edad, <u>te</u> darás cuenta <u>de</u> que las cosas no <u>son</u> como parecen.
>   [A]   [B]   [C]   [D]

1. You read the entire sentence carefully. You are not able to locate the error immediately. Look at each option carefully.

2. You notice that Choice **A** is a verb, but you do not locate the subject immediately. Look for a clue to identify the subject.

3. Choice **B** is a pronoun. You deduce that if *te* is used as an object pronoun, the subject must be *tú.* You look back to Choice **A,** and see that the verb agrees with the subject. You think that is correct.

4. You proceed to work with Choice **C**. It is the preposition *de.* You know that this preposition is part of the expression *darse cuenta de;* therefore, you know it is correctly used.

5. Go on to Choice **D**. It is a form of the verb *ser.* You observe that the subject of this sentence is *las cosas,* so the verb from *son* agrees with it.

6. You have gone through the entire sentence and find no problem with it. Look again. Think about which choice you are not completely sure is correct. Choice **A** makes you think that there is a problem. You realize that the first action is an event that has not happened yet because it follows the conjunction *cuando*. Thus, the subjunctive is needed, but the form given in the sentence is the present tense of the indicative. You conclude that Choice **A** is the correct answer.

Sample Error Recognition Sentences: Questions, Answers, and Explanations

Below are two sets of sample Error Recognition exercises. Follow the directions and, after you finish with the first set, see "Answers and Explanations for Set 1," below. Make sure that you understand the reason for each correct answer. Repeat the process with **Set 2**.

Set 1

1. Juanito no <u>es</u> <u>un</u> médico, <u>sino</u> un excelente abogado <u>especialista</u> en casos médicos.

[A] [B]   [C]   [D]

2. Para <u>pintando</u> un <u>buen</u> cuadro, <u>el</u> artista necesita <u>mucha</u> inspiración.

[A]   [B]   [C]   [D]

3. Cuando <u>conoces</u> a Ramón <u>verás</u> que <u>es</u> un hombre muy simpático <u>e</u> inteligente.

[A]   [B]   [C]   [D]

4. A pesar de su fama, Ernesto no <u>tuvo</u> la oportunidad de <u>leer</u> <u>la</u> poema que <u>había escrito</u>

[A]   [B] [C]   [D]

   para la ocasión.

5. El partido de fútbol <u>estaba</u> <u>tan</u> lejos de mi casa que no <u>pude</u> llegar <u>a</u> tiempo para el

[A]   [B]   [C]   [D]

   comienzo.

6. Desde <u>que</u> Fernando <u>era</u> pequeño, le <u>gustaba</u> muchísimo <u>jugando</u> a la pelota.

[A]   [B]   [C]   [D]

7. <u>Siendo</u> yo niña, viví en <u>algunas</u> países donde se <u>hablaban</u> <u>varios</u> idiomas.

[A]   [B]   [C]   [D]

8. Ese <u>es</u> uno de <u>los</u> dramas que me <u>hacen</u> llorar <u>muchos</u>.

[A]   [B]   [C]   [D]

9. Aunque Carmen es <u>tan baja como</u> Begoña, <u>luce</u> más alta <u>porque</u> siempre lleva tacones

[A]   [B]   [C]

   <u>demasiados</u> altos.

[D]

10. <u>Hubieron</u> <u>varios</u> accidentes ayer, debido <u>al</u> <u>mal</u> tiempo.

[A]   [B]   [C] [D]

44

Answers and Explanations for Set 1

1. **B.** Omit the indefinite article after the verb *ser* when referring to occupations or professions.

2. **A.** Use the infinitive after the preposition *para* to denote purpose. Although *pintando* may seem attractive, it is incorrect; remember that, in Spanish, the infinitive, not the gerund, form of a verb follows a preposition.

3. **A.** Use the subjunctive after the adverb *cuando* if the action of the verb has not yet taken place.

4. **C.** *Poema* is an exception to the gender-formation rule; it is a masculine noun.

5. **A.** Use the verb *ser* instead of *estar* when referring to an event taking place.

6. **D.** After *gustar,* use only the infinitive form of the verb, not the gerund.

7. **B.** Because the noun *países* is masculine, maintain gender agreement by using *algunos* instead of *algunas*.

8. **D.** *Mucho* is an adverb in this sentence; therefore, it is invariable. The following sentence, on the other hand, contains an example of *mucho* being used as an adjective: *Hay muchos chicos que en el salón.*

9. **D.** *Demasiado* is an adverb that modifies the adjective *altos;* therefore, it is invariable.

10. **A.** Use the past tense of *hay* (*hubo*). The plural forms of the verb *haber* are never used to denote the existence or the presence of something. For example, although the subjects of the following sentences are plural, the forms of *haber* are singular: *Hay dos sillas en el salón* and *Había muchas chicas en la fiesta.*

Set 2

1. Si <u>eres</u> <u>bueno</u> estudiante, tus padres <u>estarán</u> orgullosos de <u>ti</u>.
   [A]   [B]   [C]   [D]

2. Cuando César y yo <u>llegamos</u> al restaurante, ya las puertas <u>habían estado</u> cerradas, y <u>mucha</u>
                     [A]   [B]   [C]
   gente se estaba <u>yendo</u> del lugar.
                   [D]

3. Jaimito, <u>diga</u> la verdad, aunque tu mamá te <u>castigue</u> <u>por</u> haber <u>roto</u> el jarrón chino.
            [A]   [B]   [C]   [D]

4. <u>Caminando</u> <u>hacia</u> la puerta de salida, <u>a</u> mano derecha, <u>encontrará</u> el paraguas que te traje.
   [A]   [B]   [C]   [D]

5. Si no <u>tuviste</u> dinero <u>para</u> la entrada, ¿por qué <u>quisiste</u> que te <u>trajéramos</u> al teatro?
         [A]   [B]   [C]   [D]

6. Ayer <u>estuvimos</u> <u>buscando</u> un libro que <u>tratara</u> sobre <u>las</u> sistemas de clonación.
        [A]   [B]   [C]   [D]

7. Angel, <u>pídeme</u> a Estela que <u>te</u> <u>acompañe</u> a <u>mi</u> graduación.
          [A]   [B]   [C]   [D]

8. Como no <u>conozco</u> muy bien a Margarita, no <u>haya querido</u> <u>invitarla</u> <u>para</u> la fiesta de mi
   [A]   [B]   [C]   [D]
   compromiso.

9. Si Alberto y Daniel <u>salieron</u> temprano ayer por la mañana <u>hacia</u> Madrid, seguramente
                        [A]   [B]

   <u>habrían llegado</u> <u>al</u> anochecer.
   [C]   [D]

10. Si no <u>tuvieras</u> <u>que</u> trabajar mañana, te <u>pidiera</u> que <u>fueras</u> conmigo al oculista.
           [A]   [B]   [C]   [D]

Answers and Explanations for Set 2

1. **B.** The adjective *bueno* drops the *-o* when it is placed before a masculine, singular noun. Remember that this rule applies only to masculine adjectives (*mal ejemplo*) not feminine ones (*buena respuesta*).

2. **B.** The passive voice is formed with the verb *ser*, not *estar*.

3. **A.** Read the context of the sentence: *aunque tu mama te castigue*. It will help you realize that the speaker is addressing Jaimito in an informal way. Also, because the name *Jaimito* is used, an informal tone is established. Use the informal command form *di* rather than the formal command form.

4. **D.** Use the *tu* form of the verb to agree with the pronoun *te*.

5. **A.** Use the imperfect rather than the preterit to indicate that *no tener dinero* was a continuous action in the past.

6. **D.** *Sistemas* is an exception to the gender-formation rule, it is actually a masculine, plural noun.

7. **A.** Use the third person singular object pronoun *le* because Angel is being told to ask Estela to go with him. Read the context carefully, and it will help you understand that *a Estela* explains who the indirect object of *pide* is. The error reads *pídeme,* but it should read *pídele.*

8. **B.** The use of the subjunctive is not appropriate in this case, since it is a fact (not an opinion, a desire, an order, or a doubt) that the person does not know Margarita.

9. **C.** Choice **A** is grammatically correct because *salieron* agrees in number with the subject: *Alberto y Daniel.* It is in the correct tense because the preterit is used to indicate an action that took place at a specific moment in the past, as suggested by the expression *ayer por la mañana.* Use the future perfect, not the conditional form in Choice **C,** to express probability in the past. (This distracter is appealing because it translates literally into English.)

10. **C.** Use the conditional form rather than the imperfect subjunctive in a conditional clause that uses *si* to express the conclusion.

Explaining Reading Comprehension Passages

This part of the exam is related to reading. It consists of several reading selections that are followed by a series of questions. The questions may deal with different aspects of reading, such as identifying the meaning of specific words within the context of the passage, the main idea of a passage, specific details about the setting, and the characters and their relationships; comparing and contrasting ideas; determining the author's intention; and making inferences about specific situations in the passage.

> The Reading Comprehension part of the AP Spanish Language Exam includes approximately 26 questions on about four or five passages. You should spend about 40 minutes on these questions.

Ability Tested

This part of the exam is related to reading, and it tests your ability to read, comprehend, and interpret a variety of literary and nonliterary texts from different Spanish-speaking regions.

Basic Skills Necessary

You need to be able to:

- Demonstrate control of an ample range of Spanish vocabulary, including idiomatic expressions from different regions where Spanish is spoken.

- Be familiar with reading strategies that will be useful in answering questions about passages in which you don't necessarily understand every word.

To understand the written Spanish language within the context of journalistic or literary texts, your vocabulary must be within the range expected for a third-level student of Spanish as a second language. You can greatly increase your Spanish vocabulary by reading the different types of selections found in newspapers, magazines, or the Internet.

To compensate for any lack of vocabulary, use your knowledge of Hispanic culture, your own life experience, and guessing strategies. In many cases, you will have to choose from among several different meanings for one word. Content knowledge of history, science, geography, the arts, and other subjects will also be very useful when you apply this knowledge in order to discover and understand the main ideas and details in a particular passage.

Although this section deals specifically with reading comprehension, your knowledge of Spanish grammar must be advanced enough to be able to follow the idea in any type of passage. Recognizing time sequences, the use of different verbal modes, and the correct usage of prepositions, especially in idiomatic expressions, will prove very helpful in this section of the exam.

Directions

In Part D of the Multiple Choice section, you will be working with several Reading Comprehension Passages, each followed by a group of five to eight multiple-choice questions. The directions are given to you in writing, in English and Spanish. Concentrate on the directions in the language you feel most comfortable with.

The following directions resemble what you will read during Part D of the Multiple Choice section of the AP Spanish Language Exam. It is important to be familiar with the directions of each section *before* you take the test so that you can use your time more efficiently during the test.

Read each of the following passages. After each passage, you will find a series of incomplete sentences or questions. From the four choices given, select the option that best completes the sentence or answers the question according to the passage.

Lee cada uno de los pasajes siguientes. Al final de cada pasaje encontrarás una serie de oraciones incompletas o preguntas. De las cuatro opciones que aparecen, escoge la que mejor completa cada oración o responde a cada pregunta de acuerdo con el fragmento leído.

Suggested Strategies for Reading Comprehension Passages

You can use many of the same strategies for Reading Comprehension Passages that you used for Cloze Passages. The list that is directly below is based on the strategies that are presented in the Cloze Passages section. Strategies that are specific to Reading Comprehension Passages are presented in subsections following this list.

- **Read the complete selection first.** It is important to perform a first reading without attempting to answer any of the questions. Reading the entire passage will give you an idea of what the passage is all about, what tense predominates throughout the narration, and what different characters appear.

- **Use your existing knowledge of the world.** Once you read the passage the first time, think about what you know about the topic or the experiences presented. For example, if you recognize that the selection is about somebody who traveled to Spain, you can use any traveling experience you've had, as well as any cultural knowledge you have about Spain.

- **Recognize cognates.** By this time, you may already know that there are many Spanish words that resemble and have the same meaning as English words. These words are called *cognates.* When you are able to recognize cognates, it is easier for you to get the general meaning of the passage and to better understand the questions and the choices.

- **Identify words by examining word formation.** In Spanish, words are grouped into *families of words.* This means that, from one simple word, other words can be formed by adding prefixes and suffixes. For example, the word *decente* (a cognate of the English *decent*) is an adjective that can be used to form other words, such as *indecente* (English *indecent*), *decencia* (English *decency*), and so on. By recognizing words that belong to the same family, you can figure out the meaning of unfamiliar words by relating them to words you do know.

- **Use the context of the passage to figure out the meaning of unfamiliar words.** When you read a text, the word *context* refers to the words that surround an unfamiliar word. The context is very useful because it limits the meaning of a word. By using the context, you can eliminate some of your options.

- **Identify the time sequence.** This strategy is important in order to be able to follow the order of events and to answer questions that deal with cause and effect.

Skim and Scan

Skimming is a technique that will help you to get a general idea of the content of a passage without doing a complete and close reading. By skimming, you will be able to predict what the passage is about before you do a close reading for details. During the skimming process, you do not need to read every word in the passage. *Scanning* is different from skimming because, while scanning, you are looking for specific information. This technique is useful when you need to find specific details, such as the definition of a term or a given situation in a sequence of narrated events.

Identify What Type of Passage You Are Reading

Passages can be narrative, descriptive, informative, or argumentative. If you are able to determine what type of text you are dealing with from the beginning, you will have an idea of what elements you will find within the passage.

- **Narrative:** A narrative text is a text where a series of events are described. You can tell that you have a narrative text when you find the following elements: characters, actions, setting, and time. If you are working with a narrative text, you know that you are going to find many verbs in different sequences, that one or more characters will be executing those actions, and so on.

- **Descriptive:** A descriptive text represents people, animals, places, or things, enabling the reader to "see" what is being described. You can tell that you have a descriptive text when there is no action and abundant adjectives make the description more detailed and vivid. If you have a descriptive text, some of the questions may ask for specific characteristics of what is being described. If two or more things are described, some questions may ask for a comparison.

- **Informative:** An informative text gives specific information about a specific issue. Informative texts may be similar to newspaper articles. You can tell that you have an informative text when you spot objective information that may help answer the journalistic questions of "who," "what," "when," "where," "why," and "how." Description and narration may be present, but they are there only to give objective information. If you have an informative text, the questions will deal with the specific data the text provides.

- **Argumentative:** Most of the time, an argumentative text presents a theory about or a position on a given issue. You can tell that you have an argumentative text when you notice that there is a thesis on a specific topic and the author presents a series of elements to defend this thesis. If you have an argumentative text, the questions will be related to the author's position and to the different ideas the author is presenting to defend that position.

Make Inferences

Many of the questions that follow the Reading Comprehension Passages require that you make inferences from what you read. Making inferences is equivalent to reading between the lines, or getting ideas that are implicit rather than explicit. To make successful inferences, you need to use logic to connect ideas that may not be sufficiently developed in the text; these may include the narrator's comments about a specific character, details given in a dialogue without much explanation, and so on.

For example, by reading the information given in this fragment: *Ahora, debido a las grandes obras de artes que ha adquirido recientemente el museo, las horas de visita se han extendido en los fines de semana para poder acomodar a los numerosos visitantes que empiezan a conocer la importancia del mismo,* you may infer that not many people visited the museum before the museum acquired the masterpieces, even though this information does not appear explicitly. Pay attention to the following elements in the sentence when making this inference:

- The word *ahora* lets you now something is different than it was before.

- The hours are extended to accommodate more people.

- People are beginning (*empiezan*) to understand the importance of the museum. This tells you that, before, it was not very well-known.

Identify Transitional Words

Knowing the meaning of Spanish transitional words and phrases is vital to following the ideas in a passage. They are used to logically connect ideas, and have different purposes, such as to explain, illustrate, compare, contrast, and so on.

The following table is a refresher on some of the more common transitional words in Spanish.

Spanish Word	English Definition	Example in a Sentence
a pesar de eso	in spite of	Le dije a Luis que no saliera y *a pesar de eso*, lo hizo.
además	besides	No tengo dinero; *además* está lloviendo, por eso no saldré.
por el contrario	on the contrary	Rosa es estudiosa; su hermana, *por el contrario* es muy perezosa.
sin embargo	however	No tiene trabajo, *sin embargo* gasta muchísimo dinero.
por eso	for this reason	El coche de Rita está roto, *por eso* la llevo a la escuela.
puesto que	since	*Puesto que* no te interesa el libro, regálamelo.
por consiguiente	therefore	No has sacado buenas notas, *por consiguiente*, tu madre va a castigarte durante esta semana.
por lo tanto	therefore	Mi hermana va a salir, *por lo tanto,* tengo que cuidar al bebé.
con tal (de) que	as long as	Te dejo usar el coche *con tal de que* lo cuides.
a fin de que	so that	*A fin de que* puedas comer temprano, voy a empezar a cocinar ahora mismo.
en seguida	at once	Dame ese vaso *en seguida*, antes de que lo rompas.
en otras palabras	in other words	Lola no hace la tarea y falta mucho a la escuela, *en otras palabras,* es una pésima estudiante.
en resumen	in short	*En resumen*, Ramón perdió la billetera sin darse cuenta.
por último	finally	Me levanté, desayuné y *por último* salí de la casa.

Understand Any Literary Figures of Speech

Some of the passages in this section of the exam are taken from short stories and novels; therefore, they may contain literary figures of speech, such as metaphors and similes. When reading a fictional text, it is important to identify such figures of speech because they may change the meaning of words that you think you know. For example, if you read: *María tenía los cabellos de oro,* you may be able to interpret the meaning of the sentence literally because you know the meaning of each word, but you also need to realize that this is a metaphor that relates to the color of Maria's hair—blond. Maria's hair is not literally made of gold (*oro*).

Here are some more examples of the types of figures of speech that you may encounter:

- **Simile:** A figure of speech that presents an explicit comparison. In Spanish, a simile generally contains the words *como* or *cual*. When you encounter a simile, it is important to decipher the figurative meaning of the element used for comparison. For example, in the following sentence: *Maria es como una abeja, nunca deja de trabajar,* it is important to know the meaning of *abeja* (honey bee) because the insect is used to reinforce a characteristic of Maria's personality: She is a hardworking person.

- **Symbol:** Broadly, a symbol is anything that signifies, or stands for, something else. To interpret passages that contain symbolism, you must make use of your own life experience and the knowledge you have acquired about symbols in other classes, such as language arts, social studies, or arts. For example, if you read: *Pedro, eres mi cruz,* you immediately know that you are in the presence of figurative language. Once again, your vocabulary is extremely important. The word *cruz* (cross) is being used symbolically to mean suffering, sacrifice, and so on. You can infer that the speaker does not have an easy relationship with Pedro because he causes the speaker strong suffering.

- **Analogy:** A comparison of similar things, with the purpose of explaining an unfamiliar situation by comparing it to a familiar one. For example, when you compare the functioning of the heart to a pump, you are making an analogy.

- **Personification:** A figure of speech in which animals and inanimate objects are attributed human characteristics. For example, you may encounter the following sentence in a passage: *Margarita estaba muy triste, y veía como la tarde lloraba también.* Although the verb *llorar* (to cry) is an action exclusive to human beings, by attributing it to the afternoon, the author conveys that it was raining. Using *lloraba* instead of *llovía* is more effective because it is a verb that is in accordance with Margarita's feelings: *estaba muy triste* (she was very sad).

- **Euphemism:** An expression used to substitute for another of equivalent meaning but that is ruder or in bad taste. With the prevalence of political correctness, numerous euphemisms creep into everyday conversation. For example: *La tercera edad* is used instead of *vejez* to refer to old age, and *madre política* is used instead of *suegra* to refer to one's mother-in-law.

- **Hyperbole:** An obvious exaggeration. It is normally used to create humor or to add emphasis. Sometimes, hyperbole is used in everyday language. For example, in the following sentence: *La fiesta de María estaba animadísima, todo el mundo estaba allí,* the author uses the expression *todo el mundo* to emphasize that there were a lot of people at the party, or that everybody in the author's circle of friends was there. Obviously, the entire world was not there.

- **Metonomy:** A figure of speech that substitutes a person, object, or idea for another person or thing closely related to it. For example, in the following sentence: *Ayer se robaron un Velázquez del Museo del Prado,* merely the name of the painter is used rather than the phrase *un cuadro de Velázquez.*

An Example of How to Read a Passage

This section presents a passage similar to one you may encounter on the AP Spanish Language Exam. The passage is broken up by text that explains what you should notice about the passage as you read it.

No parece posible que haya pasado tanto tiempo ya, pero fue en 1992 que nos enteramos que ya no podíamos quedarnos en Montevideo. Los jefes de mi papá habían venido desde los Estados Unidos para decirnos que ya no había fondos para sostener a nuestra familia, y que debíamos de regresar a los Estados Unidos dentro de tres meses. ¡Sólo tres meses! Mis padres, sabiendo que nuestros corazones se quebrarían, decidieron esperar una semana para darnos las malas noticias.

When you read this paragraph, you should notice that the author does not feel that so much time has passed. This idea is conveyed by the expression *no parece posible que haya pasado tanto tiempo.* This expression is important to take into consideration because it helps you grasp the author's feeling about the story he or she is going to narrate. It also gives you a clue about what type of passage this is: a narration. Also notice that, in this passage, you learn that the family has been living in a foreign country for a while (you do not know exactly how long), and you may infer that the kids were happy living there because the parents did not want to let them know immediately that they had to leave.

Juanito tenía 12 años; yo casi era quinceañera. Nuestra niñez la habíamos pasado en los barrios sombrados de Carrasco, en la campiña tranquila de San Gregorio, y en las playas hermosas de Punta del Este. Asistíamos a un colegio internacional, y allí teníamos amigos de cada rincón del mundo. Los jefes americanos nos habían prometido que yo terminaría la secundaria con esos amigos. Pero ahora sabíamos que esa promesa no la iban a cumplir. El próximo día, Juanito y yo fuimos al colegio e intentamos ser valientes.

Even though this is a narrative passage, in this particular paragraph, the author briefly describes her brother and herself. You now know that the author is a female because she uses the word *quinceañera,* which is feminine, to refer to herself. She also describes her childhood, which took place in the different sceneries of Uruguay. You see that the family probably moved around the country, but the author's memories are all positive, as implied by her choice of words, especially the adjectives: *sombrados, tranquila,* and *hermosas.* It is in this paragraph that you can reach the conclusion that the family spent quite some time in Uruguay because the author speaks of spending her childhood there.

Esa noche, Juan no regresó a casa a tiempo. Yo, mirando la tele, ni siquiera me di cuenta. Pero mi mamá no tardó en preocuparse. "¿Dónde está Juanito?" me preguntó. "El ensayo nunca dura hasta esta hora."

"No sé, Mamita," le respondí. "Seguro que ya está por llegar. No te preocupes." Y, con esa indiferencia al peligro característica de la juventud, seguí con mi telenovela.

De pronto, sonó el timbre. Cuando abrí la puerta, mi hermanito me dijo, en una voz muy pequeña, "Me han robado." Incrédula, me empecé a reír. Y Juanito comenzó a llorar.

Ese día, nuestra familia cambió para siempre. Los libros, la mochila, las zapatillas . . . esas cosas las podíamos reemplazar fácilmente. Pero la inocencia . . . la inocencia es preciosa, y cuando te la roban, jamás la puedes recobrar.

In the last paragraphs of the passage, the author changes again to narration, and she focuses on a particular night: the night of the day she and her brother found out their family would have to leave Uruguay before they had planned to. The author narrates the story of her brother being robbed, an event not related to the departure of the family from Uruguay. The narration is interrupted with brief dialogues that add more veracity to the story. The incident fits in with the narration because both situations cause the kids to lose a little bit of their innocence as they discover the ugly part of life and that not everything is good, nice, or happy. The author emphasizes the fact that, once a person has a bad experience, that person is never again the same.

Now try to answer these sample questions:

---

1. De la lectura podemos inferir que para los niños, vivir en Montevideo era una experiencia

    A. aburrida.

    B. placentera.

    C. desagradable.

    D. sin importancia.

You already know that your vocabulary is important in this type of exercise. Also, remember that questions appear in chronological order, so, to answer this question, go to the beginning of the passage. The question mentions the word *Montevideo;* this may help you locate the information that is necessary in order to answer the question correctly. The question also tells you that the answer is not explicit in the passage because it says *podemos inferir;* therefore, the answer is "hidden." The word *experiencia* is a cognate, and the verb *vivir* is a high-frequency word that does not present difficulty in regard to meaning. The question is, "How did the kids feel about living in Montevideo?" If you go to the first paragraph, you see that the parents did not want to tell the kids that they would have to leave the city because this *les quebraría el corazón* (would break their hearts). You can then infer that living in Montevideo was a pleasure for them, so the correct answer is Choice **B**.

---

2. ¿Por qué tenía la familia que irse de Montevideo?

    A. Porque el papá estaba enfermo del corazón.

    B. Porque ya la niña iba a cumplir 15 años.

    C. Porque el país estaba en guerra con los Estados Unidos.

    D. Porque la situación financiera no lo permitía.

This question is asking for a reason or an explanation. The vocabulary in the question does not present serious difficulties because most of the words in it are high frequency. Go back to the first paragraph to see if you find the answer there, since the paragraph begins by talking about the fact that the family must leave the city. In the second sentence, you see that the author mentions that someone came from the United States with some news. The news concerns their situation in Montevideo: There are no more funds to support the family, so they must return to the United States. Now go back and look at all the options and try to identify at least one word that is related to money. In Choice **D,** you see the word *financiera,* a word related to the English *finance.* Thus, you know that Choice **D** is the correct answer. Choice **A** and Choice **B** may distract you because they contain words present in the reading: *corazón* and *15* (related to *quinceañera*), but these words are not related to the reason the family had to leave Montevideo.

---

3. De acuerdo con el pasaje, podemos afirmar que la estancia de los niños en Uruguay había sido

    A. breve.

    B. extensa.

    C. quieta.

    D. temporal.

To understand this question, it is important to know the meaning of the word *estancia.* This word is related to the verb *estar,* and it means *stay.* The four choices are adjectives to modify that noun. The question is, "Was their stay in Uruguay long, brief, quiet, or temporary?" If you go back to the second paragraph, you see that the author mentions that she and her brother spent their childhood there; therefore, you know that it was not a brief stay, so you can eliminate Choice **A.** And even though the author uses adjectives that would make you think of quietness, it is clear that the family visited or lived in different places in Uruguay; thus, you may eliminate Choice **C.** Be cautious with Choice **D.** The family's stay in Uruguay was not temporary because, even though they may have moved from one place to another, they were in Uruguay itself for quite a long period of time. This knowledge brings you to the correct answer: Choice **B.**

Sample Reading Comprehension Passages: Questions, Answers, and Explanations

Below are two sample Reading Comprehension Passages. Follow the directions, and, after you finish with the first sample, see "Answers and Explanations for Sample 1" (below). Make sure that you understand the reason for each correct answer. Repeat the process with Sample 2.

Sample 1

    La desaparición de especies animales, aun de aquellas que parecían más fuertes y resistentes a los cambios de ambiente, es un fenómeno muy antiguo pero del que sólo hoy empezamos a darnos cuenta con cierta claridad. En los museos de ciencias naturales vemos esqueletos de animales prehistóricos como mamuts, plesiosaurios o dinosaurios, que por evolución de la especie misma, por el cambio de condiciones ambientales o por la aparición de rivales más feroces, han dejado de existir en los lugares que parecían ser su "habitat" ideal.

    De los dinosaurios han quedado magníficos exponentes en el Dinosaur National Monument en Tejas, el mejor depósito de fósiles de este tipo. Allí los paleontólogos han encontrado restos de 14 especies de dinosaurios, algunos de los cuales alcanzaban sólo el tamaño de una gallina, mientras que otros excedían en extensión y altura a todos los animales conocidos. Pero no hace falta visitar Tejas para ver restos similares. De allí se han sacado más de 30 esqueletos completos que se encuentran ahora en diferentes museos del mundo.

Muchos animales prehistóricos dejaron de existir debido a un cambio radical de la estructura de la tierra. Los desbordamientos de mares, la solidificación de tierras húmedas y las terribles alteraciones de la temperatura modificaron el ambiente y eliminaron las fuentes de alimentación de ciertas especies. Después de muchas eras geológicas, apareció el ser humano, una nueva seria amenaza para muchas especies animales.

En poco tiempo el hombre ha llegado a ser el animal grande más numeroso de la tierra. Hace 10.000 años había sólo 10 millones de individuos en el mundo entero. Hace 2.000 años esa población aumentó a 300 millones. En el año 1980 se contaban unos cuatro billones de seres y para fines del siglo esa cifra habrá aumentado en un 50%. El efecto de esta superpoblación humana sobre la vida animal es cada vez más profundo y grave.

Todos los animales necesitan, para mantenerse, alimento, agua y un lugar dónde vivir. Cada especie tiene un diferente habitat ideal, pero puede adaptarse a ligeras variaciones del ambiente. Sin embargo, hay animales que por su evolución sólo pueden comer cierta clase de frutas o las hojas de un tipo especial de árbol. Por eso quitarles de repente ese alimento o modificarles radicalmente su habitat especial, como se ha hecho muchas veces, es lo mismo que exterminarlos. El ser humano, por su superior inteligencia, constituye la única especie animal que ha podido adaptarse a toda clase de ambientes. Pero al extenderse por toda la tierra, ha ejercido una negativa influencia sobre la vida preexistente en esas regiones.

1. El pasaje afirma que en realidad la extinción de los animales

   A. nunca se ha investigado.

   B. es más antigua de lo que creemos.

   C. es un hecho sin importancia.

   D. se debe solamente a cambios ambientales.

2. Según los fósiles encontrados, ¿cómo eran los dinosaurios?

   A. De diferentes tamaños.

   B. Parecidos a las gallinas.

   C. De 14 metros de altura.

   D. De 30 tipos diferentes.

3. ¿Qué causó la desaparición de muchas especies prehistóricas?

   A. La aparición del ser humano.

   B. La competencia con otros animales.

   C. Un cambio drástico en la estructura terrestre.

   D. La falta de evolución de las mismas.

4. ¿Por qué representa el ser humano un peligro para el resto de la vida animal?

    A. Por la rapidez con que se multiplica.

    B. Por su inteligencia.

    C. Por su falta de adaptación.

    D. Por su habilidad para evolucionar.

5. ¿Qué problema específico tienen algunas especies de animales?

    A. No soportan ciertas temperaturas.

    B. No tienen un habitat ideal.

    C. No pueden cambiar su dieta.

    D. No tienen inteligencia para sobrevivir.

Answers and Explanations for Sample 1

1. B. Animal extinction has occurred since ancient times (*la desaparición de especies animales . . . es un fenómeno muy antiguo*). After you discover that this passage is about science and ecology, and you bring forth the knowledge you have about those subjects, you can easily eliminate Choices **A** and Choice **C**. Now take a look at the word *antigua* and notice its similarity to the English word *antique*. Although *antigua* and *antique* are not exact cognates, they do have the same meaning. You know that the adjective *antique* means very old, so you know that the correct answer is Choice **B**.

2. A. Dinosaurs were animals of different sizes (*algunos de los cuales alcanzaban sólo el tamaño de una gallina mientras que otros excedían en extensión y altura a todos los animales conocidos*). Remember that the order of the questions follows the progression of the passage. In this passage, you find a clue to the correct answer in the second paragraph. Disregard Choice **C** because you can conclude that *tipo* is a synonym of *especies* in the text. Your background knowledge will come in handy when you remember that not all dinosaurs were extremely large animals, as Choice **D** states.

3. C. The disappearance of many prehistoric animals was caused by a drastic change in the Earth's structure (*muchos animales prehistóricos dejaron de existir debido a un cambio radical de la estructura de la tierra*). *Drástico* and *radical* are cognates that will help you focus on the correct answer. Your knowledge of history will allow you to eliminate Choice **A** as a fact that happened much later on, as stated in the last line of the paragraph: *después de muchas eras geológicas*.

4. A. Human beings present a danger to the rest of the animals on the planet because of the alarming rate at which we reproduce (*el efecto de esta superpoblación humana sobre la vida animal es cada vez más profundo y grave*).

5. A. Some species cannot change their eating habits, and this creates a problem for them (*hay animales que por su evolución sólo pueden comer cierta clase de frutas o las hojas de un tipo especial de árbol*). Here, the important word is *comer.* If you relate *comer* to *dieta* (a cognate of the English *diet*), you will be able to choose the correct answer. The other choices contain cognates that will help you in the elimination process.

Sample 2

Aunque muchos países han experimentado el fenómeno de la inmigración, el número de personas que han emigrado a los Estados Unidos supera el de casi todas las demás naciones en conjunto. Como resultado de la inmigración, los Estados Unidos cuenta hoy con más judíos que Israel, con más individuos de origen irlandés que Irlanda y más de origen lituano que Lituania. En Nueva York, Chicago, Filadelfia y Los Ángeles podemos encontrar gente de casi cualquier nacionalidad y cultura, viviendo a veces en barrios donde la primera lengua no es la inglesa.

El problema que tal diversidad étnica presenta es el de mantener la variedad cultural sin lesionar la unidad nacional. Y el milagro de los Estados Unidos es precisamente haber podido crear cierto balance entre ambos extremos. El impacto social y cultural de la inmigración constante y en ciertos momentos masiva se evidencia en muchos aspectos de la vida norteamericana. Si por un lado la tendencia del extranjero es la americanizarse, por el otro estos grupos raciales y nacionales modifican la realidad norteamericana con ideas y actitudes traídas de otros países.

Los extremos del proceso aparecen claramente expresados en frases del lenguaje corriente que todos conocemos. La imagen de América como crisol o *melting pot* en que las razas y las nacionalidades se han fundido como los metales de una aleación implica la idea de una fusión total y nueva. Pero a esa imagen del crisol hay que oponer la imagen de América como olla o *stew pot*. En ella se cuecen alimentos de distinto color y sabor pero cada uno conserva mucho de su naturaleza original. Esta imagen de la olla acentúa el carácter pluralístico de una sociedad que es más una vinculación libre de grupos que una integración total.

A primera vista, estas dos imágenes parecen contradictorias. Sin embargo, no lo son porque representan etapas sucesivas de un mismo fenómeno o proceso. Cuanto más antiguo es el grupo inmigratorio, más fácil es la integración completa. Desde luego, resulta aún más fácil cuando se trata de grupos inmigratorios nacionales y no raciales. Constituyen grupos nacionales aquellos que derivan de un país y mantienen su lengua y sus costumbres, pero que son racialmente semejantes a los hombres del país al que emigran. Los grupos raciales, en cambio, se diferencian del núcleo central por características físicas, además de las propias de los grupos nacionales.

1. Según este pasaje, ¿en qué país es mayor la inmigración?

   A. En Israel.

   B. En los Estados Unidos.

   C. En Irlanda.

   D. En Lituania.

2. ¿Qué problema presenta la variedad étnica?

    A. Mantener la lengua oficial.

    B. Encontrar un equilibrio entre lo nacional y lo extranjero.

    C. Aceptar la variedad cultural.

    D. Dañar la unión nacional.

3. ¿Qué efecto tiene la inmigración continua y masiva en los Estados Unidos?

    A. La desaparición de la lengua oficial.

    B. La desintegración de la población nacional.

    C. La modificación de la realidad nacional.

    D. La discriminación racial.

4. ¿A qué se refieren las palabras *crisol* y *olla* dentro del contexto de la lectura?

    A. A dos comidas extranjeras.

    B. A dos procesos culturales.

    C. A dos versiones de América.

    D. A dos ideas multiculturales.

5. ¿Cómo se consigue el carácter pluralístico de la sociedad norteamericana?

    A. Manteniendo separadas las variantes étnicas.

    B. Preparando una aleación.

    C. Rechazando la inmigración.

    D. Prohibiendo la americanización.

6. ¿Qué rasgo tienen los grupos nacionales semejante a los del país donde emigran?

    A. La lengua.

    B. La raza.

    C. Las costumbres.

    D. La cultura.

Answers and Explanations for Sample 2

When you read this passage, think of any information you may have acquired about the phenomenon of immigration in your social studies and English classes, from current news, or from your own experience. You may know of or have personally met immigrants. You probably have a lot of outside knowledge about this topic to help you with this passage.

1. **B.** More people have emigrated to the United States than to almost all other countries combined (*el número de personas que han emigrado a los Estados Unidos supera el de casi todas las demás naciones en conjunto*).

2. **B.** Ethnic variety presents the challenge of maintaining a balance between what's national and what's foreign (*el problema que tal diversidad étnica presenta es el de mantener la variedad cultural sin lesionar la unidad nacional*).

3. **C.** Immigration changes the national reality in the United States (*estos grupos raciales y nacionales modifican la realidad norteamericana*).

4. **B.** *Crisol* (melting pot) and *olla* (stew pot) refer to the cultural processes that immigrants experience when they move to a new place.

5. **A.** Different national or racial groups interact freely with one another while maintaining their unique identities (*esta imagen de la olla acentúa el carácter pluralístico de una sociedad que es más una vinculación libre de grupos que una integración total*).

6. **B.** Members of national groups are similar in appearance to the men and women native to the country to which they have emigrated (*grupos nacionales . . . son racialmente semejantes a los hombres del país al que emigran*).

> **The Web site www.cliffsnotes.com/extras contains lots of additional content that will help you tackle Reading Comprehension passages.**

Explaining Paragraph Fill-Ins

Paragraph Fill-Ins are the first part of the Free Response section of the AP Spanish Language Exam. The Free Response section tests your writing and speaking abilities, as well as your active usage of Spanish grammar and vocabulary. Within each of this section's two main parts (Part A: Writing Skills and Part B: Speaking Skills), different types of exercises test different skills and require you to perform different tasks. A total of five exercises (three for writing and two for speaking) are included in this section of the exam, and you will have a total of 80 minutes to complete both the writing and the speaking parts. The Free Response section accounts for 50% of your overall AP Spanish Language Exam score.

The Writing Skills part of the exam consists of three different exercises:

- One Paragraph Fill-Ins exercise
- One set of Discrete Sentence Fill-Ins
- One Essay

The time allotted for the entire Writing Skills part is 60 minutes. During this time, you can work on all three Writing Skills exercises. This part makes up 30% of your total AP Spanish Language Exam score. Paragraph Fill-Ins and Discrete Sentence Fill-Ins together account for 7.5% of your score, and the Essay for 22.5%.

Paragraph Fill-Ins

This part of the exam addresses your knowledge of Spanish grammatical structures. You will be given a passage containing approximately 10 blanks. You must fill in the blanks with the correct form of the words given in parentheses in order for the paragraph to read correctly, logically, and grammatically. The words you fill in must be spelled correctly, with the correct accent marks, to receive credit.

There are approximately 10 Paragraph Fill-In questions on any given version of the AP Spanish Language Exam. You should spend about 8 minutes on these questions.

Ability Tested

This part is related to language structure and syntax, and it measures not only your knowledge of Spanish grammar patterns, but also your control of certain rules, such as the plural and feminine formations of nouns and adjectives, the accentuation of words, and so on. Your spelling skills are also tested in this exercise.

Basic Skills Necessary

You need to be able to:

- Demonstrate control of complex Spanish structures.
- Be familiar with accentuation rules.
- Be able to spell difficult words.
- Recognize word types, such as adjectives, adverbs, and pronouns.

In this exercise, you are most likely to encounter answers that present some kind of difficulty in usage, spelling, accentuation, or word form. Among the most common responses are:

- Irregular verbs that may require changes in the stem for certain tenses. Remember that most irregular verbs are used rather frequently (including *hacer, tener, salir, poner,* and many others).
- Regular verbs that require spelling changes in order to maintain a specific sound that is present in the infinitive. For example, all verbs ending in *-car, -gar,* and *-zar* undergo spelling changes in the first person singular of the preterit. Many of these types of verbs are used frequently in both written and spoken Spanish (including *educar, sacar,* and *tocar; jugar, pegar,* and *entregar;* and *empezar, almorzar,* and *tropezar*).
- Verbal forms that require a written accent. If you study and review verb patterns, you will know that many forms of the preterit, as well as all the imperfect forms of verbs ending in *-er* and *-ir,* require written accent marks (for example, *salí* and *salía).*
- Adjectives placed before a singular masculine noun, which require the omission of the final *-o,* such as *primer, tercer,* and so on.
- Plural nouns that require spelling changes, such as *lápices* (from *lápiz*).
- Adverbs that are easily confused with adjectives and that do not require gender/number agreement, such as *demasiado,* which remains invariable in front of an adjective (for example, *Rosa es demasiado alta para su edad*).
- Object pronouns that require you to identify the nouns they refer to in the context of the passage.

In Part V, you can find a summary of grammatical topics that you need to master in order to be successful on this part of the exam.

Directions

In Part A.1 of the Free Response section, you will be working with a passage from which about 10 words have been omitted. The words necessary to complete the passage are given to you numbered and in parentheses. You must change the form of the word to make it logically and grammatically correct within the context of the passage, and write it in the space provided. The directions are given to you in writing, in English and Spanish. Concentrate on the directions in the language you feel most comfortable with.

The following directions resemble what you will read during Part A.1 of the Free Response section of the AP Spanish Exam. It is important to be familiar with the directions of each section *before* you take the test so that you can use your time more efficiently during the test.

Read the following passage completely. Then read it a second time, and write on the line provided after each number the appropriate form of the word given in parentheses that will complete the fragment correctly, logically, and grammatically. Correct spelling and accent marks are necessary to receive credit. Only one word is allowed in each blank. In some instances, you may find that a change of the word in parentheses is not necessary, but you still need to write the word in the blank to receive credit.

Lee el siguiente pasaje completamente. Luego vuélvelo a leer y escribe en la línea de la derecha, después de cada número, la forma apropiada de la palabra que está entre paréntesis, para completar el fragmento de forma correcta y lógica. La ortografía y los acentos deben ser correctos para recibir crédito. Solamente se permite una palabra para cada espacio. En algunas ocasiones es posible que la palabra sugerida no necesite ningún cambio; si es así, debes escribir la palabra en el espacio en blanco para recibir crédito.

Suggested Strategies for Paragraphs Fill-Ins

In this part of the exam, your success depends on your knowledge of Spanish grammar and your control of spelling and accentuation; therefore, you should be very well acquainted with Spanish grammar, spelling, and accentuation rules. Also, the reading strategies suggested in previous sections will come in handy because, in this exercise, your answers need to be correct within a particular context.

Remember that each blank requires only *one* Spanish word, so you should not write answers such as the reflexive *se cayó*. Make sure to spell and accentuate each word correctly. Finally, although some words may not require any change, you must write the word in the space provided to receive credit. You will not receive credit for answers such as "stays the same," "no change," and so on.

There may be cases, especially with verbs, in which more than one word form may be correct. In these cases, you may choose to write one form or all, but if one of the multiple answers you write is incorrect, you will lose credit for that question. To avoid this problem, just write the form that you feel is the best, or the one that presents the least spelling and/or accentuation difficulties. For example, if you know that either *hablara* or *hablase* would be a correct answer, go with *hablara,* which is easier to spell than *hablase* because of the potential confusion between *c* and *s*.

The following list goes into more detail on effective strategies.

- **Read the passage completely.** Besides getting a general idea of what the passage is about, you may come across other clues, such as the tense used, the subject of a sentence, and so on. Identifying cognates and frequently used words will help you get an idea of the content of the passage.

- **Look at each missing word individually.** When you look at a word omitted from the paragraph, notice what type of word it is and, from there, determine what to do with it. For example, if you notice that the omitted word is a verb, immediately try to identify the subject of the verb and determine what tense you must use in order to keep the sequence of verbs grammatically and logically correct. The type of word that has been omitted determines the rest of the process you will follow to get the correct answer.

- **Notice the tense in which the passage is narrated.** Depending on the tense that predominates in the paragraph, you will be able to determine the tense of the missing verbs. Remember that, if you observe that the passage is written in the past tense, your answers will most likely be in the preterit or the imperfect of the indicative or subjunctive modes. Look for a sequence of actions that may help you determine the tense required in your answer. For example, in the following sentence, if you identify *encendió* and *salió* as parts of a sequence of actions, you can determine that *abrazar* must be in the preterit, too: *Ana (abrazar) la idea sin pensarlo, encendió la luz del pasillo y salió sin ser vista.* Compound tenses are not possible answers because you are allowed to write only one word.

- **Determine the point of view of the narration.** Knowing whether the passage is narrated in first or third person will help you select the correct forms of adjectives, verbs, and pronouns because you will know exactly to whom (or what) those words are related. If your passage includes a dialogue, look for clues in the context to determine whether to use the formal *usted* or the informal *tú* in your answer.

- **Identify any existing relation between the omitted word and the words that surround it.** This is one of the most valuable strategies because a word in a paragraph will take the form needed to agree with other words that relate to it. For example, if you know that your answer is a form of an adjective, you can determine the correct form to use by finding out what noun it modifies. For example, with *las flores (azul),* the answer is the feminine plural form of the adjective *azul.* Because *azul* has only one ending for the feminine and masculine forms, you will need to remember that *-es* is the correct plural form for this adjective. If your answer is a verb, you must first establish a time sequence, then determine the subject of the sentence, to arrive at the correct form of the word. Look for other clues as well: If the omitted word is an adjective, and you're not sure about the gender of the noun that it modifies, see whether an article accompanies the noun in question. This article will give away the gender and number of the noun.

- **Check your spelling on each answer.** Misspelled words won't earn you credit, so pay close attention to the word given in parentheses and make only the necessary spelling changes. For example, if your omitted word is a form of the adjective *bueno,* make sure that you write your answer with a *b,* not a *v.*

- **Identify predictable spelling changes.** This strategy applies mostly to verbs. In Spanish, verbs are classified into groups that follow certain patterns. Be familiar with the changes different groups of verbs undergo so that your spelling errors are kept to a minimum. For example, know that, in verbs that finish in *-ucir*, you must insert a *z* before the *c* in the first person singular of the present tense (so from *traducir*, you get *traduzco*). Memorizing some of the most common verbs and the changes they take is helpful.

Sample Paragraph Fill-Ins: Questions, Answers, and Explanations

Set 1

Desde (1) momento fue Ena más poderosa que yo; me esclavizó, me sujetó a ella. Me hizo maravillarme con su vitalidad, con su fuerza, con su belleza. Según iba (2), yo la contemplaba con el mismo asombro que si (3) crecer en un cuerpo todos (4) anhelos no realizados. Yo (5) con la salud, con la alegría, con el éxito personal que me había sido negado y (6) vi crecer en Ena desde que (7) una niñita. Usted sabe, Andrea, que mi hija es como (8) irradiación de fuerza y vida . . . Comprendí, humildemente, el sentido de mi existencia al ver en ella (9) mis orgullos, mis fuerzas y mis deseos mejores de perfección realizarse (10) mágicamente.

1. _____ (aquel)

2. _____ (crecer)

3. _____ (ver)

4. _____ (mi)

5. _____ (soñar)

6. _____ (lo)

7. _____ (ser)

8. _____ (un)

9. _____ (todo)

10. _____ (tanto)

Answers and Explanations for Set 1

1. **aquel.** *Aquel* remains in the masculine, singular form to show agreement.

2. **creciendo.** Use the gerund combination of *ser* + gerund.

3. **viera/viese.** Use the imperfect subjunctive in a dependent noun clause when the verb in the main clause is in the imperfect.

4. **mis.** The possessive must show agreement in number. The word following the blank is *anhelos,* a plural noun. You can arrive at this conclusion even if you are not familiar with the meaning of the word *anhelos* (which means *wishes* or *desires*).

5. **soñaba.** Use the imperfect to describe continuous actions in the past.

6. **los.** The article must show agreement in number. This is a direct object pronoun that refers to the nouns *la salud, la alegría,* and *el éxito personal.*

7. **era.** Use the imperfect to describe continuous conditions in the past.

8. **una.** The definite article must show agreement in gender and number. Nouns that end in *-ción* are feminine. Knowing this rule of grammar will help you score well, whether you are familiar with the meaning of the word or not.

9. **todos.** *Todo* must show agreement in number.

10. **tan.** *Tanto* is reduced when modifying an adverb.

Set 2

Recorrió su cotidiano itinerario y se (1) con pocos transeúntes, el tormentoso ambiente y la lluvia hacía (2) el caminar por las calles. (3) iban con prisa. La tarde era cada vez más (4) e invitaba al recogimiento en el hogar. La lluvia, de continuar así, (5) ser torrencial en (6) rato. Ganaba ya la calle donde estaba (7) su casa, junto a una vieja mezquita que los cristianos, tras la conquista de la ciudad, a finales del siglo XI, (8) en iglesia, la iglesia de Santo Tomé, cuando el (9) relámpago de la tormenta cruzó el cielo, (10) todo por un instante.

1. _____ (cruzar)

2. _____ (incómodo)

3. _____ (Todo)

4. _____ (destemplado)

5. _____ (poder)

6. _____ (poco)

7. _____ (emplazado)

8. _____ (convertir)

9. _____ (primero)

10. _____ (iluminar)

Answers and Explanations for Set 2

1. **cruzó.** Continue using the preterit to indicate an action completed in the past. This verb is part of a sequence of actions in the past; in this case, there are two actions in the sequence: *recorrió* and *se cruzó*.

2. **incómodo.** *Incómodo* remains in the masculine singular form to show agreement.

3. **todos.** *Todo* is used in the plural form to mean *all*. The verb that follows this subject is *iban*, a plural form. Thus, the subject is plural as well.

4. **destemplada.** The adjective must show gender agreement with the noun *tarde*, which is feminine and singular.

5. **podría.** Use the conditional to indicate probability. Read the entire passage first to determine that the conditional should be used in this sentence.

6. **poco.** *Poco* remains in the masculine singular form to show agreement.

7. **emplazada.** The adjective must show gender agreement with the noun *casa*, which is feminine and singular.

8. **convirtieron.** Use the preterit to indicate an action completed in the past. The phrase *a finales del siglo XI* signals a specific moment when the action was completed in the past. As such, this verb requires the preterit form.

9. **primer.** Drop the *-o* when the adjective is followed by a masculine, singular noun.

10. **iluminándolo.** Use the gerund to express the cause of the action. Notice that the direct object pronoun *lo*, which refers to *todo*, is attached to the verbal form.

Explaining Discrete Sentence Fill-Ins

This part of the exam addresses your knowledge of Spanish grammatical structures that deal specifically with verbs. You will be given 10 sentences in which a verb has been omitted. You must fill in the blanks with the correct form of the verb given in parentheses to make each sentence grammatically correct. To receive credit, each word you fill in must be spelled correctly, with the correct accent marks.

> There are 10 questions of this type on any given AP Spanish Language Exam. You should spend about 7 minutes on these questions.

Ability Tested

This part of the exam is related to verb usage and conjugation. To be successful, you must have a good command of not only simple verbal patterns, but also of ones that require a knowledge of sequences of verbs, usage of verbs in subordinate clauses, and so on. You should also be able to conjugate regular and irregular verbs in all tenses and modes, using the correct spelling and observing accentuation rules.

Basic Skills Necessary

You need to be able to:

- Conjugate regular and irregular verbs in any tense or mode.
- Determine the tense and/or mode required by the sequence of time.
- Determine the mode required by the main clause in a complex sentence.
- Spell and accentuate any verbal form correctly, including the forms of the infinitive, the imperative, and the gerund that carry a pronoun at the end.
- Determine the subject of the verbal form.

This type of exercise is most likely to require answers that present some kind of difficulty in usage, spelling, and/or accentuation. Among the most common responses are:

- Irregular verbs that may require changes in the stem for certain tenses. Most irregular verbs are used rather frequently (including *hacer, tener, salir,* and *poner*).
- Regular verbs that require spelling changes to maintain a specific sound present in the infinitive, such as verbs ending in *-car, -gar,* and *-zar,* which change in the first person singular of the preterit and other tenses. For example, *sacar, jugar,* and *empezar* change to *saqué, jugué,* and *empecé* in the preterit and to *saque, juegue,* and *empiece* in the subjunctive.

- Verbal forms that require a written accent. For example, many forms of the preterit and all forms of the imperfect of -er and -ir verbs require written accent marks: *salí, salía, salíamos,* and so on.

- Compound verbal forms that contain an irregular past participle. Examples include *hemos dicho, han descubierto,* and *habías visto.*

- Reflexive verbs that require the usage of special pronouns.

- Imperative verbs in both affirmative and negative for informal and formal treatments.

The Grammar Review in Part V covers verbs in Objectives 10 through 18.

Directions

In Part A.2 of the Free Response section, you will be given 10 sentences in which a verb has been omitted. The verb necessary to fill each blank is given to you numbered and in parentheses. You must conjugate the verb in the tense and mode that is appropriate to make the sentence grammatically correct, then write the correct form of the verb in the space provided. The directions are given to you in writing, in English and Spanish. Concentrate on the directions in the language you feel most comfortable with.

The following directions resemble what you will read during Part A.2 of the Free Response section of the AP Spanish Language Exam. It is important to be familiar with the directions of each section *before* you take the test so that you can use your time more efficiently during the test.

In the following set of sentences, one verb is missing. On the line after the number, write the correct form and tense of the verb, taking into consideration the context of the sentence. In some cases, you may have to use more than one word, but you need to use a tense of the verb given in parentheses.

En el siguiente grupo de oraciones falta un verbo. Escribe en la línea después de cada número la forma y el tiempo correcto del verbo, tomando en consideración el contexto de la oración. En algunos casos vas a necesitar más de una palabra, pero es necesario que uses un tiempo del verbo que aparece entre paréntesis.

Suggested Strategies for Discrete Sentence Fill-Ins

Read each sentence carefully and locate the verb that is missing. Remember that, to be correct, your answer needs to be not only grammatically correct, but also correctly spelled and accentuated. Be aware that in this exercise, unlike in the Paragraph Fill-Ins, you may use more than one Spanish word in your answer, so make sure that you do not leave out any necessary reflexive pronouns. As in the Paragraph Fill-Ins, a verb may not require any change, but you must still write it in the space provided to receive credit. You will not receive credit for answers such as "stays the same," "no change," and so on.

There may be cases in which more than one form of the verb in parentheses is correct. In these cases, you may choose to write one form or all, but if one of the multiple answers you write is incorrect, you will lose credit for that question. To avoid this problem, just write the verbal form that you feel is the best, or the one that presents the least spelling and/or accentuation difficulties. For example, if you know that either *hablara* or *hablase* would be a correct answer, go with *hablara,* which is easier to spell than *hablase* because of the potential confusion between *c* and *s*.

In this part of the exam, your success depends on your ability to use and conjugate verbs in any tense or mode, and on your control of spelling and accentuation; therefore, you should be very well acquainted with all type of Spanish verbs, time sequence, tenses and modes, and spelling and accentuation rules for verbal forms.

The list below goes into more detail about possible strategies for this section of the exam:

- **Read each sentence completely.** This will give you a general sense as to whether the sentence is simple or complex, whether it contains any subordinate clauses, and so on.

- **Locate the missing verb.** At first glance, you should be able to recognize whether the verb is regular or irregular. If it is a reflexive verb, it will end with the syllable *-se*.

- **Identify the subject of the sentence and the subject of any subordinate clause.** This is necessary in order to conjugate your verb in the correct person and number.

- **Identify any object.** In the sentence, you may encounter either direct or indirect objects that will later be replaced by a pronoun attached to a verbal form. If you leave out the pronoun, your answer will be considered incorrect. The same holds true for reflexive verbs.

- **Try to recognize a time sequence.** Each sentence should contain either another verb or a time expression that will give you a clue in regard to the tense you need to select.

- **Determine what type of sentence you have.** Knowing what is expressed in a sentence is essential to correctly conjugating the verb. Sentences that express a direct order require the imperative form of the verb. Remember that the negative form of a command is the same as the present subjunctive. Sentences that express desires, emotions, or indirect orders require the subjunctive mode and not the indicative, which is used to talk about facts.

- **Be aware of the idea expressed by the verb in the main clause of a complex sentence.** If you are dealing with a complex sentence, check the verb of that sentence to see whether, because of the idea it indicates, it requires the usage of the subjunctive in the dependent clause.

- **Check the spelling for each answer.** Misspelled verbal forms won't earn you credit; therefore, pay close attention to the verb given in parentheses and make only the necessary spelling changes. Make sure that you copy the verb correctly, and do not introduce any unnecessary changes. For example, if your omitted word is a form of the verb *huir,* make sure that you write your answer with an *h*.

- **Identify predictable spelling changes.** In Spanish, verbs are classified in groups that follow certain patterns. To keep your spelling errors at a minimum, be aware of the changes different groups of verbs undergo. For example, verbs that finish in *-ucir* get a *z* before the *c* in the first person singular of the present tense (so from *traducir,* you get *traduzco*).

Memorizing some of the most common verbs and the changes they take is very helpful. Remember that verbs that contain prefixes are conjugated in the same way as the primitive verb. This means that the verb *componer* is conjugated exactly like *poner*, which is the verb from which the former is derived.

- **Take notice of punctuation to help you determine the correct answer.** A comma following a noun usually indicates that a form of the imperative has been omitted.

Examples of How to Work through Discrete Sentence Fill-Ins

Here are some examples of how to work through Discrete Sentence Fill-Ins. Remember that all the answers are verbal forms.

Suppose you come across the following sentence:

> La semana pasada (1) a leer una novela y todavía no la he terminado. (empezar)

1. First, read the sentence completely and determine what verb is missing. In this case, it is *empezar*. This verb presents difficulties in some tenses because it is a stem-changing verb (the second *e* changes to *ie*) and because it sometimes undergoes an orthographic change (from *z* to *c*) in order to keep the correct sound. So, once you know what form you need to write in the space provided, remember to take these factors into consideration.

2. When you read the sentence, the first words that you encounter give you a clue about the proper tense to use: *La semana pasada* is a time expression. Immediately, you can eliminate the possibility of using the present, the future, the subjunctive, or the conditional because you know that this action already happened. The imperfect can also be eliminated because the time expression suggests a specific time in the past.

3. Now, you must find the subject of the sentence so that you can select the verbal form that maintains the agreement in person and number with the subject. If no specific pronoun is mentioned (such as in this sentence), the only way to find the subject is to examine any other conjugated verbal form. The second part of this sentence contains *he terminado*, which tells you that the subject is *yo*. Thus, the correct answer is *empecé*. Notice that, in this case, the stem change is not relevant, but the orthographic change is necessary. To spell this verbal form correctly, you must also remember the pattern of accentuation of conjugated verbs.

Here is another example:

> Si mis padres (2) mucho dinero, iría a una universidad privada. (tener)

1. The missing verb in this sentence is *tener*, a verb that is irregular in some tenses and forms. With this is mind, start looking for clues in the context to pinpoint the correct form to fill in the blank.

2. Notice that this sentence starts with the word *si*. You know that this word is used in sentences in which the conditional is used and that, in general, this word introduces contrary-to-fact situations. In this type of situation, the first verb is always in the imperfect subjunctive and the second verb is in the conditional. In this sentence, the missing verb is the first one in the sequence. The second verb is *iría,* a conditional form of *ir.* Thus, you can determine that the missing verb is in the imperfect subjunctive.

3. In this sentence, finding the subject does not present much difficulty because it appears at the beginning of the sentence and next to the missing verb. The subject is *mis padres;* therefore, the missing verb will be in the third person plural form: *tuvieran.* As this sentence demonstrates, it is vital that you master frequently used irregular verbs.

One more example:

> Sonia no quiere que su hija (3) de la casa después de las diez de la noche. (salir)

1. *Salir* is another frequently used irregular verb. Read the sentence to determine what tense is appropriate in the context of the sentence and to find the subject of the sentence (*Sonia*). To spell the missing verbal form correctly, you must recall in what cases this verb is irregular.

2. Notice the form of the verb *querer;* because this verb expresses desire, it generally introduces a dependent clause that contains the subjunctive. When you come across a verb like this, the next step is to look for the word *que.* In this case, it is located right after the verb. Now you are certain that the form that you need to write in the blank is a form of the subjunctive. To keep the logic of the sequence given by the verb *quiere,* use a form of the present subjunctive.

3. Finally, to pinpoint the correct form of the verb, determine the subject of the dependent clause. In this sentence, it is *su hija.* This requires third person singular; therefore, the answer is *salga.*

Sample Discrete Sentence Fill-Ins: Questions, Answers, and Explanations

Set 1

1. Rosa, (1) del cuarto de una vez.

1. _____ (salir)

2. En la reunión de ayer, Héctor (2) un poema muy hermoso.

2. _____ (leer)

3. Si fueras un poco más inteligente, (3) tus tareas todos los días.

3. _____ (hacer)

73

4. Si el tiempo (4), iríamos a la playa.

4. _____ (componerse)

5. Eduardo dijo que (5) temprano para evitar complicaciones de tránsito.

5. _____ (salir)

6. Si sigues (6), nunca te van a creer.

6. _____ (mentir)

7. A estas horas ya Luz y Lorena (7) de la universidad.

7. _____ (graduarse)

8. Yo continúo (8) con varias organizaciones benéficas.

8. _____ (contribuir)

9. Es imprescindible que (9) tus propios libros.

9. _____ (elegir)

10. Pablo, (10) el trabajo que te mandé, inmediatamente.

10. _____ (hacer)

Answers and Explanations for Set 1

1. **sal.** Use the imperative form to indicate that a command is given. Notice the comma after *Rosa,* which is an indication that the imperative form is required. (This context does not indicate whether the register is formal or informal. *Salga* is a possible answer as well.)

2. **leyó.** Use the preterit to indicate that the action was completed in the past. *En la reunión de ayer* is a clue that indicates a specific time in the past and, thus, the need to use the preterit.

3. **harías.** Use the conditional after an if clause that uses the imperfect subjunctive. The subjunctive is used in contrary-to-fact clauses. This clue will help you determine that the conditional needs to be used in the main clause.

4. **se compusiera.** Use the subjunctive in an if clause when the main clause uses the conditional.

5. **saldría.** Use the conditional after verbs of communication (*decir*).

6. **mintiendo.** *Seguir* + gerund means *to keep on doing something*.

7. **se habrán graduado.** Use the future perfect to indicate that an event will be completed in the future before some point in time in the future. Notice the expression *a estas horas ya,* which indicates that an event probably has taken place.

8. **contribuyendo.** *Continuar* + gerund means *to be still doing something*.

9. **elijas.** Use the present subjunctive after impersonal expressions. The expression *es imprescindible que* includes the verbal form *es,* which is a form of the present tense.

10. haz. Use the imperative form to indicate that a command is given. The comma following the proper noun *Pablo* indicates the need for the imperative form. (This context does not indicate whether the register is formal or informal. *Haga* is a possible answer as well.)

Set 2

1. Es injusto que Ana pretenda que yo (1) todas las respuestas.

1. _____(buscar)

2. Leticia, ¿cómo (2) ese premio tan importante?

2. _____(obtener)

3. El gobierno de los Estados Unidos siempre (3) en causas humanitarias.

3. _____(contribuir)

4. Si el perro (4), fue porque lo pisaste.

4. _____(gruñir)

5. Anoche Anita (5) muy tarde.

5. _____(dormirse)

6. Quería que (6) por mi casa para darte tu regalo de cumpleaños.

6. _____(pasar)

7. (7) muchos años que Manuel trabajaba en esa fábrica, pero al final se jubiló.

7. _____(Hacer)

8. (8) estos exámenes, me di cuenta de que Arturo no estaba en clase hoy.

8. _____(Corregir)

9. Por favor, Sr. Pérez, (9) las causas del asesinato.

9. _____(investigar)

10. Doña Tecla, no (10) tacaña y dele una limosna al pobre.

10. _____(ser)

Answers and Explanations for Set 2

1. busque. Use the subjunctive following *ser* + adjective + *que*. The use of the subjunctive in this sentence is determined by *pretenda,* a verb that expresses a wish or desire and is followed by *que*. Notice that the subject *Ana* is different from *yo,* which is the subject of the answer, *busque*.

2. obtuviste. Use the preterit to indicate that the action was completed in the past. The context allows for *obtuvo* as a possible answer as well.

3. **contribuye.** Use the present tense to indicate a repetitive action.

4. **gruñó.** Use the preterit to indicate that the action was completed in the past.

5. **se durmió.** Use the preterit to indicate that the action was completed in the past. Notice the expression of time *anoche,* which indicates a specific time or moment in the past requiring the use of the preterit.

6. **pasaras, pasases.** Use the imperfect subjunctive when the verb in the main clause is in the imperfect and indicates a wish or desire, as is the case of *querer.*

7. **hacía.** Use the imperfect *hacía* + expression of time + *que* to label an action that was continuing in the past when something else happened.

8. **corrigiendo.** The use of the gerund is equivalent to English phrases beginning with *while.*

9. **investigue.** Formal commands use the present subjunctive. Notice the comma after the formal treatment *Sr. Pérez,* which indicates that a form of the imperative is needed.

10. **sea.** Negative formal commands use the present subjunctive. *Doña* is a formal treatment used to address a female and requires the formal imperative form of *ser.*

Explaining Essay Questions

This part of the exam measures your competency in writing in Spanish. You are given a specific topic and are asked to write a well-organized essay in Spanish of a minimum of 200 words.

There is only one Essay on each AP Spanish Language exam. The time allotted to complete the Essay is 45 minutes.

Ability Tested

The Essay is designed to test your ability to express your thoughts in an accurate and articulate fashion in written Spanish. Your knowledge of complex grammatical structures, the precision and richness of your vocabulary, and your spelling and ability to follow other conventions of the written language are all taken into consideration when determining your total score on this part of the exam. Therefore, your grammar skills and the range of your vocabulary play a very large role in this part.

Basic Skills Necessary

You need to have:

- Good spelling and accentuation skills.
- Good control of syntax in order to express complex thoughts about a topic of general interest in a variety of modes.
- An ample range of vocabulary in order to write about any given topic.
- Knowledge of essay organization and punctuation rules.

Directions

In this part of the Free Response section of the exam, you will be given a topic on which to write a composition. The directions are given to you in writing, in English and Spanish. Concentrate on the directions in the language you feel most comfortable with.

The following directions resemble what you will read during this part of the Free Response section of the AP Spanish Language Exam. It is important to be familiar with the directions in each section *before* you take the test so that you can use your time more efficiently during the test.

Write a well-organized essay in Spanish of at least 200 words and about the topic given below. Your score will be based on organization, range and appropriateness of vocabulary, and grammatical accuracy. It is recommended that you use the first five minutes to organize your ideas.

Escribe un ensayo bien organizado, en español y de una extensión de al menos 200 palabras, sobre el tema que aparece a continuación. Tu calificación estará basada en la organización, la riqueza y la precisión del vocabulario y la corrección gramatical. Se te recomienda que utilices los primeros cinco minutos para organizar tus ideas.

Suggested Strategies for Essay Questions

In this part of the exam, your success depends on how well you express yourself in written Spanish. You should be able to profit from your previous knowledge and apply the same organizational strategies that you have learned for writing essays in your English classes, such as creating an overall structure for your essay and writing good paragraphs.

- **Read the questions carefully and completely.** As you will see in the sample essays that are provided later in this section, the essay topic is sometimes given to you in an elaborate fashion. The question may be four or five lines long, and it gives you very specific directions as to what to write about. The question can facilitate your ideas and organization because the way it is written guides you as to how to write your composition.

- **Make sure that you understand what the topic is.** Even though you may not understand every single word in the question, find a few words (cognates, for example) that give you a clue about the theme.

- **Use the time suggested in the directions to organize your ideas.** Using any type of prewriting activity could save you time later. By using a Venn diagram, for example, you gather all the information you have about the topic. Try to do your prewriting in Spanish so that you already have the basic vocabulary with which to work.

A Venn diagram is a graphic organizer that is useful if the essay question deals with any sort of comparison. The diagram consists of two or more overlapping circles. In the area that belongs to all circles, you write the ideas or characteristics that the elements you are comparing have in common. In the areas that do not overlap, you write the characteristics of each element that are different from the other elements. The following figure illustrates a Venn diagram.

Another graphic organizer that may be helpful when writing your essay is a word wheel. The word wheel helps you collect ideas or vocabulary related to the topic of your essay. The following figure illustrates a word wheel.

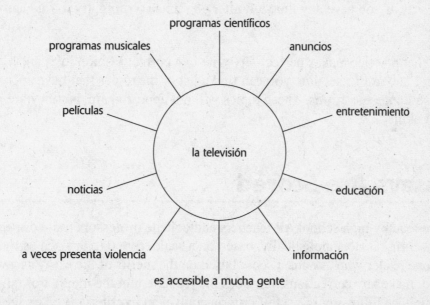

- **Make sure that your essay has a clear and defined organization that consists of an introduction, a body, and a conclusion.** Remember, the directions point out that your essay must be well organized. Writing an essay without a clearly defined organizational structure may result in a lower score.

- **Do not paraphrase the question in your introduction.** Your introduction must contain the topic sentence. By reading the topic sentence, the reader should be able to know what you are writing about.

- **Make sure that the paragraphs that make up the body of your essay are organized and consistent with your introduction.** If the essay is repetitive and not well focused, your score will be lower.

- **Include examples that support what you are saying.** In most cases, the essay topic itself instructs you to support your opinion with examples. Examples should be incorporated following any statement you make about the topic.

- **Write a logical conclusion.** Finish your essay with a conclusion. The conclusion should not be a repetition of what you said before. After writing a coherent essay, arrive at a conclusion that summarizes your ideas or your opinion.

- **Do not waste time correcting mistakes.** If you want to erase a word or a phrase, just cross it out.

- **Write as clearly as possible with blue or black ink, or with a ballpoint pen.** It is extremely important that the reader be able to fairly evaluate the way you express your ideas in Spanish, without having to waste time deciphering your handwriting. If a student's handwriting is impossible to read, the reader cannot know what the writer is saying in regard to content or even whether the writer is spelling correctly.

- **Do not write your essay on the insert where the question is printed.** You will not have time to recopy in the exam booklet, and your work will not be evaluated.

- **Proofread only if you have time.** Most of the time, there is no time to copy a clean version of your essay. If you have any time left after you finish writing, try to find and correct any mistakes.

Do not forget that practice makes perfect. To write in a correct fashion in Spanish, you need a lot of practice. Later in this section, you can find a list of the topics that have appeared in previous AP Spanish Language exams. These topics will not appear again, but they are good to write on to test your skills.

How Essays Are Scored

The essays are read by high school AP teachers and college professors trained specifically for this task. The scoring is done holistically, based on a scale from 0 to 9. Each essay is read and evaluated by one reader who assigns a score based on the merits of the essay as a whole. The reader does not make any corrections, nor does the reader count the number of mistakes the essay may have. The following is a set of criteria equivalent to criteria used by the readers to evaluate essays.

High Score (9)

This essay demonstrates an excellent command of the Spanish language in written expression. To receive this score, the essay must be well organized and treat the given topic thoroughly. It must show correct usage of complex grammatical structures, and the vocabulary must be varied, rich, and precise. The writer uses Spanish idiomatic expressions correctly. General conventions of the written language such as spelling, accentuation, and punctuation are generally correct. There may be occasional errors of syntax and vocabulary.

Medium-High Score (7–8)

This essay shows a good to very good command of the Spanish language in written expression. To receive this score, the essay must present a good organizational structure and deal with the given topic. The essay must reflect some evidence that the writer is able to use some complex syntax. It should show very good control of elementary grammatical structures and simple verb usage. The vocabulary must be appropriate and of a considerable range. This essay demonstrates good use of the conventions of the written language. There may be a few errors of syntax and vocabulary.

Medium Score (4–6)

This essay shows a basic to good command of the Spanish language in written expression. To receive this score, the essay must show some relevancy to the given topic. It is poorly organized but shows that the writer is competent in using elementary structures and simple verb tenses, although the writer commits numerous errors when using more complex syntax. The vocabulary is somewhat appropriate but limited and, at times, there is evidence of second-language interference. It may contain frequent errors of spelling and other conventions of the written language.

Medium-Low Score (2–3)

This essay suggests that the writer is not competent in Spanish written expression. The essay does not exhibit any organizational structure. There are numerous grammatical errors, even in the usage of simple structures and regular verbs; occasionally, however, a complex structure may be correct. The vocabulary is limited, and there is significant second-language interference. Errors of spelling and other conventions of the language are abundant.

Low Score (0–1)

This essay demonstrates that the writer is not competent in Spanish written expression. Grammatical errors are constant and impede communication. The vocabulary is extremely limited, and second language interference is frequent. Numerous errors in spelling and other conventions of the language make it difficult to understand the content. The essay may contain nothing to earn points. A blank page, any off-task writing, or an essay written in English all fall into this category.

Previous Essay Topics

The following is a list of the themes that have appeared in the AP Spanish Language Exam over the past 14 years. These are just the topics—the real questions cannot be reproduced because they are copyrighted material. Although the themes are not repeated, these topics can help you practice writing essays and can help you improve your vocabulary and grammar skills. Write your essays in a similar setting to where you would take the actual exam and following the same strategies that you would use in the actual exam.

1988: La preocupación por mantenerse saludable y en buena forma física, y la importancia de una buena dieta y un régimen de ejercicios para tener una buena salud.

1989: Los beneficios que pueden obtenerse al dar una mayor importancia al estudio de varias lenguas, desde el punto de vista personal, social, político y comercial.

1990: Aspectos necesarios para mantener una buena relación entre los adolescentes y los adultos.

1991: Una explicación personal de lo que es la felicidad.

1992: La juventud ante los problemas de importancia mundial.

1993: La importancia de tener sentido del humor.

1994: El mundo en el siglo XXI.

1995: Los aspectos de la vida moderna que afectan más a los adolescentes.

1996: Una cápsula de tiempo para guardar las cosas más interesantes y representativas de la época.

1997: Un momento importante de la infancia.

1998: Los niños y la televisión. Papel de los padres en este tema.

1999: La carrera universitaria. Irse fuera de la ciudad o quedarse.

2000: El papel de la fantasía en la vida.

2001: Una persona que haya tenido una gran influencia en tu vida.

2002: El éxito. Significado que tiene para cada persona.

An Example of How to Write an Essay

In order to produce a good essay, you should take a systematic approach. You have only 45 minutes to organize your ideas and write your essay during the AP Spanish Language Exam. If you develop a system of a few steps and practice using it, you will end up making a better use of the allotted time. The directions given in the exam suggest that you use the first five minutes to plan your essay and the rest of the time to write and correct it.

The first step is to read and understand the question. Suppose your essay topic is the following:

La televisión en nuestros tiempos ocupa un lugar importante en la vida diaria; sin embargo, a pesar de las ventajas que la televisión puede ofrecer, también tiene desventajas. En un ensayo bien organizado de 200 palabras o más expresa tu opinión sobre este tema.

Ideally, you will completely understand the content of the question, but this may not always happen.

As you read the question, notice the words that you are able to understand easily. Pay special attention to any cognates you may find. In the sample topic, you immediately know that the question deals with television (*televisión*). As you continue reading, you find the words *ocupa* and *importante* (also cognates). By now, you may already realize that the first part of the question is about television being important to people. You next find a transition phrase: *sin embargo*. This phrase will help you shape your ideas on what you are writing about: Even though television is important, there is something about it that is not so good. You keep looking for more clues to complete your thoughts, and you find two other cognates: *ventajas* and *desventajas*. Although they are far from each other within the sentence, you now know that, regardless of the rest of the words in the question that you may or may not know, you must write an essay on the advantages and disadvantages of television. In the second sentence, you find two more cognates: *expresa* and *opinión*. Now you get the entire picture: You must express your opinion about the advantages and disadvantages of television.

Once you know what you have to write about, you need to do some sort of prewriting activity to organize all the ideas that come to your mind about the topic. For this particular example, a T-chart may be helpful. A T-chart is a two-column graphic organizer framed with a T-shape, as illustrated below.

Ventajas	Desventajas
Accesible a mucha gente	Toma el tiempo de otras actividades
Tiene noticias	Algunos programas son violentos
Es educativa	Puede ser mala influencia para los
Nos entretiene	niños
Conocemos productos nuevos	Es mala para los ojos
Podemos escuchar música	

As you see, once you finish your T-chart, your ideas are organized and you are ready to write your essay.

When writing your essay, it is of vital importance that you structure it well because organization is one of the aspects taken into consideration by readers as they evaluate essays. It is recommended that you use a standard format that consists of an introduction, a body, and a conclusion. For the sample topic given above, a well-organized essay should have at least four paragraphs: one for the introduction, two for the body (one to discuss the advantages and one to discuss the disadvantages), and one for the conclusion.

In the first paragraph, take a position in regard to television; this is your thesis statement. In general, do you think television is good or bad? Do you think it is more positive or negative in people's daily lives?

In the second and third paragraphs, discuss the advantages and disadvantages of television. In the last paragraph, conclude whether television is good or bad. Your conclusion must agree with your thesis statement. Once you are finished, if you have any time left, go back and read your work, and try to correct any spelling or accentuation errors.

Sample Essay: Questions, Answers, and Explanations

Sample 1

Con los adelantos técnicos, hoy en día, se hace más común que las personas vivan más tiempo. Sin embargo, hay quien piensa que una sociedad donde hay un gran número de ancianos puede presentar un problema para los más jóvenes. En un ensayo bien organizado comenta tu opinión sobre este tema. Para respaldar tu opinión usa ejemplos concretos.

High-Scoring Essay

Los adelantos técnicos de los últimos años han dado lugar a nuevas maneras de alargar la vida de los seres humanos. Cada día, nuevos tipos de cirugía y diferentes clases de medicamentos son utilizados para curar enfermedades que antes causaban la muerte prematura. Aunque desde el punto de vista humano esto es muy bueno, socialmente puede presentar un problema.

Este tema es un poco problemático. Por un lado, es lógico que las personas quieran vivir más tiempo y con mejor salud. Por otra parte, si las personas dejan de trabajar cuando tienen sesenta y cinco años, y luego viven hasta los noventa, ellos van a poner en ruina la seguro social. La sociedad por sus gastos.

Otro problema es donde poner a los viejos. Muchas familias no quieren tener a sus viejos en va a ser de mayoría anciana, y nosotros los jóvenes tendremos que pagar casa, o no tienen nadie para cuidarlos y lo ponen en casas de cuidado para los mayores. Esto tampoco es justo para los ancianos porque a veces ellos sufren maltratos y piensan que los parientes no los quieren.

En conclusión, este tema presenta un conflicto, porque los ancianos merecen amor y respeto, pero para los jóvenes y la sociedad, tener una población vieja grande es un problema.

Analysis of the High-Scoring Essay

This essay clearly demonstrates excellence in written expression. There is abundant evidence of the writer's control of complex grammatical structures (*si las personas dejan de trabajar cuando tienen . . .*). The range of verb forms and tenses used is more than appropriate to deal with this specific topic: present, imperfect (*antes causaban la muerte prematura*), future (*los jóvenes tendremos que pagar*), and present perfect (*han dado lugar*) of the indicative, as well as present subjunctive with an impersonal expression (*es lógico que las personas quieran vivir*), passive voice (*son utilizados*), and verb + preposition + infinitive (*si las personas dejan de trabajar*). The essay is very well organized, and the writer makes good use of transitional words and phrases (*cada día, aunque, por un lado*). There is ample evidence of a wide vocabulary (*medicamentos, prematura, ruina, maltratos*). Notice the use of circumlocution in *en casas de cuidados para los mayores* rather than using an English word or phrase to communicate the idea that the exact Spanish word *asilo* would express. The writer shows very good control of spelling and other conventions of the written language. **Score: 9**

Medium-Scoring Essay

Es cierto que con los adelantos técnicos, hoy en día, es normal que la gente vive más tiempo. A mí me parece que es verdad que cuando hay muchos ancianos en una sociedad pueden haber muy muchos problemas, por que ellos paran de trabajando y los jóvenes tienen que mantener ellos.

En los últimos años, ciencia ha permitido que miles ancianos alargen su vida. Por medio de la cirugía y tratamientos, los ancianos pueden vivir una mejor vida, y más larga. Pero no han tomado en cuenta lo que es esto para nosotros los jóvenes. Según que pasan los años, la juventud es la que tiene que ayudar a pagar los gastos de manteniendo los ancianos. Ahora hay muchos homes y esto es una signal que la gente está viviendo demasiado. Ante la gente sólo esperó a vivir por cincuenta años, no más. Ahora los doctores ayudan los ancianos a quedarse vivos por más tiempo. Un otro problema de personas viviendo demasiado tiempo es quien cuida a ellos, las personas más jovenes tienen que trabajar para soportar sus viejos y no pueden cuidar a ellos, por eso ponen a los ancianos en casas especiales. En conclusión, a mí me parece que las personas tienen que vivir solamente el tiempo que necesita y no hacer nada para vivir tanto tiempo y causar problemas a su parientes.

Analysis of the Medium-Scoring Essay

This essay shows some control of basic grammar structures (*a mí me parece que; los ancianos pueden vivir mejor*), even though there are some errors (*un otro problema* rather than *otro problema; ciencia* rather than *la ciencia*), including errors in subject and verb agreement (*en una sociedad pueden haber muy muchos problemas* rather than *en una sociedad puede haber muchos problemas*). There are some evident mistakes in the usage of more complex patterns, such as the usage of the indicative rather than the subjunctive mode with an impersonal expression followed by *que* (*es normal que la gente vive*). There are some redeeming features, such as the correct use of the verb *parecer*, but in general, the essay maintains basic, but not advanced, grammatical usage. It also shows a lack of control in the use of verbs following prepositions (*ellos paran de trabajando*). There is an evident interference from English (*homes, signal, un otro problema*). This essay shows a limited vocabulary. There is good organization. Spelling and accentuation are generally correct, although there are some errors in spelling-change verbs (*alargen*). This essay shows that the writer possesses more than a basic command of the language. **Score: 6**

Medium-Low-Scoring Essay

Ahora tenemos los adelantos técnicos, y mucho gente viva demasiado. Esto traer problemas a joven como yo. Por ello no a trabajar asta esta muy viejo, pero necesita el dinero por pagando sus prescriptions.

El gente major necesita que cuiden para ellos. Necesita gente joven para que lleve a ellos a comprar cosa por que ellos ya no puede drive. La abuela sigue a molestar su niño para llevar a ella a lugar diferente.

Otra problema con gente majores es que nunca deja a mi a ir donde quiero. Siempre piensa la calle hay mucho problema. También cuando ellos está enfermo tienes que cuidar a ellos.

En conclusión, yo creo que gente muy majores solamente da problema a gente joven. Esa es mi opinion.

Analysis of the Medium-Low-Scoring Essay

This essay shows very little control of the most basic grammatical structures, as shown by phrases such as *mucho gente viva demasiado*. Apparently, the writer does not know the gender of the noun *gente,* which is a high-frequency word. It is also evident that he or she lacks control of verb usage. Many verbs are given in the infinitive form (*traer, trabajar*). There is also strong English interference (*drive, prescriptions*). The vocabulary is very limited, and the essay has poor organization. The essay is also shorter than 200 words. This suggests that the writer was limited by the lack of control of grammar structures and/or of vocabulary. The essay suggests that the writer is not competent in Spanish written expression. **Score: 2**

Sample 2

En los últimos tiempos, los deportistas profesionales se han convertido en algunas de las personas mejor pagadas del mundo. ¿Crees que es justo que se la pague más a alguien que trabaja "jugando," que a alguien que ha obtenido un título universitario y realiza una función dentro de la sociedad? Basa tu respuesta en ejemplos concretos.

High-Scoring Essay

Cada profesión tiene su valor, para algunas personas las carreras que tienen que ver con la medicina son las más importante porque de ellos depende la salud y la vida de los seres humanos. Sin embargo, es cierto que la sociedad en general opina que las profesiones deportivas son las más importantes.

Yo creo que no es justo lo que está pasando en nuestros tiempos con respecto a los sueldos de los deportistas profesionales. Esos salarios tan altos de los deportistas profesionales, me parece que ponen en ridículo a los profesionales universitarios. Por ejemplo, vamos a comparar a un jugador de baloncesto profesional y a un profesor universitario. El jugador fue escogido por su equipo recién graduarse de la escuela secundaria, seguramente nunca asistió a la universidad. El profesor tiene un doctorado de una universidad prestigiosa y trabaja para otra institución universitaria. El jugador trabaja jugando baloncesto, solamente hace divertir a los demás con su juego. Además, solamente trabaja durante los meses de entrenamiento y temporada, unos cuantos meses. El profesor, en cambio, trabaja enseñando y preparando a los futuros profesionales, normalmente trabaja como nueve meses de cada año, y cuando no enseña, hace investigaciones y prepara sus próximos cursos. También, seguramente escribe libros y artículos profesionales. El jugador gana tres millones de dólares al año. El profesor, si tiene unos años de experiencia y con un poco de suerte, llegara a los ochenta mil.

En conclusión, con esta escena, es lógico que los profesionales universitarios se sientan estúpidos, porque tuvieron que estudiar mucho en la universidad para conseguir su título, hacen algo para servir a su sociedad y sin embargo, les pagan una miseria. Esto, definitivamente, no es justo.

Analysis of the High-Scoring Essay

This essay clearly demonstrates excellence in written expression. There is abundant evidence of the writer's control of complex grammatical structures (*me parece que ponen . . .*). The range of verb forms and tenses used is more than appropriate to deal with this specific topic: present, preterit, as well as present subjunctive (*es lógico que . . . se sientan estúpidos*), passive voice (*fue escogido por su equipo*), and verb + infinitive, although some errors appear (such as *recién graduarse de la escuela primaria* and *hace divertir a los demás con su juego*). There is a very good use of prepositions (*hacer algo para servir*). The essay is very well organized, and the writer makes good use of transitional words or phrases (*sin embargo, yo creo, me parece, además*). There is ample evidence of a wide vocabulary (*poner en ridículo, salario, entrenamiento, temporada*) despite some repetition (*deportistas profesionales*). The writer shows very good control of spelling and other conventions of the written language. **Score: 9**

Medium-Scoring Essay

Me encantaría ser un jugador profesional de beisbol, yo ha jugado el deporte toda mi vida y pienso que es un deporte muy difícil a jugar, por eso es que los profesionales ganan tanto dinero. Claro que es justo que los jugadores profesionales reciben la cantidad de dinero que ellos quieren. Ellos sirven a la sociedad para se entrener.

Los peloteros profesionales son como los actores de cine. La gente quiere ver la pelicula y tienen que pagar en el cine, y con este dinero le pagan a los actores.

Otras profesiones también deberian ganar más dinero de lo que les pagan ahora, pero no creo que es justo que no le paguen a los deportistas, porque ellos trabajan muy duro para ser mejor, aunque no han ido a la universidad, algunos son educados.

Para terminar, yo quiero decir que aunque hay profesiones que necesitan que le suban el sueldo, no se debe hablar mal de los deportistas porque ellos hacen algo importante para la sociedad que es ayudarnos a divertirnos un poco.

Analysis of the Medium-Scoring Essay

This essay shows good competence in written expression. Although it is relevant to the given topic, its organization is only adequate. The vocabulary is appropriate to the topic (*jugador, béisbol, entretener, dinero*), and there is evidence that the writer has control of simple structures. There are, however, errors in the more complex structures, such as the formation of the compound tenses (*yo ha jugado* rather than *yo he jugado*), the usage of the indicative rather than the subjunctive mode with impersonal expressions followed by *que* (*es justo que . . . reciben*), and the use of reflexive verbs (*se entrener* rather than *entrenarse*). There are some redeeming features, such as the correct use of conditional forms (*encantaría, debería*), but in general the essay maintains basic, but not advanced, grammatical usage. It also shows a lack of control in the use of verbs following prepositions (*difícil a jugar*). Spelling and accentuation are generally correct. **Score: 5**

Low-Scoring Essay

Deportistas hoy ganar mucho. Es fair ellos tienen playing el mucho de tiempo. Con el sol y rain. Yo va estar el futballista famosa para tiene mucho dinero.

Gente no think esta fair cuando fuiste a la university y esta pobre, perro deportista también va a university por un poco tiempo, asi que no hay problema.

En conclussion yo creo que no tiene problema para deportista aser mucho dinero y no fui al colegio todo el tiempo.

Analysis of the Low-Scoring Essay

This essay shows that the writer possesses practically no control of the most basic Spanish grammatical structures. This is demonstrated by the sentence: *deportistas hoy ganar mucho.* The sentence lacks the definite article before the noun, and the verb is used in an impersonal form. This suggests that the writer is not even able to conjugate a regular verb in the present tense. Grammatical errors are so abundant that they impede communication. The excessive interference of the English language (*fair, playing, rain, think*), as well as the repetition of some basic Spanish words (*dinero, problema, tiempo*), suggests that this student lacks the vocabulary necessary to complete this task. The essay is short and has practically no structure. This essay demonstrates that the writer is not competent in Spanish written expression. **Score: 1**

The Web site www.cliffsnotes.com/extras has lists of idiomatic expressions and classified vocabulary, both of which can help you boost your Essay score.

Explaining Picture Sequences

Picture Sequences are part of the Speaking Skills section of the exam. This part of the exam consists of two different exercises:

- One Picture Sequence
- One set of Directed Response questions

The time allotted for this part is 20 minutes. You do not have control over the time on this part because it is paced by a master tape. This part makes up 20% of your total AP Spanish Language Exam score, with the Picture Sequence and Directed Response section each being worth 10%.

Picture Sequences

This part of the exam measures your competency in speaking Spanish. You will be given a set of six pictures; in your own words, you must tell the story suggested by the sequence of pictures.

There is only one Picture Sequence on any given AP Spanish Language Exam. You will have two minutes to study the pictures and two minutes to talk about them.

Ability Tested

This exercise is designed to measure your abilities using the spoken language within a specific situation. As you will see in the set of rubrics used to evaluate this type of exercise, your command of language structure, your vocabulary, your fluency, and your pronunciation are all taken into consideration in scoring your response.

Basic Skills Necessary

You need to have:

- Good pronunciation and intonation.
- A good command of Spanish language structure in order to describe what you see in the pictures and to narrate a story in a coherent and thorough fashion.
- An ample range of vocabulary in order to be able to speak about any topic.

- Control of the usage of all parts of speech, including transitional words, in order to produce a fluent and cohesive sample of speech.

- The ability to appropriately use formulas for polite and familiar greetings, leave-taking, apologies, and so on.

Directions

In Part B.1 of the Free Response section of the exam, you will be working with a set of six pictures that tell a story. The directions are given to you orally, in English and Spanish. There will also be some short directions, in English and Spanish, printed above the first frame of the sequence. Concentrate on the directions in the language you feel most comfortable with.

The following directions resemble what you will hear during Part B.1 of the Free Response section of the AP Spanish Language Exam. It is important to be familiar with the directions for each section *before* you take the test so that you can use your time more efficiently during the test.

The pictures on this page represent a story. You have two minutes to organize your ideas and two minutes to tell the story. Try to talk about all of the pictures and move smoothly from one to the other. Remember, you should use as much of the allotted time as possible. Your score will be based on the appropriateness and grammatical correctness of your answer, as well as on your vocabulary, pronunciation, and fluency.

Los dibujos que ves en esta página sugieren una historia. Tienes dos minutos para organizar tus ideas y dos para contar la historia. Al contar la historia trata de hablar de todos los dibujos y de moverte con fluidez de uno a otro. Recuerda que debes de usar la mayor cantidad del tiempo que te dan. Tu calificación se basará no solamente en la precisión y corrección gramatical de tu respuesta, sino también en el vocabulario, la pronunciación y la fluidez del discurso.

Begin to think about the story. (Two minutes elapse.) You have two minutes to tell the story. Start speaking as soon as you hear the beep. BEEP. (Two minutes elapse.) Stop your recorder.

Suggested Strategies for Picture Sequences

One of the most important elements in this type of exercise is time. Use your preparation time wisely. Make sure that you look at all the pictures, and prepare what you are going to say about each one. Think about how you are going to connect them to one another to keep your story fluent. Once you hear the signal to begin speaking, do not spend too much time on any one frame; rather, try to distribute the time equally. Make an effort to speak during the entire allotted time.

The following list goes into more detail:

- **Use the preparation time to study the six frames.** It is important to look at each picture individually and have an idea of what you are going to say about it. Do not try to write down the story; if you do, you will waste the preparation time and will not be able to prepare to speak about the entire sequence.

- **Make mental notes on the vocabulary that you may be able to use for each frame.** Or go one step further and write down some words to guide you through your response. Consider the setting of your story: Describe the place, talk about the weather, and look for details that may help you speak about each picture, such as time of day, facial expressions, and so on. If you do not remember a specific word in Spanish, describe the action or the object that you want to identify in the picture. This is called circumlocution; it will help you avoid using English words and get your idea across in Spanish.

- **Think of the story in Spanish.** If you are able to think of a basic vocabulary with which to tell the story, as suggested in the previous strategy, you probably will be able to tell the story in Spanish—that is, without translating from your English thoughts. On the other hand, if you prepare your story in English and plan to translate it into Spanish, you risk compromising the fluency of your speech because you may have to stop speaking in order to carry on your mental translation. This will result in a waste of time.

- **Refer to each picture while telling the story.** Although you may spend more time on one picture than on another, make sure that you refer to each of them because each contains certain elements that will help you build a better and more fluid story.

- **Select the verbal tenses that you are more comfortable with.** Although it is important that the verbs be correct, you have the choice of telling the story in the tense you like. The preterit tense presents problems for most students because of the irregularity of many verbs. Also, deciding whether the preterit or the imperfect tense should be used can be a challenge. Using the present or the future tense may eliminate some of these problems.

- **Correct yourself.** If you realize that you have made a mistake, go ahead and correct yourself. Self-correction will earn you points because, by identifying your mistakes, you demonstrate that you know what you are saying.

- **Use your imagination and creativity.** The purpose of this exercise is to elicit a sample of your speaking abilities, and although you must keep yourself within the limits of the story, certain resources will make the story more interesting. You may use adjectives to add richness to your vocabulary and, at the same time, give more originality to your story. You may also introduce yourself into the story by choosing to take the role of the main character; in that way, you can include feelings and emotions to make the story come alive while showing that you are familiar with a variety of structures and expressions.

- **Do not forget the final twist.** In most cases, the story has a twist at the end. This may come as some sort of surprising ending, such as the occurrence of the unexpected or the discovery of a hidden detail. By adding this twist to the story, the test writers are giving you the opportunity to use a series of language elements, such as the subjunctive tense, the expression of certain emotions, and so on.

- **Indicate that you are finished.** Once you are finished, you should indicate that you are done so that your story does not seem to be incomplete or cut. Say something such as, "*He terminado,*" or, "*Eso es todo,*" so that the person who is evaluating your work will know that you have said all you have to say about the story.

- **Try to be as relaxed as possible.** Being nervous will cause you to forget the vocabulary you need and to make grammatical mistakes. Your voice will also be affected, and you probably will not be able to maintain fluency and good pronunciation and intonation.

How to Practice for the Picture Sequence Section

To be successful in this part of the test, you need to practice. Because you probably do not have to do anything quite like Picture Sequences in your Spanish classes in school, it is even more crucial that you practice for this section.

You need to practice not only by doing Picture Sequences, but also by recording your practice. By doing so, you will be able to compare what you planned to say and what you actually said. This will help you visualize yourself speaking Spanish so that, eventually, thinking in Spanish will come naturally to you. Recording your practice will also make you more confident with the technical aspect of the exercise, such as pressing the correct buttons, adjusting the volume, and so on. By practicing telling stories, you will also get the sense of how long two minutes is. Many students are not able to administer their time appropriately; as a result, they either stop talking long before the two minutes have elapsed or they run out of time and their story remains incomplete.

The second strategy for practicing for Picture Sequences is vocabulary acquisition. Learn as much vocabulary as you can in preparation for the exam. Vocabulary is crucial in this exercise because your objective is to orally communicate what you have to say about the pictures. There are no definite lists or topics you should give more importance to than others, though, because the Picture Sequences deal with a different situation each year. The best solution to this is to try to get an ample range of vocabulary that will allow you to talk about any specific topic.

You can find lists of classified vocabulary at **www.cliffsnotes.com/extras** that may be useful when dealing with this type of exercise. The classified vocabulary lists provide you with many high-frequency Spanish words that may be used in any context of a Picture Sequence to add to a narration of events. These lists will help you produce a Picture Sequence response that shows a variety of vocabulary and that is more elaborate because you will be able to talk about details and characteristics that you observe in the pictures.

To give you an idea of what the lists of classified vocabulary look like, below is the Personal Attributes list. As every Picture Sequence has people in it, you can certainly expect to be able to use some of these words.

Los Atributos Personales	Personal Attributes	Los Atributos Personales	Personal Attributes
ágil	nimble	inteligente	intelligent
alegre	happy	joven	young
alto	tall	lento	slow
anciano	elderly	listo	clever
bajo	short	loco	mad; crazy
bizco	cross-eyed	manco	one-armed
bobo	dumb; silly	mentiroso	liar
calvo	bald	moreno	dark
canoso	gray-haired	mudo	dumb; mute
ciego	blind	negro	black
cojo	lame	nervioso	nervous
corpulento	stout	pálido	pale
cortés	polite; courteous	pequeño	small
cuerdo	sane	perezoso	lazy
culto	well-educated; refined	pesado	heavy
delgado	slim; thin	rápido	quick
descortés	impolite	rubio	fair; blonde
diligente	diligent; laborious	saludable	healthy
distraído	absent-minded	sensato	judicious; prudent
elegante	elegant	sensible	sensitive
embustero	liar	sordo	deaf
enfermo	ill; sick	tener pecas	to have freckles
esbelto	slender	tener una cicatriz	to have a scar
feo	ugly	terco	stubborn
flaco	skinny	testarudo	stubborn
gordo	fat	tonto	foolish
grande	big	triste	sad
grosero	rude	tuerto	one-eyed
grueso	fat	viejo	old
guapo	handsome	zurdo	left-handed
hermoso	beautiful		

93

Picture Sequence Scoring

Your speech sample is evaluated by high school AP teachers and college professors trained specifically for this task. The global evaluation of each sample is based on a scale from 0 to 9 and takes into consideration the sustained level of performance in the sample. Each sample is evaluated using a set of rubrics established beforehand. The following is a set of criteria equivalent to the rubrics used to evaluate the Picture Sequence exercise.

High Score (9)

This is a sample that demonstrates excellent oral expression. The characteristics of this sample may include an excellent command of complex structures, rich and precise vocabulary, a high level of fluency, and excellent pronunciation. The story is detailed and rich, and it covers the sequence thoroughly. There may be a few errors in grammar, vocabulary, or pronunciation.

Medium-High Score (7–8)

This is a sample that demonstrates very good oral expression. The characteristics of this sample may include a good command of complex structures, although there may be some errors; the speaker demonstrates a good vocabulary and level of fluency. The story is very well narrated, and the speaker has very good pronunciation.

Medium Score (5–6)

This is a sample that demonstrates good oral expression. The characteristics of this sample may include a good command of simple structures, although there may be some errors. The range of vocabulary used is adequate, but there may be some Anglicisms; fluency is affected by some hesitation. The story is told in an adequate fashion, and the speaker's pronunciation is good.

Medium-Low Score (3–4)

This is a sample that suggests a lack of competence in oral expression. This sample is characterized by poor control of simple grammatical structures, including serious and frequent errors. The speaker demonstrates a narrow range of vocabulary, and some Anglicisms are present; fluency is very limited. The story is poorly told and may need some interpretation. Although fair, the speaker's pronunciation may affect comprehension.

Low Score (1–2)

This is a sample that demonstrates a lack of competence in oral expression. This sample is characterized by a weak usage of grammatical structures, a limited vocabulary, the frequent use of Anglicisms, and very little fluency. The sample, although relevant to the sequence, is fragmented and requires interpretation. Pronunciation is poor and renders comprehension difficult.

No Score (0)

This is an off-task sample, containing obscenities, singing, or nonsense utterances; a narrative totally unrelated to the Picture Sequence; a blank tape (no answer); or phrases stating that the student is not able to produce an acceptable sample.

Sample Picture Sequences

Sample 1

The six drawings on the next page represent a story. Use the pictures to tell the story, according to your interpretation.

Los seis dibujos que aparecen en la próxima página representan una historieta. Utiliza los dibujos para contar la historia, según tu propia interpretación.

PLAY TRACK 7 ON CD 1

Sample 2

The six drawings on the next page represent a story. Use the pictures to tell the story, according to your interpretation.

Los seis dibujos que aparecen en la próxima página representan una historieta. Utiliza los dibujos para contar la historia, según tu propia interpretación.

PLAY TRACK 7 ON CD 1

Explaining Directed Response Questions

This part of the exam measures your competency in speaking Spanish. You will be given a series of five Directed Response questions that will require you to provide spontaneous replies. All the questions deal with the same topic. The topic normally deals with universal matters or situations that students are familiar with (such as friendship, school or work, free time, food, travel, and so on). The questions are arranged from simple to complex. The first question may be in the present tense, and the rest of them will probably use more complex structures, such as the preterit, the subjunctive, or the conditional tense. Each response is evaluated individually. The instructions and the questions are given by the master tape only. You will not be able to read them because they are not printed in the exam booklet. Your answer will be recorded on a tape.

The time to complete the five Directed Response questions is paced by the master tape. Each question is asked twice, and you have 20 seconds to respond to each question.

Ability Tested

This exercise is designed to measure your skills in answering specific questions orally in Spanish. As you will see in the set of criteria used to evaluate your responses to these questions, comprehension of the questions, command of language structure, vocabulary, fluency, and pronunciation are all taken into consideration in scoring your response.

Basic Skills Necessary

You need to have:

- Good pronunciation and intonation.
- A good command of Spanish grammatical structures and verbs tenses in order to provide the correct response.
- An ample range of vocabulary in order to understand and respond to questions about any general topic.
- A good comprehension of the spoken language.
- The ability to appropriately use formulas for polite and familiar greetings, leave-taking, apologies, and so on.

Directions

In Part B.2 of the Free Response section of the exam, you will be working with a set of five questions that deal with a specific topic. You will first hear a practice question. Do not answer the practice question, but pay close attention to it and mentally prepare a response. This practice question will give you an idea about the theme or topic that the question will address. When you hear the question a second time, give your answer out loud. The directions are given to you orally, in English only.

The following directions resemble what you will hear during Part B.2 of the Free Response section of the AP Spanish Language Exam. It is important to be familiar with the directions for each section *before* taking the test so that you can use your time more efficiently during the test.

In this section, you will be asked to respond to a series of questions in Spanish. Each question will be asked twice. Try to understand each question because you will be graded on your comprehension of the questions, as well as on your pronunciation and grammatical accuracy. Try to answer each question with full sentences and as extensively as possible. Do not worry if, when you are told to stop, you have not finished answering. The time allotted to respond to each question is 20 seconds. For each question, wait until you hear a beep to begin speaking.

Examples of Possible Questions

In the Directed Response section, you must orally answer five questions related to the same topic. The following are examples of topics and sets of questions that you may encounter in the exam:

La salud

1. ¿Te consideras una persona de buena salud? ¿Por qué?

2. ¿Qué crees que es necesario para mantener una buena salud?

3. Convence a tu mejor amigo para que deje de comer alimentos poco saludables.

4. ¿Cómo crees que ha influido la tecnología en la salud?

5. Según tu opinión, ¿hay alguna relación entre la condición física y el carácter de una persona? ¿Por qué?

Descripción de ti mismo

1. ¿Te consideras una persona atlética o intelectual? ¿Por qué?

2. ¿Cuáles son algunas de las actividades que no te gusta realizar?

3. ¿Cuáles son algunas cosas a las que les tienes mucho miedo?

4. ¿Te consideras amigo de los animales? ¿Por qué?

5. Si pudieras escoger el lugar para vivir toda tu vida, ¿cuál escogerías y por qué?

El trabajo

1. ¿Qué trabajos detestas realizar en la casa?

2. ¿Qué tipo de trabajo has realizado para cumplir con tus horas comunitarias?

3. ¿Es fácil conseguir un buen trabajo en el lugar donde vives?

4. Si pudieras escoger tu trabajo ideal, ¿cuál escogerías y por qué?

5. En tu opinión, ¿qué es más importante para escoger un trabajo, el sueldo o el tipo de trabajo? ¿Por qué?

Tu ciudad

1. Describe el lugar donde vives.

2. ¿Cuál es el sitio más atractivo para ti en el lugar donde vives? ¿Por qué?

3. Si pudieras escoger entre vivir en la playa o en las montañas, ¿cuál de las dos escogerías y por qué?

4. Convence a un amigo tuyo que en el sitio donde vives hay muchas cosas para divertirse.

5. Cuando termines la secundaria, ¿te gustaría irte del lugar donde vives? ¿Por qué?

Las artes

1. ¿Tienes talento para algún arte en especial? ¿Cuál?

2. ¿Cuál es tu artista de cine favorito? ¿Por qué?

3. ¿Por qué crees que es tan difícil triunfar en el mundo artístico?

4. ¿Consideras que las artes son más o menos importantes que las ciencias? ¿Por qué?

5. Eres representante de un cantante famoso. Convence a un empresario para que le dé un buen contrato a tu representado.

Los animales

1. De todos los animales domésticos, ¿cuál prefieres y por qué?

2. Cuando eras pequeño, ¿te dejó tu mamá tener una mascota? ¿Por qué?

3. Convence a tu amigo para que te regale un gatito de los que tiene en su casa.

4. Si estuviera en tus manos, ¿qué harías para proteger a los animales callejeros?

5. ¿Crees que los circos y las corridas de toro son un ejemplo de violencia en contra de los animales? ¿Por qué?

Suggested Strategies for Directed Response Questions

It is important to listen to each question carefully because your comprehension of each question is the first step to providing an appropriate answer. Answer in complete sentences and elaborate your answers as much as possible. Remember that you are allowed to correct yourself if you realize that you have made a mistake. If you have not finished giving your answer when the speaker starts talking again, just stop speaking and listen to the next question. The following list goes into more detail:

- **Start talking as soon as possible.** Any silence on your part after any question may indicate that you are translating the question into English because you are not fluent in Spanish.

- **Use introductory phrases to start your answer.** You may begin your answers with expressions such as *en mi opinión, yo creo,* or *por lo que he visto.* Using an introductory phrase will give you some extra time to prepare your answer.

- **Try to pick a couple of words you understand from the question.** If you do not understand the entire content of the question, picking a couple of words and saying something related to the topic may earn you partial credit. Listening for context clues is a process similar to reading for context clues.

- **Answer each question using a complete sentence.** You may even write down some words to guide you through your response. Do not take too much time writing the answer, though, or you will waste time that you may need for the next question.

- **Do not worry about telling the truth.** Be creative. Your goal is to answer the question appropriately, so you may fib if necessary. For example, if you know that you are being asked about the weather in your city, and you do not remember a word that describes the climate of your area, you may give a climatic description of any region. You just need to talk in Spanish; if you remain silent, there is nothing to get credit for.

- **Correct yourself.** If you realize that you have made a mistake, go ahead and correct yourself. Self-correction will earn you points because, by identifying your mistakes, you demonstrate that you know what you are saying.

- **Try to be as relaxed as possible.** Being nervous will cause you to forget the vocabulary you need and to make grammatical mistakes. Your voice will also be affected, and you probably will not be able to maintain fluency and good pronunciation and intonation.

Directed Response Scoring

Your speech sample is evaluated by high school AP teachers and college professors trained specifically for this task. Each answer is evaluated individually, using a set of rubrics established beforehand. The following is a set of criteria equivalent to the rubrics used to evaluate the Directed Response exercise.

Excellent (4)

The response clearly shows that the student is competent in the spoken language. The question is answered thoroughly with ease of expression and a high level of fluency. The vocabulary used is of a wide range. Pronunciation is very good, and there are practically no grammatical errors.

Very good to good (3)

The response shows that the student is competent in the spoken language. The question is answered well with ease of expression and good fluency. The vocabulary used is of a good range. Pronunciation is good, and there may be a few grammatical errors.

Acceptable (2)

The response suggests that the student is competent in the spoken language. The question is answered in an adequate manner, and there is some fluency. Occasional hesitation is present, and the student may correct himself or herself. The vocabulary used is adequate to the response, but there may be some second-language interference, as shown by the presence of Anglicisms. Pronunciation problems may interfere with communication. Grammatical structures contain some errors.

Weak to poor (1)

The response suggests that the student is not competent in the spoken language. The answer is inadequate or incomplete due to a lack of resources, and fluency is limited. The vocabulary is not sufficient to give an appropriate response. The language is fragmented, and grammatical structures show a limited command of the spoken language. Poor pronunciation interferes with communication.

Unacceptable (0)

The response shows that the student is incompetent in the spoken language. It is clear that the student does not understand the question or is not able to give an appropriate answer. The answer may be incomprehensible. There may be no answer at all or the student may say something such as, *"No comprendo la pregunta."* The recording may contain sounds and utterances that make no sense.

Sample Directed Response Questions

Sample 1

LISTEN TO TRACK 8 ON CD 1

Sample 2

LISTEN TO TRACK 9 ON CD 1

A transcript of the CD is on the Web at www.cliffsnotes.com/extras.

PART III

DIAGNOSTIC TEST

Use this test to get a general feel for your strengths and weaknesses.

Answer Sheet for the Diagnostic Test

(Remove this sheet and use it to mark your answers)

PART A	PART B	PART C	PART D
1 Ⓐ Ⓑ Ⓒ Ⓓ	12 Ⓐ Ⓑ Ⓒ Ⓓ	22 Ⓐ Ⓑ Ⓒ Ⓓ	31 Ⓐ Ⓑ Ⓒ Ⓓ
2 Ⓐ Ⓑ Ⓒ Ⓓ	13 Ⓐ Ⓑ Ⓒ Ⓓ	23 Ⓐ Ⓑ Ⓒ Ⓓ	32 Ⓐ Ⓑ Ⓒ Ⓓ
3 Ⓐ Ⓑ Ⓒ Ⓓ	14 Ⓐ Ⓑ Ⓒ Ⓓ	24 Ⓐ Ⓑ Ⓒ Ⓓ	33 Ⓐ Ⓑ Ⓒ Ⓓ
4 Ⓐ Ⓑ Ⓒ Ⓓ	15 Ⓐ Ⓑ Ⓒ Ⓓ	25 Ⓐ Ⓑ Ⓒ Ⓓ	34 Ⓐ Ⓑ Ⓒ Ⓓ
5 Ⓐ Ⓑ Ⓒ Ⓓ	16 Ⓐ Ⓑ Ⓒ Ⓓ	26 Ⓐ Ⓑ Ⓒ Ⓓ	35 Ⓐ Ⓑ Ⓒ Ⓓ
6 Ⓐ Ⓑ Ⓒ Ⓓ	17 Ⓐ Ⓑ Ⓒ Ⓓ	27 Ⓐ Ⓑ Ⓒ Ⓓ	
7 Ⓐ Ⓑ Ⓒ Ⓓ	18 Ⓐ Ⓑ Ⓒ Ⓓ	28 Ⓐ Ⓑ Ⓒ Ⓓ	
8 Ⓐ Ⓑ Ⓒ Ⓓ	19 Ⓐ Ⓑ Ⓒ Ⓓ	29 Ⓐ Ⓑ Ⓒ Ⓓ	
9 Ⓐ Ⓑ Ⓒ Ⓓ	20 Ⓐ Ⓑ Ⓒ Ⓓ	30 Ⓐ Ⓑ Ⓒ Ⓓ	
10 Ⓐ Ⓑ Ⓒ Ⓓ	21 Ⓐ Ⓑ Ⓒ Ⓓ		
11 Ⓐ Ⓑ Ⓒ Ⓓ			

CUT HERE

CUT HERE

Section I: Multiple Choice Questions

Part A: Dialogue and Narratives

You will hear a dialogue. At the end of it, you will hear several questions about what you have just heard. From the choices printed below, select the one that best responds to each of the questions.

Ahora vas a oír un diálogo. Al final del mismo escucharás unas preguntas sobre lo que has escuchado. De entre las opciones que aparecen impresas debajo, escoge la que mejor responda a cada una de las preguntas.

Dialogue

PLAY TRACK 10 ON CD 1

1.   A.   Que tome un jugo.

    B.   Que le ponga bronceador.

    C.   Que infle una balsa.

    D.   Que se meta en el agua.

2.   A.   Quemarse con el sol.

    B.   Inflar la balsa.

    C.   Molestar a los demás.

    D.   Meterse al agua.

3.   A.   Que beba un refresco.

    B.   Que se ponga bronceador.

    C.   Que tenga cuidado con las olas.

    D.   Que no lo moleste más.

You will hear a short narrative. At the end of it, you will hear several questions about what you have just listened to. From the choices printed below, select the one that best responds to each question.

Ahora vas a oír una narración corta. Al final de la misma escucharás unas preguntas sobre lo que has escuchado. De entre las opciones que aparecen impresas debajo, escoge la que mejor responda a cada una de las preguntas.

GO ON TO THE NEXT PAGE

Short Narrative

PLAY TRACK 11 ON CD 1

4. **A.** A los niños solamente.

   B. A todos los seres humanos.

   C. Al ganado vacuno.

   D. A las personas que los atacan a ellos.

5. **A.** El terror que le tienen los humanos.

   B. La transmisión de una enfermedad entre animales.

   C. La muerte de muchas personas.

   D. Las marcas que dejan a sus víctimas.

6. **A.** Sangre.

   B. Un veneno.

   C. Animales voladores.

   D. Plantas silvestres.

You will hear a longer selection. It is about five minutes in length. You may take notes, although you will not receive a grade for these notes. At the end of the selection, you will answer several questions about what you have just listened to. Select the best answer for each question from the choices printed below. Base your selections on the information you have heard.

Ahora vas a oír una selección más extensa. Su duración es de aproximadamente cinco minutos. Debes tomar apuntes en el espacio disponible en esta página, aunque los mismos no serán calificados. Al final de la selección, tendrás que contestar varias preguntas sobre lo que acabas de escuchar. De entre las opciones que aparecen impresas debajo, escoge la que mejor responda a cada una de las preguntas, teniendo en cuenta la información que has escuchado.

Longer Narrative

PLAY TRACK 12 ON CD 1

7. ¿De dónde proviene el nombre de Veracruz?

   A. De las culturas prehispánicas.

   B. De la conmemoración del Viernes Santo.

   C. De las tradiciones del tiempo de Moctezuma.

   D. De la plata que se almacenaba en la ciudad.

8. ¿Cuál es una de las grandes tradiciones de Veracruz?

   A. Tomar café en el Malecón.

   B. Usar vestimenta jarocha.

   C. Echarse un clavado.

   D. Tomarse una nieve.

9. ¿Qué se puede encontrar en el mercado de artesanías?

   A. Buques cargueros.

   B. Nieve de coco.

   C. Trajes de manta.

   D. Dulces tradicionales mexicanos.

10. ¿Qué hay que hacer para que un clavadista se eche al agua?

    A. Rezarle a la Virgen de Guadalupe.

    B. Tirar una moneda.

    C. Tomarse un café.

    D. Sentarse en el Zócalo.

11. ¿Qué es el Zócalo?

    A. Un mercado de artesanías.

    B. Un área de Veracruz de mucho ambiente.

    C. El puerto de Veracruz.

    D. El santuario de la Virgen de Guadalupe.

Part B

Cloze Passage

Each of the following passages contains numbered blanks, which indicate that words or groups of words are missing. There are four options to fill in each blank, but only one is correct.

In order to determine the general meaning of the passage, read quickly through it first. Then read it again and select the option that best fills each blank according to the context of the complete passage.

Cada uno de los siguientes pasajes contiene espacios en blanco numerados para indicar que faltan palabras o grupos de palabras. Hay cuatro opciones para llenar cada espacio, pero solamente una es correcta.

Para poder determinar el sentido general del pasaje, léelo rápidamente; luego léelo de nuevo y selecciona la opción que mejor complete cada espacio de acuerdo con el contexto total del pasaje.

La ciudad de México, la (12) grande del mundo, la más contaminada y la más (13) poblada, se ha convertido en una (14) ecológica. Treinta mil fábricas y 3.5 millones de vehículos (15) día con día la nube tóxica que cubre (16) entero la gran metrópoli. La ciudad de México, antaño la región más transparente, es el (17) lugar en el mundo en donde se puede llegar a contraer hepatitis con (18) aspirar el aire que todo ser humano requiere para subsistir. (19) de agua al monstruo urbano le cuesta a la ciudad mitad de su producción energética. La capital del Imperio Azteca, construida (20) un lago y un subsuelo arenoso, es materia de investigación para los científicos que observan (21) el hundimiento natural provocará que el agua contaminada finalmente alcance los lagos subterráneos.

GO ON TO THE NEXT PAGE

12. A. como
    B. más
    C. tan
    D. tanto

13. A. densamente
    B. pobremente
    C. inútilmente
    D. vagamente

14. A. maravilla
    B. pesadilla
    C. semilla
    D. tablilla

15. A. alimentan
    B. alimenten
    C. alimentarán
    D. alimentarían

16. A. con
    B. para
    C. por
    D. sin

17. A. mismo
    B. solo
    C. tanto
    D. único

18. A. casi
    B. sólo
    C. también
    D. tampoco

19. A. Abastecer
    B. Abasteciendo
    C. Abastecido
    D. Abastecida

20. A. debajo
    B. entre
    C. hacia
    D. sobre

21. A. cómo
    B. cuál
    C. cuyo
    D. que

Part C

Error Recognition

In the following sentences, select the underlined part of the sentence that is necessary to change to make the sentence grammatically correct.

En las oraciones que aparecen a continuación, escoge la parte subrayada que habría que cambiar para que la oración sea gramaticalmente correcta.

22. <u>Hacía</u> muchos años que no <u>visitaba</u>
      [A]   [B]

    Madrid, y <u>la</u> encontré <u>muy</u> cambiada
            [C]   [D]

    que me sorprendió muchísimo.

23. Con <u>tantos</u> problemas, me fue
         [A]

    imposible <u>decirle</u> a mis alumnos que no
            [B]

    <u>habían pasado</u> <u>el</u> examen final.
      [C]   [D]

24. Al <u>tener que</u> abandonar <u>la</u> embarcación,
[A]   [B]

los pasajeros no <u>pudieron</u> disfrutar <u>de la</u>
[C]   [D]

viaje.

25. <u>Nuestros</u> eminentes estadistas
[A]

<u>han determinado</u> que la economía
[B]

<u>mejorará</u> dentro de unos <u>poco</u> meses.
[C]   [D]

26. <u>El</u> agua de <u>esta</u> ciudad no <u>está</u> potable,
[A]   [B]   [C]

no <u>la</u> bebas.
[D]

27. Si <u>me dices</u> otra mentira, no <u>volveré</u> a
[A]   [B]

creer en <u>te</u> <u>nunca</u> más.
[C]   [D]

28. <u>Mantenme</u> al tanto de la situación,
[A]

<u>para que</u> cuando yo <u>regrese</u> me <u>puedas</u>
[B]   [C]   [D]

contar los detalles.

29. <u>Al</u> tratar de salir <u>del</u> coche, Aida <u>le</u>
[A]   [B]   [C]

rompió un brazo y hubo que <u>llevarla</u> al
[D]

hospital.

30. <u>Después de</u> <u>tanta</u> llover, el cielo <u>se</u>
[A]   [B]   [C]

aclaró y hasta <u>salió</u> el sol.
[D]

Part D

Reading Comprehension

Read each of the following passages. After each passage, you will find a series of incomplete sentences or questions. From the four choices given, select the option that best completes the sentence or answers the question according to the passage.

Lee cada uno de los pasajes siguientes. Al final de cada pasaje encontrarás una serie de oraciones incompletas o preguntas. De las cuatro opciones que se te dan, escoge la que mejor complete cada oración o responda a cada pregunta de acuerdo con el fragmento leído.

En las últimas décadas, después de los avances conseguidos en gran parte por los esfuerzos del feminismo, las actitudes con respecto a la mujer han cambiado y también las ideas de muchas mujeres sobre ellas mismas. Antes, la sociedad tendía a creer que el papel apropiado de la mujer era siempre el de casarse, de dar a luz, criar hijos y cuidar de la casa y del marido. Por eso presionaba a la mujer en este sentido. Si una mujer aspiraba a afirmar su personalidad a través de una carrera o de una profesión, su único camino era permanecer soltera y entonces se le miraba como a persona rara. Algo parecido ocurría con la mujer casada que no quería tener hijos; la sociedad la consideraba como a un ser extraño. Es decir, la mujer no era ni siquiera libre para elegir su estado civil, su profesión o para decidir si tendría hijos o no. Muchas jóvenes infelices se casaron así sin amor, simplemente por la presión que la sociedad y la familia ejercían sobre ellas. Y hasta años recientes, mujeres que hubieran preferido ciertas carreras, no podían seguirlas porque la sociedad les bloqueaba el camino, al considerar estas carreras aptas sólo para hombres.

GO ON TO THE NEXT PAGE

Para mostrar cuánto han cambiado las ideas de las mujeres sobre ellas mismas, echemos una ojeada a la encuesta efectuada en noviembre de 1983 por el diario *The New York Times*. Muestra que las norteamericanas encuestadas prefieren el trabajo fuera de casa al trabajo en el hogar. Es decir, quieren ganar un salario o sueldo, como lo hacen la mayoría de los hombres. La encuesta revela dos datos sorprendentes: El 58% de las mujeres interrogadas afirman que seguirían trabajando aunque tuviesen recursos económicos como para no tener que hacerlo; únicamente el 26% considera que la maternidad es uno de los objetivos máximos en la vida de una mujer. Sin duda, hace veinte o treinta años, esta misma encuesta habría dado resultados muy distintos, porque en aquel entonces la mujer tenía muchas menos opciones o alternativas en la vida.

31. ¿Qué ha logrado el feminismo?

   A. Que las mujeres no tengan hijos.

   B. Que las mujeres tengan ideas diferentes sobre sí mismas.

   C. Que las mujeres cambien su personalidad.

   D. Que las mujeres permanezcan solteras.

32. Según la lectura, ¿qué debía hacer toda mujer hace algún tiempo atrás?

   A. Afirmar su personalidad.

   B. Casarse y tener hijos.

   C. Buscar un trabajo.

   D. Cambiar su estado civil.

33. Según el pasaje, ¿cuáles eran las consecuencias si una mujer se quedaba soltera?

   A. La sociedad pensaba que era rara.

   B. La sociedad le negaba el estado civil.

   C. No podía tener hijos.

   D. Podía seguir la profesión que quisiera.

34. ¿Por qué no podían las mujeres seguir ciertas carreras?

   A. Porque tenían que dar a luz.

   B. Porque no podían afirmar su personalidad.

   C. Porque tenían que cuidar al marido.

   D. Porque eran carreras consideradas sólo para hombres.

35. Los datos de la encuesta indican que la mayoría de las mujeres

   A. prefiere tener un empleo.

   B. quiere quedarse en la casa.

   C. no necesita trabajar.

   D. considera que la maternidad es un objetivo muy importante.

IF YOU FINISH BEFORE TIME IS CALLED, CHECK YOUR WORK ON THIS SECTION ONLY. DO NOT WORK ON ANY OTHER SECTION IN THE TEST.

Section II: Free Response

This section consists of two main parts, and each part contains more than one type of exercise. The total time allotted to complete it is one hour and 20 minutes.

Part A: Writing Skills

This part tests your writing skills in Spanish, and it consists of three different exercises: paragraph fill-ins, discrete sentence fill-ins, and an essay.

Paragraph Fill-Ins

Read the following passage completely. Then read it a second time, and write on the line provided after each number the appropriate form of the word given in parentheses that will complete the fragment correctly, logically, and grammatically. Correct spelling and accent marks are necessary to receive credit. Only one word is allowed in each blank. In some instances, you may find that a change of the word in parentheses is not necessary, but you still need to write the word in the blank to receive credit.

Lee el siguiente pasaje completamente. Luego vuélvelo a leer y escribe en la línea de la derecha, después de cada número, la forma apropiada de la palabra que está entre paréntesis, para completar el fragmento de forma correcta y lógica. La ortografía y los acentos deben ser correctos para recibir crédito. Solamente se permite una palabra para cada espacio. En algunas ocasiones es posible que la palabra sugerida no necesite ningún cambio; si es así, debes escribir la palabra en el espacio en blanco para recibir crédito.

(1) tarde me pareció Román trastornado. Por (2) vez tuve frente a él la misma sensación de desequilibrio que me (3) siempre tan desagradable la permanencia junto a Juan. En el curso de aquella conversación que (4) hubo momentos en que toda la cara se (5) iluminaba de malicioso (6) humor, otras veces me miraba (7) fruncido el ceño, (8) intensos los ojos como si realmente (9) apasionante para él lo que me (10).

1. _____ (Aquel)

2. _____ (primer)

3. _____ (hacer)

4. _____ (tener)

5. _____ (le)

6. _____ (bueno)

7. _____ (medio)

8. _____ (tanto)

9. _____ (ser)

10. _____ (contar)

GO ON TO THE NEXT PAGE

Discrete Sentence Fill-Ins

In the following set of sentences, one verb is missing. Write on the line after the number the correct form and tense of the verb, taking into consideration the context of the sentence. In some cases, you may have to use more than one word, but you need to use a tense of the verb given in parentheses.

En el siguiente grupo de oraciones falta un verbo. Escribe en la línea después de cada número la forma y el tiempo correcto del verbo, tomando en consideración el contexto de la oración. En algunos casos vas a necesitar más de una palabra, pero es necesario que uses un tiempo del verbo que aparece entre paréntesis.

11. A Juanito no le gusta que lo (11) con su hermano.

11. _____(comparar)

12. Como Ángel (12) un accidente anoche, la fiesta se canceló.

12. _____(tener)

13. El profesor dijo que mañana no (13) clases de matemáticas.

13. _____(haber)

14. Colón no (14) a América si no hubiera sido tan ambicioso.

14. _____(descubrir)

15. Hace treinta años, (15) de moda las minifaldas.

15. _____(estar)

16. ¿Cuánto crees que (16) el jarrón chino que vimos ayer?

16. _____(costar)

17. Si hubieras tenido cuidado, no (17) tantos platos.

17. _____(romper)

18. Yo siempre (18) en sacar buenas notas.

18. _____(esforzarse)

19. (19) un poco, olvidarás tus penas.

19. _____(Divertirse)

20. Señores González, (20) sus documentos al juez.

20. _____(mostrar)

Essay

> **NOTE:** During the AP Spanish Language Exam, you will be given a booklet in which to write the essay. For this practice test, use any lined paper.

Write a well-organized essay in Spanish of at least 200 words about the topic given below. Your score will be based on organization, range and appropriateness of vocabulary, and grammatical accuracy. It is recommended that you use the first five minutes to organize your ideas.

Escribe un ensayo bien organizado, en español y de una extensión de al menos 200 palabras sobre el tema que aparece a continuación. Tu calificación estará basada en la organización, la riqueza y la precisión del vocabulario y la corrección gramatical. Se te recomienda que utilices los primeros cinco minutos para organizar tus ideas.

Desde pequeños nos han enseñado que no se debe decir mentiras. Sin embargo, hay ocasiones en que la vida nos obliga a decir lo que se llaman "mentiras piadosas." En un ensayo bien organizado, comenta tu opinión sobre diferentes tipos de mentiras. En tu comentario incluye ejemplos que demuestren cuándo o cuándo no debe una persona mentir y por qué.

Part B: Speaking Skills

The instructions for this section will be given to you by the Master CD. This section consists of two different exercises: a picture sequence story and directed response questions. Your voice will be recorded during this section of the exam. The instructions are mostly in English, but there are some questions in Spanish to which you must respond.

Picture Sequence

PLAY TRACK 13 ON CD 1

The six drawings below represent a story. Use the pictures to tell the story, according to your interpretation.

Los seis dibujos que aparecen a continuación representan una historieta. Utiliza los dibujos para contar la historia, según tu propia interpretación.

GO ON TO THE NEXT PAGE

Directed Response

PLAY TRACK 14 ON CD 1

IF YOU FINISH BEFORE TIME IS CALLED, CHECK YOUR WORK ON THIS
SECTION ONLY. DO NOT WORK ON ANY OTHER SECTION IN THE TEST.

Answer Key for the Diagnostic-Test

Section I: Multiple Choice Questions

Dialogue

1. C
2. A
3. A

Short Narrative

4. C
5. B
6. B

Long Narrative

7. B
8. A
9. D
10. B
11. B

Cloze Passage

12. B
13. A
14. B
15. A
16. C
17. D

18. B
19. A
20. D
21. A

Error Recognition

22. D
23. B
24. D
25. D
26. C
27. C
28. A
29. C
30. B

Reading Comprehension Passage

31. B
32. B
33. A
34. D
35. A

Section II: Free Response Questions

Paragraph Fill-Ins

1. aquella
2. primera
3. hacía
4. tuvimos
5. le
6. buen
7. medio
8. tan
9. fuera/fuese
10. contaba

Discrete Sentence Fill-Ins

11. comparen
12. tuvo
13. hay/habrá
14. habría descubierto
15. estaban
16. costaría
17. habrías roto
18. me esfuerzo
19. Divirtiéndote
20. muestren

Essay

At the end of the Diagnostic Test section you will find a guide to scoring essays together with essay samples, their scores, and an analysis of each essay.

Answers and Explanations for the Diagnostic Test

Section I: Multiple Choice Questions

Dialogue

1. C. In the beginning of the dialogue, Cecilia clearly states that she wants Arturo to inflate the float (*balsa*). Choice **D** may be attractive, but it is incorrect because Cecilia wants to get in the water herself; she doesn't want Arturo to get in the water.

2. A. Arturo states that he doesn't want to get sunburnt (*coger una insolación*). One way of figuring out the meaning of the word *insolación* is to relate it to a low-level word (in this case, that word is *sol,* which means *sun* in Spanish).

3. A. Arturo tells Cecilia to drink some lemonade (*¿Por qué no tomas un poco de limonada?*) to cool herself off. The clue here is to recognize the play on words with *refrescar.*

Short Narrative

4. C. Although children and adults are mentioned because they are afraid of vampires, the narrative states that the truth is that bats attack only cattle (*ganado vacuno*).

5. B. Although the narrative mentions the terror that vampires cause in children and adults, the narrative states that the main problem with bats is that they transmit disease (*transmiten la rabia bovina*).

6. B. Choice **A** is attractive because you may assume that, because vampires are attracted to blood, this is the way to kill them. However, the narrative says that once the bats are caught with nets, they are sprayed with poison (*veneno*) in order to get rid of them.

Long Narrative

7. B. Although Moctezuma is mentioned in the beginning of the narrative, the narrative states that the name Veracruz comes from *Viernes Santo, día de la Verdadera Cruz.*

8. A. Even though eating ice cream (Choice **D**) and diving (Choice **C**) are mentioned as traditions in the narrative, the biggest tradition is to drink some coffee on the Malecón (*visitar Veracruz y no ir al Malecón a tomar un café es como no haber conocido una de las grandes tradiciones del lugar*).

9. D. In the marketplace, one can find traditional Mexican candies (*dulces tradicionales mexicanos*).

10. B. In order for the *clavadistas* to dive, one must throw a coin into the water (*si les arrojan al agua una moneda se echan un clavado en la profundidad del mar para recogerla*).

11. A. *El Zócalo* is described as one of the liveliest places in Mexico (*Junto al Zócalo están los portales más vivos de todo México*).

Cloze Passages

12. **B.** In order to fill in this blank, look at the pattern established by using *la más* later in the sentence.

13. **A.** The adverb *densamente* is used to describe the density of the population.

14. **B.** *Pesadilla* is chosen to describe the ecological nightmare that is Mexico City.

15. **A.** The use of the present tense indicates the immediacy of the action.

16. **C.** The preposition *por* is used in common expressions such as *por entero*.

17. **D.** *Único,* when used before a noun, means *only* as opposed to *unique* (which is what it means when it is used after a noun).

18. **B.** *Sólo* is used as the shortened form of *solamente,* which means *only*.

19. **A.** In Spanish, the infinitive form of the verb may be used as a noun.

20. **D.** The preposition *sobre* is used to show that the Aztec Empire was built on top of a lake.

21. **A.** The interrogative *cómo* is used within the sentence to explain the manner in which the water is polluted.

Error Recognition

22. **D.** *Muy* is an adverb used to express the superlative of an adjective. To make the sentence correct, the adverb *tan* should be used in order to express the idea that the city has changed so much that it surprised the narrator.

23. **B.** The pronoun attached to the end of *decir* should be *les* to agree with the noun it replaces (*alumnos*).

24. **D.** The noun *viaje* is masculine, singular; therefore, the contraction *del* must be used before the noun.

25. **D.** The indefinite adjective *poco* must agree in gender and number with the noun it modifies (*meses*), which is masculine and plural.

26. **C.** The verb *ser* rather than *estar* must be used when giving a description.

27. **C.** The prepositional pronoun *ti* must be used after a preposition (*en*). *Te* is a direct object pronoun.

28. **A.** It is necessary to use the direct object pronoun *te* instead of *me* because, according to the context of the sentence, the second person is the one who needs to keep informed.

29. **C.** Aida broke her arm; therefore, the third person reflexive pronoun *se* must be used, rather than the indirect object pronoun *le*.

30. **B.** In this sentence, *tanto* is used as an adverb modifying the verb *llover;* therefore, it is invariable.

Reading Comprehension Passage

31. B. Feminism has changed the way women think of themselves (*las actitudes con respecto a la mujer han cambiado y también las ideas de muchas mujeres sobre ellas mismas*).

32. B. Not long ago, women were expected to marry, raise a family, and keep house (*el papel apropiado de la mujer era siempre el de casarse, de dar a luz, criar hijos y cuidar de la casa y del marido*).

33. A. At one time, society considered single women strange (*entonces se le miraba como a persona rara*).

34. D. Some career choices were reserved for men only (*la sociedad les bloqueaba el camino, al considerar estas carreras aptas sólo para hombres*).

35. A. According to the survey, most women prefer to work outside the home (*las norteamericanas encuestadas prefieren el trabajo fuera de casa al trabajo en el hogar*).

Section II: Free Response Questions

Paragraph Fill-Ins

1. aquella. The demonstrative must show agreement in gender and number with the noun (*tarde*).

2. primera. The adjective and the noun (*vez*) must agree in gender and number.

3. hacía. Use the imperfect to describe events in the past.

4. tuvimos. Use the preterit to indicate that the action was completed in the past.

5. le. Use the indirect object pronoun to talk about Juan's face.

6. buen. *Bueno* drops the *-o* when used before a masculine, singular noun.

7. medio. *Medio* remains in the masculine, singular form to show agreement.

8. tan. *Tanto* is reduced to *tan* when modifying adjectives or adverbs.

9. fuera/fuese. Use the imperfect subjunctive in dependent noun clauses when the verb in the main clause is in the imperfect.

10. contaba. Use the imperfect to describe a continuous action in the past.

Discrete Sentence Fill-Ins

11. comparen. Use the subjunctive following the expression *gustar que*.

12. tuvo. Use the preterit to indicate that the action was completed in the past.

13. hay/habrá. The present tense as well as the future tense may be used to express future time. Notice that this is a case of the impersonal use of *haber* to refer to the presence or existence of something, so only the third person singular form is correct.

14. **habría descubierto.** Use the conditional perfect to describe the result of an action.

15. **estaban.** Use the imperfect to indicate a continuous action in the past.

16. **costaría.** Use the conditional when the main verb expresses belief (such as *creer*).

17. **habrías roto.** Use the conditional perfect after an if clause that uses the subjunctive. The second person singular is required because, although the subject is omitted, the previous verb hints that the subject is *tú*.

18. **me esfuerzo.** Use the present tense to indicate a repeated or continuous action.

19. **divirtiéndote.** The use of the gerund is equivalent to English phrases beginning with *by* (such as *by having fun*). The second person singular is required because, although the subject is omitted, the second verb hints that the subject is *tú*.

20. **muestren.** Formal commands use the present subjunctive. The formal command is required because the speaker sets the formal tone by addressing the other person(s) by a title (in this case, *Señores*).

Sample Answers for Essay Question

High-Scoring Essay

Aunque desde pequeños nuestros padres nos hayan enseñado a no decir mentiras, a veces nos damos cuenta de que ellos alguna vez han dicho una que otra mentira. Son las llamadas "mentiras piadosas."

Yo no creo que hay ninguna diferencia entre una mentira y una "mentira piadosa." Las dos son iguales, porque con una mentira se oculta la verdad. Sin embargo, la diferencia principal, en mi opinión, es qué verdad se está ocultando. No es lo mismo mentir, para encubrir a una persona que ha cometido una falta y está tratando de evadir el castigo, que mentir cuando se le oculta a una persona una verdad que puede hacerle mucho daño.

Por ejemplo, si sabes que alguien ha robado algo, y dices que no lo sabes o dices que fue otra persona, lo que estás haciendo es encubrir a alguien que ha cometido un delito. Pero las "mentiras piadosas" son las que se dicen para no hacer sufrir a otra persona. Quizás sabes que alguien tiene una enfermedad grave, y no lo sabe, tú le dices una mentira para evitar que esa persona se desanime y piense que se va a morir.

En conclusión, yo creo que mentir no es bueno, sobre todo cuando se convierte en un hábito o ayuda a la gente a hacer cosas malas, pero si mintiendo, yo puedo evitar el sufrimiento de una persona que quiero, yo miento.

Analysis of the High-Scoring Essay

This essay demonstrates a relevant and very well-developed treatment of the given topic. It also has very good organization, and ease of expression is demonstrated. There is ample evidence that the writer has control of complex structures, such as the usage of the subjunctive rather than of the indicative (*nos hayan enseñado*), the usage of the gerund (*estás haciendo, si mintiendo*), and the usage of perfect tense (*ha robado, ha cometido*). The range of vocabulary is very ample (*encubrir, evadir, delito, desanimar, sufrimiento*). Spelling and other conventions of the language are correct. **Score: 9**

Medium-Scoring Essay

Yo no estoy en acuerdo que hay varios tipos de mentiras. Porque mentir quiere a decir que no estás diciendo verdad, y mi mama siempre dice que la gente siempre tiene que decir la verdad, porque es pescado decir mentira.

Es verdad que la gente dice mentiras por diferentes razones y que unas veces es mas malo que otros. Si tu dice mentiras para que una persona no va a la cárcel, porque un crimen que cometió, es más malo que decir a tu mama que no tienes dinero, y tienes dos pesos. Yo creo que la gente dice "mentiras piadosas" porque tiene mucho miedo a decir la verdad a unos otros, porque no quiere que causan un suffering a los parientes o los amigos. Yo creo que tienes que ser valiente y decir todo, aunque sea muy mal.

En conclusión yo no creo que tienen diferentes tipos de mentiras, porque cuando dices mentiras no dices la verdad y esto es lo mas importante.

Analysis of the Medium-Scoring Essay

This essay shows some control of basic grammar structures, although there are some errors in the use of irregular comparative (*más malo*). There are also errors of lack of agreement between noun and pronoun (*unas veces es más malo que otros*). There are some evident mistakes in the usage of more complex patterns, such as the usage of the indicative, rather than the subjunctive, mode (*para que una persona no va a la cárcel*). Also, the use of prepositions shows some lack of control (*estoy en acuerdo, quiere a decir*). There are some redeeming features, such as the correct use of the subjunctive (*aunque sea*), but in general the essay maintains a basic grammatical usage. There is an evident interference from English (*decir la verdad a unos otros, suffering*). This essay shows limited vocabulary. There is adequate organization, but the essay is not extensive. There are some errors of spelling (*pescado*), and a few accent marks are missing. This essay shows that the writer possesses more than a basic command of the language. **Score: 5**

PART IV

THREE FULL-LENGTH PRACTICE TESTS

If you struggle with the listening sections of the exams, go to www.cliffsnotes.com/extras on the Web to find a script of the Audio CDs.

Answer Sheet for Practice Test 1

(Remove this sheet and use it to mark your answers)

CUT HERE

PART A

1 Ⓐ Ⓑ Ⓒ Ⓓ
2 Ⓐ Ⓑ Ⓒ Ⓓ
3 Ⓐ Ⓑ Ⓒ Ⓓ
4 Ⓐ Ⓑ Ⓒ Ⓓ
5 Ⓐ Ⓑ Ⓒ Ⓓ
6 Ⓐ Ⓑ Ⓒ Ⓓ
7 Ⓐ Ⓑ Ⓒ Ⓓ
8 Ⓐ Ⓑ Ⓒ Ⓓ
9 Ⓐ Ⓑ Ⓒ Ⓓ
10 Ⓐ Ⓑ Ⓒ Ⓓ
11 Ⓐ Ⓑ Ⓒ Ⓓ
12 Ⓐ Ⓑ Ⓒ Ⓓ
13 Ⓐ Ⓑ Ⓒ Ⓓ
14 Ⓐ Ⓑ Ⓒ Ⓓ
15 Ⓐ Ⓑ Ⓒ Ⓓ
16 Ⓐ Ⓑ Ⓒ Ⓓ
17 Ⓐ Ⓑ Ⓒ Ⓓ
18 Ⓐ Ⓑ Ⓒ Ⓓ
19 Ⓐ Ⓑ Ⓒ Ⓓ
20 Ⓐ Ⓑ Ⓒ Ⓓ
21 Ⓐ Ⓑ Ⓒ Ⓓ
22 Ⓐ Ⓑ Ⓒ Ⓓ
23 Ⓐ Ⓑ Ⓒ Ⓓ
24 Ⓐ Ⓑ Ⓒ Ⓓ
25 Ⓐ Ⓑ Ⓒ Ⓓ
26 Ⓐ Ⓑ Ⓒ Ⓓ
27 Ⓐ Ⓑ Ⓒ Ⓓ
28 Ⓐ Ⓑ Ⓒ Ⓓ

PART B

29 Ⓐ Ⓑ Ⓒ Ⓓ
30 Ⓐ Ⓑ Ⓒ Ⓓ
31 Ⓐ Ⓑ Ⓒ Ⓓ
32 Ⓐ Ⓑ Ⓒ Ⓓ
33 Ⓐ Ⓑ Ⓒ Ⓓ
34 Ⓐ Ⓑ Ⓒ Ⓓ
35 Ⓐ Ⓑ Ⓒ Ⓓ
36 Ⓐ Ⓑ Ⓒ Ⓓ
37 Ⓐ Ⓑ Ⓒ Ⓓ
38 Ⓐ Ⓑ Ⓒ Ⓓ
39 Ⓐ Ⓑ Ⓒ Ⓓ
40 Ⓐ Ⓑ Ⓒ Ⓓ
41 Ⓐ Ⓑ Ⓒ Ⓓ
42 Ⓐ Ⓑ Ⓒ Ⓓ
43 Ⓐ Ⓑ Ⓒ Ⓓ
44 Ⓐ Ⓑ Ⓒ Ⓓ
45 Ⓐ Ⓑ Ⓒ Ⓓ
46 Ⓐ Ⓑ Ⓒ Ⓓ
47 Ⓐ Ⓑ Ⓒ Ⓓ
48 Ⓐ Ⓑ Ⓒ Ⓓ

PART C

49 Ⓐ Ⓑ Ⓒ Ⓓ
50 Ⓐ Ⓑ Ⓒ Ⓓ
51 Ⓐ Ⓑ Ⓒ Ⓓ
52 Ⓐ Ⓑ Ⓒ Ⓓ
53 Ⓐ Ⓑ Ⓒ Ⓓ
54 Ⓐ Ⓑ Ⓒ Ⓓ
55 Ⓐ Ⓑ Ⓒ Ⓓ
56 Ⓐ Ⓑ Ⓒ Ⓓ
57 Ⓐ Ⓑ Ⓒ Ⓓ
58 Ⓐ Ⓑ Ⓒ Ⓓ
59 Ⓐ Ⓑ Ⓒ Ⓓ
60 Ⓐ Ⓑ Ⓒ Ⓓ
61 Ⓐ Ⓑ Ⓒ Ⓓ
62 Ⓐ Ⓑ Ⓒ Ⓓ
63 Ⓐ Ⓑ Ⓒ Ⓓ

PART D

64 Ⓐ Ⓑ Ⓒ Ⓓ
65 Ⓐ Ⓑ Ⓒ Ⓓ
66 Ⓐ Ⓑ Ⓒ Ⓓ
67 Ⓐ Ⓑ Ⓒ Ⓓ
68 Ⓐ Ⓑ Ⓒ Ⓓ
69 Ⓐ Ⓑ Ⓒ Ⓓ
70 Ⓐ Ⓑ Ⓒ Ⓓ
71 Ⓐ Ⓑ Ⓒ Ⓓ
72 Ⓐ Ⓑ Ⓒ Ⓓ
73 Ⓐ Ⓑ Ⓒ Ⓓ
74 Ⓐ Ⓑ Ⓒ Ⓓ
75 Ⓐ Ⓑ Ⓒ Ⓓ
76 Ⓐ Ⓑ Ⓒ Ⓓ
77 Ⓐ Ⓑ Ⓒ Ⓓ
78 Ⓐ Ⓑ Ⓒ Ⓓ
79 Ⓐ Ⓑ Ⓒ Ⓓ
80 Ⓐ Ⓑ Ⓒ Ⓓ
81 Ⓐ Ⓑ Ⓒ Ⓓ
82 Ⓐ Ⓑ Ⓒ Ⓓ
83 Ⓐ Ⓑ Ⓒ Ⓓ
84 Ⓐ Ⓑ Ⓒ Ⓓ
85 Ⓐ Ⓑ Ⓒ Ⓓ
86 Ⓐ Ⓑ Ⓒ Ⓓ
87 Ⓐ Ⓑ Ⓒ Ⓓ
88 Ⓐ Ⓑ Ⓒ Ⓓ
89 Ⓐ Ⓑ Ⓒ Ⓓ
90 Ⓐ Ⓑ Ⓒ Ⓓ

CUT HERE

Section I: Multiple Choice Questions

This section consists of four different parts: Part A, Part B, Part C, and Part D.

Total time: 1 hour and 30 minutes

Number of questions: 90

Percent of total grade: 50

Part A

Time: Approximately 30 minutes

The time for the questions below is paced by the tape.

You will hear a few dialogues. At the end of each, you will hear several questions about what you have just listened to. From the choices printed below, select the one that best responds to each question.

Ahora vas a oír algunos diálogos. Al final de cada uno escucharás unas preguntas sobre lo que has escuchado. De entre las opciones que aparecen impresas, escoge la que mejor responda a cada una de las preguntas.

Get ready to listen to the first dialogue.

Dialogue 1

PLAY TRACK 15 ON CD 1

1. A. Ella ya no va al gimnasio.

    B. Ella cambió su horario de hacer ejercicios.

    C. Ella consiguió un trabajo de maestra.

    D. Ella ya terminó sus horas comunitarias.

2. A. Se mantiene en la línea.

    B. Se pone muy nerviosa.

    C. Trabaja con niños pequeños.

    D. Asiste a la universidad.

3. A. Cuidar niños pequeños.

    B. Mantener su figura.

    C. Terminar sus estudios.

    D. Ver a Miguel.

4. A. Ya no va nunca.

    B. A las once de la mañana.

    C. A las doce del día.

    D. A las cinco de la tarde.

Dialogue 2

PLAY TRACK 16 ON CD 1

5. **A.** De negocios,

   B. De novios.

   C. De vacaciones.

   D. De estudios.

6. **A.** El no sabe.

   B. Donde diga su novia.

   C. A un lugar muy turístico.

   D. A las islas griegas.

7. **A.** Porque a su novia no le gusta la playa.

   B. Porque es un lugar poco romántico.

   C. Porque hace demasiado calor.

   D. Porque hay mucha gente allí en el verano.

Dialogue 3

PLAY TRACK 17 ON CD 1

8. **A.** De que la graduación sea en tres semanas.

   B. De que Leonardo esté en la biblioteca tan tarde.

   C. De que Leonardo esté estudiando medicina.

   D. De que Leonardo haya llenado unos formularios.

9. **A.** Tiene mucho trabajo de la escuela.

   B. No se puede graduar en tres semanas.

   C. No podrá estudiar la carrera que le gusta.

   D. No tiene dinero para ir a la universidad.

10. **A.** Profesor de biología.

    B. Escultor.

    C. Profesor de artes plásticas.

    D. Médico.

You will hear a few short narratives. At the end of each, you will hear several questions about what you have just listened to. From the choices printed below, select the one that best responds to each question.

Ahora vas a oír algunas narraciones cortas. Al final de cada una escucharás algunas preguntas sobre lo que has escuchado. De entre las opciones que aparecen impresas, escoge la que mejor responda a cada una de las preguntas.

Get ready to listen to the first narrative.

Narrative 1

PLAY TRACK 18 ON CD 1

11. **A.** Animales fósiles parientes de las arañas.

B. Un tipo de dinosaurio fosilizado.

C. Un tipo de animal marino fosilizado.

D. Los posibles antepasados del hombre.

12. **A.** Fueron los primeros organismos pluricelulares.

B. Fueron los primeros que tuvieron el cuerpo dividido en tres partes.

C. Fueron los primeros que vivieron fuera del agua.

D. Fueron los únicos que se fosilizaron.

13. **A.** Parece que están vivos.

B. Parece que no tienen cerebro.

C. Dan la imagen de una explosión.

D. Parecen objetos de coleccionistas.

Narrative 2

PLAY TRACK 19 ON CD 1

14. **A.** Que la escritura se originó en Egipto.

B. Que la escritura es más antigua de lo que se creía.

C. Que la escritura nació en Mesopotamia.

D. Que la escritura fue desarrollada por los sumerios.

15. **A.** Inscripciones sumerias.

B. Tabletas de escritura cuneiforme.

C. Vasijas de Mesopotamia.

D. Nuevos datos sobre la escritura egipcia.

16. **A.** A que la escritura egipcia es la más antigua.

B. A que los sumerios usaban inscripciones en tinta.

C. A que la escritura cuneiforme es mesopotámica.

D. A que los pueblos antiguos no se comunicaban con escritura.

You will hear a longer selection. It is about five minutes in length. You may take notes, although you will not receive a grade for these notes. At the end of the selection, you will answer several questions about what you have just heard. Select the best answer for each question from the choices printed on the exam. Base your selections on the information you have heard.

Ahora vas a oír una selección más extensa. Su duración es de aproximadamente cinco minutos. Debes tomar apuntes en el espacio disponible en esta página, aunque los mismos no serán calificados. Al final de la selección, tendrás que contestar varias preguntas sobre lo que acabas de escuchar. De entre las opciones que aparecen en el examen, escoge la que mejor responda a cada una de las preguntas, teniendo en cuenta la información que has escuchado.

GO ON TO THE NEXT PAGE

Longer Narrative 1

PLAY TRACK 20 ON CD 1

17. ¿Cuándo se fundó San Agustín?

  A. En 1500.

  B. En 1565.

  C. En 1586.

  D. En 1640.

18. ¿De dónde proviene el nombre de la ciudad?

  A. Era el nombre del rey de España.

  B. Del calendario religioso.

  C. Así se llamaba el conquistador que la fundó.

  D. Era el nombre de un pirata famoso.

19. ¿Por qué fue importante San Agustín durante el período colonial español?

  A. Porque sobrevivió las guerras del siglo XVIII.

  B. Porque era la única estación militar en la frontera noreste del Imperio Español.

  C. Porque fue parte de la adquisición de la Florida.

  D. Porque tenía las construcciones más antiguas.

20. ¿Qué recuerda The Oldest Wooden Schoolhouse?

  A. Las invasiones extranjeras.

  B. El saqueo de los piratas.

  C. La falta de educación.

  D. Las condiciones de vida de los habitantes.

21. ¿Qué es la coquina?

  A. Un tipo de construcción de San Agustín.

  B. Una mezcla de cal, concha y arena.

  C. Un tipo de concha.

  D. Un edificio viejo de San Agustín.

22. ¿En qué está inspirado el estilo del castillo de Zorayda?

  A. En un castillo árabe de Granada.

  B. En la isla de Anastasia.

  C. En construcciones del Medio Oriente.

  D. En el estilo moderno floridano.

23. ¿Qué protege a la ciudad de San Agustín?

  A. El castillo de Zorayda.

  B. La Misión del Nombre de Dios.

  C. Los cañones del castillo de San Marcos.

  D. La familia Musallem.

You will hear another selection. It is about five minutes in length. You may take notes, although you will not receive a grade for these notes. At the end of the selection, you will answer several questions about what you have just heard. Select the best answer for each question from the choices printed on the exam. Base your selections on the information you have heard.

Ahora vas a oír otra selección. Su duración es de aproximadamente cinco minutos. Debes tomar apuntes en el espacio disponible en esta página, aunque los mismos no serán califica-dos. Al final de la selección, tendrás que contestar varias preguntas sobre lo que acabas de es-cuchar. De entre las opciones que aparecen en el examen, escoge la que mejor responda a cada una de las preguntas, teniendo en cuenta la información que has escuchado.

Longer Narrative 2

PLAY TRACK 21 ON CD 1

24. ¿Qué es lo único a que le tiene miedo El Cordobés?

    A. Al número trece.

    B. A la virgen.

    C. A los toros.

    D. A ponerse viejo.

25. ¿Cuánto cobró El Cordobés por una corrida?

    A. Trece mil dólares.

    B. Quinientos dólares.

    C. Veinte duros.

    D. Un millón de pesetas.

26. ¿Por qué se sentía El Cordobés como un fracasado antes de ser torero?

    A. Era muy pobre.

    B. No sabía leer.

    C. Había sido herido varias veces.

    D. Estaba preso en Carabanchel.

27. ¿Por qué fue preso El Cordobés?

    A. Por robar un cochinillo.

    B. Por rebuscar maíces.

    C. Por echarse a torear en la Plaza de Madrid.

    D. Por recoger remolachas.

28. ¿Qué pasaba cuando El Cordobés toreaba por televisión?

    A. Todo se paralizaba.

    B. La gente hablaba mal de él.

    C. Un profesor lo enseñaba a leer.

    D. La gente quería que le firmara un libro.

GO ON TO THE NEXT PAGE

Part B

Suggested time: 10 minutes

Cloze Passages

Each of the following passages contains numbered blanks, which indicate that words or groups of words are missing. There are four options to fill in each blank, but only one is correct.

In order to determine the general meaning of the passage, read quickly through it first. Read it again and select the option that best fills each blank according to the context of the complete passage.

Cada uno de los siguientes pasajes contiene espacios en blanco numerados para indicar que faltan palabras o grupos de palabras. Hay cuatro opciones para llenar cada espacio, pero solamente una es correcta.

Para poder determinar el sentido general del pasaje, léelo rápidamente; luego léelo de nuevo y selecciona la opción que mejor complete cada espacio de acuerdo con el contexto total del pasaje.

La Condesa casi nunca (29) del palacio. Contemplaba el jardín (30) el balcón plateresco de su alcoba, y con la sonrisa amable de las devotas linajudas, (31) pedía a Fray Angel, su capellán, que (32) las rosas para el altar de la (33) . Era muy piadosa la Condesa. (34) como una priora noble retirada en las estancias tristes y silenciosas de (35) palacio, con los ojos vueltos (36) el pasado . . . Descendía de la casa de Barbanzón, una de las más antiguas . . . La Condesa guardaba (37) reliquias aquellas páginas infanzonas aforradas en velludo carmesí, que de los (38) pasados hacían gallarda remembranza con sus grandes letras floridas . . .

29. A. salía	**31. A.** lo	
B. sale	**B.** la	
C. salió	**C.** le	
D. saldrá	**D.** se	
30. A. desde	**32. A.** corte	
B. de	**B.** cortó	
C. hasta	**C.** cortase	
D. hacia	**D.** cortará	

33. A. capilla

    B. casilla

    C. cestilla

    D. mesilla

34. A. Vive

    B. Vivía

    C. Vivió

    D. Ha vivido

35. A. mi

    B. tu

    C. su

    D. sus

36. A. a

    B. con

    C. desde

    D. hacia

37. A. como

    B. cuyas

    C. tan

    D. cual

38. A. siglos

    B. momentos

    C. estaciones

    D. épocas

Mi primera víctima (y cuántas más no han caído ya) fue nuestro propio perro, (39) nombre, demasiado denigrante, demasiado perruno, no quiero declarar aquí. Ahora que (40) pienso bien, creo que su nombre (41) parte principalísima en el desenlace. Quizá si se (42) de otro modo yo (43) en él. El nombre de un perro es (44) importante como el perro mismo. Un hombre, una mujer, pueden, si les da la (45), y por motivos a cual más extraño y pintoresco, (46) otro apelativo . . . Pero un perro tiene que sufrir su nombre de por vida, (47) que tome la (48) de lanzarse a la calle y convertirse en un perro vagabundo, huesoso, innominado . . .

39. A. cuya

    B. cuyo

    C. cual

    D. que

40. A. el

    B. lo

    C. la

    D. se

41. A. tiene

    B. tenía

    C. tuvo

    D. haya tenido

42. A. ha llamado

    B. había llamado

    C. haya llamado

    D. hubiera llamado

GO ON TO THE NEXT PAGE

43. A. he reparado

B. haya reparado

C. había reparado

D. habría reparado

44. A. más

B. menos

C. mucho

D. tan

45. A. gama

B. gana

C. ganga

D. gansa

46. A. buscarse

B. marcarse

C. quitarse

D. sacarse

47. A. a menos

B. al menos

C. al tanto

D. por tanto

48. A. decisión

B. dedicación

C. salvación

D. solución

Part C

Suggested time: 10 minutes

Error Recognition

In the following sentences, select the underlined part of the sentence that needs to be changed in order to make the sentence grammatically correct.

En las oraciones que aparecen a continuación, escoge la parte subrayada que habría que cambiar para que la oración sea gramaticalmente correcta.

49. Yo <u>estaba</u> hablando <u>por teléfono</u> cuando
     [A]   [B]
<u>se oyeron</u> unos golpes <u>tan</u> fuertes en la
  [C]   [D]
puerta.

50. Se <u>han recibido</u> varios informes de
     [A]
compañías <u>cuyas</u> finanzas se <u>hallan</u>
       [B]   [C]
en <u>mal</u> situación.
   [D]

51. Pedro se <u>interrogó</u> a <u>él</u> mismo <u>sobre</u> el
       [A]   [B]   [C]
éxito <u>de la</u> misión.
   [D]

52. <u>Cuando</u> Bernardo terminó de <u>contando</u>
  [A]   [B]
su historia, todos se <u>habían quedado</u>
               [C]
dormidos, debido a <u>la</u> lentitud del
             [D]
relato.

53. No es la <u>primer</u> vez que María <u>se cae</u> <u>de</u>
       [A]   [B] [C]
la escalera, <u>rodando</u> por sus peldaños.
         [D]

54. Todos <u>esperaban</u> esas palabras <u>del</u> jefe
     [A]   [B]
<u>por</u> volver, aunque en realidad no lo
 [C]
<u>desearan</u>.
  [D]

55. En la escuela <u>habían</u> chicos violentos
[A]

con <u>los que</u> Mario tenía que <u>pelearse</u>
[B]   [C]

<u>de vez</u> en cuando.
[D]

56. El abogado <u>me</u> escuchó con paciencia
[A]

<u>hasta</u> que <u>terminaba</u> de contarle lo que
[B]   [C]

<u>había sucedido</u> con mis maletas.
[D]

57. Aunque <u>supe</u> desde hace tiempo que él
[A]

<u>llegaría</u> a eso de las dos <u>de</u> la tarde, yo
[B]   [C]

lo esperaba con inquietud desde <u>el</u>
[D]

amanecer.

58. A pesar <u>de que</u> no <u>conocí</u> mucho a
[A]   [B]

Roberto, en pocos días <u>me</u> puse al tanto
[C]

de <u>su</u> situación.
[D]

59. Cecilia no <u>encontraba</u> palabras <u>para</u>
[A]   [B]

agradecerle <u>a</u> Lucía <u>tantos</u> atenciones.
[C]   [D]

60. <u>Al</u> unirse al equipo de béisbol, Orlando
[A]

<u>sólo</u> quería conseguir amistades <u>nuevos</u>
[B]   [C]

porque se <u>sentía</u> muy solo.
[D]

61. Como el sol <u>le</u> molestaba en <u>sus</u> ojos
[A]   [B]

<u>tuvo</u> que comprarse unos lentes <u>más</u>
[C]   [D]

oscuros.

62. <u>Por</u> aquella época, se <u>veía</u> que <u>tanta</u> Ana
[A]   [B]   [C]

como Roberto, no <u>podían</u> olvidar lo
[D]

sucedido.

63. No existe <u>ningún</u> ley que <u>prohíba</u> que
[A]   [B]

los residentes <u>viajen</u> a <u>otros</u> países de
[C]   [D]

Europa.

Part D

Suggested time: 40 minutes

Reading Comprehension Passages

Read each of the following passages. After each passage, you will find a series of incomplete sentences or questions. From the four choices given, select the option that best completes the sentence or answers the question according to the passage.

Lee cada uno de los pasajes siguientes. Al final de cada pasaje encontrarás una serie de oraciones incompletas o preguntas. De las cuatro opciones que aparecen, escoge la que mejor completa cada oración o responda a cada pregunta de acuerdo con el fragmento leído.

GO ON TO THE NEXT PAGE

El hambre tiene distintas causas pero en general todas están relacionadas con el subdesarrollo económico. Un clima duro y la falta de buena tierra cultivable pueden ser causas determinantes de la pobreza. Pero una tierra pobre y desértica puede tornarse fértil, sin embargo, con el uso de modernas técnicas de cultivo, entre ellas el riego artificial, como ha ocurrido en Israel. En ciertas regiones de África, Asia y Latinoamérica, los campesinos cultivan la tierra con métodos y con procedimientos que poco han cambiado a través de los siglos. Es decir, en muchos países la pobreza y el hambre están relacionadas no sólo con las condiciones económicas sino también con el atraso tecnológico.

En los países del tercer mundo millones de personas mueren cada año de hambre o de enfermedades producidas por la desnutrición. Centenares de millones más viven desnutridas por la escasez de alimentos que les impide el consumo mínimo necesario para mantener la salud. La deficiencia alimenticia resta vitalidad a otros millones de personas y la falta de proteínas afecta el cerebro de muchos niños, causándoles un retraso mental.

No bastan para solucionar el problema las organizaciones humanitarias de los países ricos. Estas organizaciones alivian el hambre endémica enviando sacos de harina, arroz, leche en polvo y otras materias alimenticias, sobre todo cuando a la pobreza crónica se agregan desastres naturales como sequías e inundaciones, o cuando ocurren conflictos armados. Tales medidas ofrecen un alivio parcial pero nunca contribuyen a una solución permanente. Para ello, sería preciso primeramente aumentar la producción de alimentos en estas regiones pobres y luego asegurar una distribución equitativa, y ello requeriría en muchos casos un profundo cambio sociopolítico. La cooperación internacional podría contribuir con sus esfuerzos a transformar la economía de estas regiones. Los países más privilegiados podrían ayudar enviando instructores técnicos para adiestrar a los agricultores locales en los modernos métodos de cultivo más idóneos para cada región. También se necesitaría una enorme cantidad de capital para efectuar una modernización profunda de la economía de esos países.

Pero la cooperación internacional a ese nivel parece todavía utópica. Lo más probable es que esas regiones del tercer mundo, cuyas poblaciones están aumentando rápidamente, seguirán viviendo a merced de la naturaleza y de la ayuda alimenticia de los países más afortunados.

64. Según el pasaje, ¿cuál es la causa principal del hambre mundial?

    A. La falta de desarrollo económico.

    B. La dureza del clima.

    C. La calidad de la tierra.

    D. El bajo número de campesinos.

65. ¿Qué causa la muerte y muchas de las enfermedades y trastornos en la población del tercer mundo?

    A. La desnutrición.

    B. La falta de medicina.

    C. La falta de agua.

    D. Los desastres naturales.

66. La ayuda de las organizaciones humanitarias no resuelve el problema totalmente porque solamente

    A. alivian el hambre endémica.

    B. cooperan mandando tecnología.

    C. ayudan cuando hay guerras.

    D. ayudan cuando ocurren desastres naturales.

67. Como primer paso para reducir el hambre mundial, el pasaje sugiere

    A. reducir el atraso tecnológico.

    B. consumir lo mínimo para conservar la salud.

    C. aumentar la producción de alimientos en el tercer mundo.

    D. invertir mucho capital en la economía de los países del tercer mundo.

68. ¿Cómo podrían ayudar los países más ricos?

    A. Enviando arroz y leche en polvo.

    B. Enseñando a los campesinos a usar métodos más modernos de cultivo.

    C. Evitando conflictos armados.

    D. Haciendo grandes cambios sociopolíticos.

69. Según la conclusión de este pasaje, la situación económica del tercer mundo

    A. dependerá de los cambios políticos.

    B. se verá afectada por cambios climáticos.

    C. mejorará radicalmente en pocos años.

    D. continuará dependiendo de otros países.

Si de verdad fueran las cigüeñas las que "trajesen los bebés," todos procederíamos de África. En realidad, esto es cierto en parte: Desde hace algunos años sabemos que el primer hombre fue un "africano," nacido hace cuatro millones de años en Olduvai, en Tanzania, o en Etiopía a lo largo del valle del Hombre, o en Kenya en las orillas del lago Turkana. Así, pues, a fin de cuentas todos procedemos del África negra, de una extensa área en donde la cigüeña pasa algunos meses del año invernando.

El área africana de la cigüeña europea es aún más vasta; se extiende al sur del Sahara de este a oeste por una gran parte del continente, llegando hasta el Transvaal y Sudáfrica.

En el continente negro, la cigüeña tiene un extraño modo de cazar. Cuando el sol incandescente provoca en la sabana grandes y repentinos incendios, la cigüeña aguarda impasible a los ratones, los reptiles y los insectos que huyen aterrados del fuego.

Los africanos llaman a la cigüeña con un nombre que significa "gran pájaro de las langostas," puesto que, en su dieta, estos dañosísimos insectos desempeñan un papel de primera magnitud. Por esta razón, en Mali es una especie protegida desde hace unos años.

Los habitantes de aquel país han partido de algunas comprobaciones. En primer lugar, que la lucha contra los enjambres de insectos llevada a cabo hasta hoy, y que se sigue haciendo, con pesticidas lanzados en gran cantidad desde aviones es eficaz, pero terriblemente peligroso, pues mueren las langostas pero también los insectos polinizadores que son útiles para la agricultura. En segundo lugar, que una vez absorbidos por el suelo los pesticidas entran en un círculo, envenenando primero la vegetación, luego los animales que se alimentan de ella y, por último, al hombre que es el último anillo de la cadena alimentaria. En tercer lugar, la cigüeña es, naturalmente, un eficaz pesticida ecológico. De ahí que se la proteja hoy. Resulta interesante observar que, en Mali, se ha promovido la "campaña cigüeña," para tutelar las dos especies de cigüeña: la cigüeña

GO ON TO THE NEXT PAGE

blanca, europea, y la cigüeña negra, africana de Abdim, que sólo vive en África. Esto sugiere una estupenda metáfora: Unámonos todos, blancos y negros para la salvación del mundo; unamos nuestras fuerzas y defendamos la vida.

Y la cigüeña es vida. Su nombre, acuñado por los sumerios en Mesopotamia hace ya decenas y decenas de siglos, alude a un símbolo mágico. En realidad, cigüeña significaría "el cascarón que da vida."

70. ¿En qué se basa la introducción de este pasaje?

    A. En un mito popular.

    B. En una creencia religiosa.

    C. En una verdad científica.

    D. En una superstición antigua.

71. ¿Qué hacen todos los años las cigüeñas en África?

    A. Buscan a los bebés.

    B. Aprenden a cazar.

    C. Pasan los meses de invierno.

    D. Provocan incendios.

72. Según este pasaje, ¿qué elemento natural juega un papel importante en la alimentación de la cigüeña?

    A. El sol.

    B. Las sabanas.

    C. Los incendios.

    D. El polen.

73. ¿Qué animal ocupa un lugar primordial en la dieta de la cigüeña?

    A. El ratón.

    B. Un reptil.

    C. Otra cigüeña.

    D. La langosta.

74. ¿Por qué está protegida la cigüeña en Mali?

    A. Para que siga trayendo bebés.

    B. Porque elimina insectos dañinos.

    C. Porque evita grandes incendios.

    D. Para que no se coma a los ratones.

75. ¿Por qué es peligroso usar pesticidas en Mali?

    A. Porque envenena a las cigüeñas.

    B. Porque se caen los aviones.

    C. Porque produce grandes incendios.

    D. Porque al final mata al hombre.

76. Según el pasaje, la "campaña cigüeña" es equivalente a

    A. la unión de los humanos para proteger al mundo.

    B. la labor que hacen algunos animales.

    C. la tradición popular africana.

    D. La preocupación de los hombres por controlar a los animales.

77. ¿Con qué se relaciona el nombre "cigüeña"?

    A. Con un hombre de Olduvai.

    B. Con el lagoTurkana.

    C. Con un símbolo mágico sumerio.

    D. Con un tipo de langosta de Mali.

Existía, hace muchos años, un rey joven y apuesto, que no había encontrado aún a una mujer capaz de despertar su amor, aunque le habían presentado las más bellas princesas casaderas de todos los reinos vecinos. Ninguna había conseguido enamorarle, pues les encontraba a todas mil defectos.

Su placer favorito era la caza, a la que dedicaba todos los ratos libres que le dejaban sus asuntos de Estado. En una cacería en que iba, como siempre, acompañado de nobles caballeros y seguido por los monteros y perros, se internó en la espesura del monte, y allí encontró a una pastora de extraordinaria belleza cuidando su rebaño, que pastaba en un verde ribazo, y, al verla, quedó enamorado de ella. Acercóse el rey a hablarle, y le preguntó cómo se llamaba, al tiempo que alababa su gran hermosura. Ella contestó que Griselda, y respondió con tal discreción que el rey, que no había estado nunca enamorado, sintió abrasarse de amor y le propuso hacerla su esposa, declarándole el sentimiento que había nacido en su alma. Ella aceptó, y el rey le impuso como previa condición a su boda que tenía que obedecerle ciegamente a cuanto él le mandara, sin que de sus labios saliera una queja, aunque le viera hacer las más extrañas cosas. La pastora se comprometió a cumplirlo y fue conducida a palacio y vestida con magníficos trajes de brocado de oro. Las bodas se celebraron con pompa y esplendor, y a la ceremonia acudieron todos los nobles del reino.

Muy feliz transcurrió el primer año de matrimonio para la pastora y el rey. Al cabo de él, la reina dio a luz un niño: "Siento decirte que tengo que matar al niño que acaba de nacer, porque un rey no puede tener descendencia con una pastora."

La madre quedó horrorizada al oírlo; pero recordó la condición que ella había aceptado antes de su boda y, dominando su dolor, replicó: "Vuestro hijo es; haced de él lo que queráis."

El rey tomó al niño de brazos de su madre y se lo entregó a un servidor para que lo matara. Griselda quedó muerta de angustia, pero sin proferir una queja.

La pastora siguió obedeciendo ciegamente los mandatos de su esposo, y pasado el segundo año nació una niña. El rey, al verla, dijo: "He de mandar matar también a tu hija, porque mi reino se opone a que yo mezcle mi sangre real con la de una pastora."

A lo que Griselda, haciendo esfuerzos inauditos por contener su pena, respondió: "Cúmplase vuestra voluntad, que hija vuestra es."

Y unos servidores de palacio sacaron a la niña de la habitación de la madre, que quedó desolada, pero sin que nadie le oyera un solo lamento.

78. ¿Qué conflicto tenía el joven monarca?

A. No encontraba mujeres solteras.
B. Tenía muchos defectos.
C. No tenía tiempo para enamorarse.
D. No encontraba una esposa de su gusto.

79. El rey dedicaba su tiempo libre a

A. jugar con sus perros.
B. cuidar su rebaño.
C. buscar novia.
D. ir de cacería.

80. ¿Quién es Griselda?

A. Una pastora bella.
B. La hija de un caballero noble.
C. Una princesa vecina.
D. La hija de un montero.

GO ON TO THE NEXT PAGE

81. ¿Cómo conoció el rey a Griselda?

    A. Por casualidad.

    B. Se la presentaron.

    C. Ella vino a su palacio.

    D. La vio en una boda.

82. Para poder casarse con el rey, Griselda siempre tendría que

    A. serle fiel.

    B. cuidar el rebaño.

    C. aceptar sus órdenes.

    D. esconder su identidad.

83. ¿Qué hace el rey con los hijos de Griselda?

    A. Se los lleva al ribazo.

    B. Los mata en cuanto nacen.

    C. Se los regala a los criados.

    D. Los manda vivir con los pastores.

84. ¿Qué hace Griselda ante las acciones de su esposo?

    A. Reacciona con violencia.

    B. Se lamenta horrorizada.

    C. Esconde su dolor y obedece.

    D. Demuestra su pena llorando.

85. ¿Qué puede inferirse sobre las cualidades morales de Griselda, según su forma de actuar?

    A. Era una mujer fiel a sus principios.

    B. Era mejor madre que esposa.

    C. No le tenía amor a sus hijos.

    D. Tenía miedo de la cólera del rey.

Había una vez un niño llamado David N., cuya puntería y habilidad en el manejo de la resortera despertaba tanta envidia y admiración en sus amigos de la vecindad y de la escuela, que veían en él—y así lo comentaban entre ellos cuando sus padres no podían escucharlos—un nuevo David.

Pasó el tiempo.

Cansado del tedioso tiro al blanco que practicaba disparando sus guijarros contra latas vacías o pedazos de botella, David descubrió un día que era mucho más divertido ejercer contra los pájaros la habilidad con que Dios lo había dotado, de modo que de ahí en adelante la emprendió con todos los que se ponían a su alcance, en especial contra Pardillos, Alondras, Ruiseñores y Jilgueros, cuyos cuerpecitos sangrantes caían suavemente sobre la hierba, con el corazón agitado aún por el susto y la violencia de la pedrada.

David corría jubiloso hacia ellos y los enterraba cristianamente.

Cuando los padres de David se enteraron de esta costumbre de su buen hijo se alarmaron mucho, le dijeron que qué era aquello, y afearon su conducta en términos tan ásperos y convincentes que, con lágrimas en los ojos, él reconoció su culpa, se arrepintió sincero, y durante mucho tiempo se aplicó a disparar exclusivamente sobre los otros niños.

Dedicado años después a la milicia, en la Segunda Guerra Mundial David fue ascendido a general y condecorado con las cruces más altas por matar él solo a treinta y seis hombres, y más tarde degradado y fusilado por dejar escapar viva una Paloma mensajera del enemigo.

86. ¿Por qué se destacaba David?

A. Porque tenía muchos amigos.

B. Porque no le gustaba la escuela.

C. Porque tenía destreza para tirar al blanco.

D. Porque no le gustaba escuchar a sus padres.

87. Del pasaje se deduce que una resortera es un objeto para

A. tirar piedras.

B. abrir latas.

C. romper botellas.

D. controlar un vehículo.

88. ¿Quiénes fueron las víctimas de la habilidad de David?

A. Sus padres.

B. Los pájaros.

C. Sus amigos.

D. Los vecinos.

89. ¿Cómo reaccionaron los padres de David al saber lo que el chico hacía?

A. Lo regañaron duramente.

B. Lo obligaron a ir a la escuela.

C. Le regalaron una alondra.

D. Le regalaron una resortera.

90. ¿Cómo afectó a David en la edad adulta la lección que le enseñaron sus padres?

A. Le propició una carrera brillante.

B. Le costó la vida.

C. Le hizo matar a muchos hombres.

D. Le facilitó una gran oportunidad.

IF YOU FINISH BEFORE TIME IS CALLED, CHECK YOUR WORK ON THIS SECTION ONLY. DO NOT WORK ON ANY OTHER SECTION IN THE TEST.

STOP

Section II: Free Response

This section consists of two main parts, Part A and Part B, and each part contains more than one type of exercise.

Total time: 1 hour and 20 minutes
Percent of total grade: 50

Part A: Writing Skills

This part tests your writing skills in Spanish, and it consists of three different exercises: paragraph fill-ins, discrete sentence fill-ins, and an essay.

Time: 60 minutes

Paragraph Fill-Ins

Suggested time: 8 minutes

Read the following passage completely. Then read it a second time, and write on the line provided after each number the appropriate form of the word given in parentheses that will complete the fragment correctly, logically, and grammatically. Correct spelling and accent marks are necessary to receive credit. Only one word is allowed in each blank. In some instances, you may find that a change of the word in parentheses is not necessary, but you still need to write the word in the blank to receive credit.

Lee el siguiente pasaje. Luego vuélvelo a leer y escribe en la línea de la derecha, después de cada número, la forma apropiada de la palabra que está entre paréntesis, para completar el fragmento de forma correcta y lógica. La ortografía y los acentos deben ser correctos para recibir crédito. Solamente se permite una palabra para cada espacio. Es posible que la palabra sugerida no necesite ningún cambio; si es así, debes escribir la palabra en el espacio en blanco para recibir crédito.

Al (1) al ábside de la Catedral me (2) en el baile de luces que (3) los faroles contra sus (4) rincones, (5) románticos y (6). Oí un áspero carraspeo como si a alguien se (7) desgarrara el pecho entre la maraña de (8). Era un sonido siniestro, (9) por los ecos, que se iba (10). Pasé unos momentos de miedo.

1. _____(llegar)

2. _____(fijar)

3. _____(hacer)

4. _____(mil)

5. _____(volverse)

6. _____(tenebroso)

7. _____(le)

8. _____(callejuela)

9. _____(cortejado)

10. _____(acercar)

Discrete Sentence Fill-Ins

Suggested time: 7 minutes

In the following set of sentences, one verb is missing. Write on the line after the number the correct form and tense of the verb, taking into consideration the context of the sentence. In some cases, you may have to use more than one word, but you need to use a tense of the verb given in parentheses.

En el siguiente grupo de oraciones falta un verbo. Escribe en la línea después de cada número la forma y el tiempo correctos del verbo, tomando en consideración el contexto de la oración. En algunos casos vas a necesitar más de una palabra, pero es necesario que uses un tiempo del verbo que aparece entre paréntesis.

GO ON TO THE NEXT PAGE

11. Quiero que (11) a Griselda; es una chica encantadora.

11. _____(conocer)

12. Ayer (12) la matrícula de la universidad con el dinero que me dio mi padre.

12. _____(pagar)

13. Cuando (13) el programa, me avisas, por favor.

13. _____(empezar)

14. Anoche (14) dos incendios en la misma calle.

14. _____(haber)

15. Cuando llegue el verano, ya todos los árboles (15).

15. _____(florecer)

16. Como la estaba esperando, Elena (16) muy de prisa.

16. _____(vestirse)

17. No creo que Rosalía (17) esas cosas de mí.

17. _____(decir)

18. (18) hacia la iglesia, verás el edificio del que te hablé.

18. _____(ir)

19. Raquel, no (19) miedo; los fantasmas no existen.

19. _____(tener)

20. Niños, (20) ropas apropiadas para ir a esquiar.

20. _____(ponerse)

Essay

Suggested writing time: 45 minutes

> **NOTE:** During the AP Spanish Language Exam, you will be given a booklet in which to write the essay. For this practice test, use any lined paper.

Write a well-organized essay in Spanish of at least 200 words and about the topic given below. Your score will be based on organization, range and appropriateness of vocabulary, and grammatical accuracy. It is recommended that you use the first five minutes to organize your ideas.

Escribe un ensayo bien organizado, en español y de una extensión de al menos 200 palabras, sobre el tema que aparece a continuación. Tu calificación estará basada en la organización, la riqueza y la precisión del vocabulario y la corrección gramatical. Se te recomienda que utilices los primeros cinco minutos para organizar tus ideas.

En los últimos tiempos se ha producido un "boom" en la tecnología, que a su vez ha causado cambios en las posibilidades del empleo. En un ensayo bien organizado comenta sobre las habilidades que son necesarias ahora para conseguir un empleo, en comparación con las que se necesitaban antes de producirse esta explosión tecnológica.

Part B: Speaking Skills

The instructions for this section will be given to you by the Master CD. This section consists of two different exercises: a picture sequence story and directed response questions. Your voice will be recorded during this section of the exam. The instructions are mostly in English, but there are some questions in Spanish to which you must respond.

PLAY TRACK 1 ON CD 2

The six drawings on the next page represent a story. Use the pictures to tell the story, according to your interpretation.

Los seis dibujos que aparecen en la próxima página representan una historieta. Utiliza los dibujos para contar la historia, según tu propia interpretación.

GO ON TO THE NEXT PAGE

Directed Response

PLAY TRACK 2 ON CD 2

IF YOU FINISH BEFORE TIME IS CALLED, CHECK YOUR WORK ON THIS
SECTION ONLY. DO NOT WORK ON ANY OTHER SECTION IN THE TEST.

Practice Test 1 Scoring Worksheet

This worksheet is designed to help you calculate your score in this practice test following similar procedures to those used by the College Board. Try to be as objective as you can while evaluating the essay and the oral questions. In the case of the essay, you may compare the sample essays given to your own work to be able to determine your own score.

Section I: Multiple Choice Section

Part A: number correct (out of 28)_____ − ($\frac{1}{3}$ × **number wrong** _____) × 1.2857 = ☐

Part B: number correct (out of 20)_____ − ($\frac{1}{3}$ × **number wrong** _____) × .9000 = ☐

Part C: number correct (out of 15)_____ − ($\frac{1}{3}$ × **number wrong** _____) × .6000 = ☐

Part D: number correct (out of 27)_____ − ($\frac{1}{3}$ × **number wrong** _____) × 1.0000 = ☐

Total weighted section I score (add the 4 boxes): _____

Section II: Free Response Section

Fill-Ins: (out of 20)_____ × .6750 = ☐

Essay: (out of 9)_____ × .9474 = ☐

Picture Sequence: (out of 9)_____ × .5294 = ☐

Directed Responses: (out of 20)_____ × 1.1250 = ☐

Total weighted section II score (add the 4 boxes): _____

Final Score

weighted section I: _____ + **weighted section II:** _____ = **final score:** _____

Probable Final AP Score

Final Converted Score	Probable AP Score
180–134	5
133–114	4
113–86	3
85–63	2
62–0	1

Answer Key for Practice Test 1

Section I: Multiple-Choice Questions

Dialogue 1
1. B
2. C
3. B
4. D

Dialogue 2
5. B
6. A
7. D

Dialogue 3
8. B
9. C
10. D

Short Narrative 1
11. A
12. B
13. A

Short Narrative 2
14. B
15. B
16. A

Long Narrative 1
17. B
18. B
19. B
20. D
21. C
22. A
23. C

Long Narrative 2

24. C
25. D
26. A
27. C
28. A

Cloze Passages

29. A
30. A
31. C
32. C
33. A
34. B
35. C
36. D
37. A
38. A
39. B
40. B
41. C
42. D
43. D
44. D
45. B
46. A
47. A
48. A

Error Recognition

49. D
50. D
51. B

52. B
53. A
54. C
55. A
56. C
57. A
58. B
59. D
60. C
61. B
62. C
63. A

Reading Comprehension Passages

64. A
65. A
66. A
67. C
68. B
69. D
70. A
71. C
72. A
73. A
74. B
75. D
76. A
77. C
78. D
79. A
80. A
81. A
82. C

83. B		**87.** A	
84. C		**88.** B	
85. A		**89.** A	
86. C		**90.** B	

Section II: Free-Response Questions

Paragraph Fill-Ins

1. llegar
2. fijé
3. hacían
4. mil
5. volviéndose
6. tenebrosos
7. le
8. callejuelas
9. cortejado
10. acercando

Discrete Sentence Fill-Ins

11. conozcas, conozca, conozcan
12. pagué, he pagado
13. empiece
14. hubo
15. habrán florecido
16. se vistió
17. diga, haya dicho
18. yendo
19. tengas
20. pónganse

Essay Question

In the section "Answers and Explanations for Practice Test 1," you will find a guide to scoring essays together with essay samples, their scores, and analysis of each essay.

Answers and Explanations for Practice Test 1

Section I: Multiple Choice Questions

Dialogue 1

1. **A.** At the very beginning of the dialogue, Ana states that she is still going to the gym (*sigo yendo al gimnasio*), but she doesn't see Miguel anymore because she had to switch classes (*tuve que cambiar mi horario de la clase de aeróbicos*). Although Choice **A** seems like an appropriate answer, Miguel only thinks Ana doesn't go to the gym anymore because he has not seen her lately.

2. **C.** Choice **D** is a good distracter because Ana mentions that she needs community service hours for college before she states what she does in the morning; however, she immediately explains that she works at a day-care center (*guardería infantil*) every morning.

3. **B.** At the beginning of the dialogue, Ana clarifies that she is still going to the gym because she likes to stay in shape (*mantener la línea*). Although Choice **A** may seem like a possibility because Miguel mentions it, the only time Ana says something is important to her is when she talks about exercising.

4. **D.** Ana clearly states that she now goes to the gym at 5:00 p.m. (*ahora voy a las cinco de la tarde*). Choice **B** and Choice **C** may be attractive because both times were mentioned in the dialogue; however, Choice **B** is referring to Ana's old aerobics class, and Choice **C** refers to the time that Ana finishes working at the day-care center.

Dialogue 2

5. **B.** Although you may be tempted to select Choice **C** due to the nature of the trip, the man states at the beginning of the conversation that he wants to surprise his fiancée with a spectacular honeymoon (*viaje de novios*).

6. **A.** Although the man mentions that his fiancée loves the beach, he says he has no fixed idea of where he wants to go (*no tengo ni idea*) at the beginning of the dialogue; that is why the clerk gives him several suggestions.

7. **D.** The man doesn't want to go to Torremolinos because it is too crowded in the summer (*en el verano va demasiada gente*). Choice **A** is contradictory to what the man stated earlier (*a mi novia le encanta la playa*), and Choice **C** is not a possible answer because there is no specific information about Torremolinos in the dialogue.

Dialogue 3

8. **B.** Choice **D** is a good distracter because, when Leonardo mentions the applications (*formularios*), Laura reacts with an expression of surprise; in reality, though, she is surprised because he has not filled them out (*no me digas que todavía no lo has hecho*).

9. **C.** Although Leonardo mentions that he has a lot of work (Choice **A**), he makes the point at the end of the dialogue that he cannot study what he wants because his father is opposed to it (*mi padre . . . quiere que sea médico como él*).

10. **D.** You learn that Leonardo's father is a doctor because that is the reason Leonardo cannot be a sculptor (*escultor*).

Short Narrative 1

11. **A.** The narrative describes trilobites as relatives of spiders and scorpions (*artrópodos fósiles emparentados con las arañas y los escorpiones*). To understand this, you must make the connection between *emparentado* and *pariente*.

12. **B.** Trilobites were the first organism to have a body that was divided into three parts. In order to answer this question, you must realize that *fue trascendente* is a synonym of *importancia*.

13. **A.** Although Choice **D** is attractive because the narrative states that the trilobite fossils have become collectors' items, the question refers to the impression they cause (*nos hace pensar que están vivos*).

Short Narrative 2

14. **B.** Although Egypt and Mesopotamia are mentioned in the narrative as parts of the world where writing may have originated, this group of people discovered that writing is at least 200 years older than it was believed to be (*es 200 años más antigua de lo que se creía*).

15. **B.** Choice **A** is attractive because the narrative mentions that the group found inscriptions, but it does not state where the inscriptions were from. In order to answer this question, you must be attentive to the word *tabletas*.

16. **A.** To select the correct option, listen for the word *conclusión* in the narrative and take note of what follows; the narrative textually states that the team concluded that the oldest writing comes from Egypt.

Longer Narrative 1

17. **B.** Although all the dates were mentioned in the narrative, only this choice refers to the founding of San Agustín.

18. **B.** The narrative states that the city's name is derived from a particular saint's day (*el 8 de septiembre de 1565, día del festival de San Agustín*); therefore, the answer involves the religious calendar.

19. **B.** The question asks about the importance of San Agustín during the colonial period; the narrative states that the city was of military significance (*fue la única estación militar importante de la frontera noreste del imperio español en América*).

20. **D.** You may be tempted to select Choice **B** because of the possible confusion between "The Oldest Wooden Schoolhouse" and "The Oldest House."

21. C. The definition of *coquina* is given as a kind of shell (*la concha de la region*). You may confuse this answer with the elements that make up the floors of the rooms.

22. A. *El Castillo de Zorayda* was inspired by a Moorish castle in Granada (*su estilo morisco estuvo inspirado en lo que su constructor viera al visitar la Alhambra en Granada, España*).

23. C. San Agustín is protected by the cannons of the castle of San Marcos (*permanece protegido por los cañones del Castillo de San Marcos*).

Longer Narrative 2

24. C. In order to answer this question, you must make the connection between the words *sólo* and *único,* which both mean *only* in English (*yo sólo le tengo miedo a los toros*).

25. D. Although *veinte duros* was also used in the text, the answer is a million pesetas (*un millón de pesetas que pesaba un kilo*).

26. A. Although this answer is not clearly stated in the narrative, you can infer it from the following statement: *desde chiquito ya empecé a robar cochinillos por los campos.*

27. C. Although stealing is an offense that could result in arrest, the narrative states that he was jailed for spontaneously jumping into the bullring (*porque me había tirado de espontáneo en la plaza de Madrid*).

28. A. Although Choice **C** and Choice **D** were both mentioned in the narrative, neither describes what would happen when El Cordobés would fight a bull (*se paraba todo cuando mis corridas salían en televisión*).

Cloze Passages

29. A. Use the imperfect to indicate a continuous action in the past.

30. A. Use the preposition *desde* to indicate the location from which the garden was seen.

31. C. Use the third person indirect object pronoun to indicate that Fray Ángel was the person receiving the action.

32. C. Use the imperfect subjunctive to indicate subordination in a clause preceded by *que.*

33. A. *Capilla* (chapel) is clearly the choice after the use of the word *altar.*

34. B. Use the imperfect to indicate an ongoing action in the past.

35. C. Use the third person possessive adjective in reference to La Condesa.

36. D. To indicate that her eyes looked toward the past, use the preposition *hacia.*

37. A. In this case, the word *como* means "like" (as used in a simile).

38. A. Because La Condesa was remembering her lineage, you can infer that centuries have gone by.

39. B. The relative pronoun *cuyo* indicates possession and agrees in gender and number with the thing possessed (in this case, *nombre*).

40. B. *Lo* is used in this construction because the direct object of the verb *pensar* is implied, but not given.

41. C. Use the preterit to indicate that the action occurred in the past and was completed in the past.

42. D. *Quizá* refers to hypothetical actions; therefore, use the past perfect subjunctive after an adverb of probability.

43. D. The statement refers to a situation that is a consequence of a previous action; therefore, use the perfect conditional.

44. D. *Tan . . . como* are the key words used in a comparative statement of equality.

45. B. *Dar la gana* is an idiomatic expression, loosely translated as "feel like."

46. A. The context of the sentence requires the use of the verb *buscarse,* which means "to look for."

47. A. Use *a menos* to mean "unless."

48. A. *Tomar la decisión* is an expression that means "make a decision."

Error Recognition

49. D. The adverb *tan* is used in comparative patterns. The context of the sentence requires *muy,* which is normally used in superlative constructions.

50. D. The word *mal* is used as an adjective; therefore, it must agree in gender and number with the noun it modifies (in this case, *situación*), which is feminine singular.

51. B. Use the prepositional pronoun *sí* after a preposition rather than the subject pronoun *él.*

52. B. *Terminar de* + infinitive is the appropriate construction for this sentence. The use of the gerund is incorrect.

53. A. *Vez* is a feminine singular noun; therefore, the numeral must agree in gender and number.

54. C. The preposition *para* is used to denote purpose or intention.

55. A. Use only the third person singular forms of *haber* in impersonal expressions to indicate the presence or existence of something.

56. C. Use the preterit rather than the imperfect to indicate that the action was completed in the past.

57. A. *Supe* means "I found out." *Sabía* is equivalent to "knew," which is the meaning required by the context of this sentence.

58. B. *Conocí* means "to meet for the first time." *Conocía* means "was acquainted with," which is the meaning required by the context of this sentence.

59. D. *Atenciones* is a feminine plural noun; therefore, the adjective *tantos* does not agree with it in gender. *Tantas* will make this sentence correct.

60. C. *Amistades* is a feminine plural noun; therefore; the adjective *nuevos* does not agree with it in gender. *Nuevas* will make this sentence correct.

61. B. Before a body part, use a definite article rather than a possessive adjective.

62. C. Here, the word *tanto* is part of an adverbial phrase (*tanto como*); therefore, it is invariable.

63. A. The noun *ley* is feminine singular; therefore, the indefinite adjective *ningún* must agree in gender and number. *Ninguna* will make this sentence correct.

Reading Comprehension Passage

64. A. To find the main cause of world hunger, look at the first line of the passage: *están relacionadas con el subdesarrollo económico.*

65. A. The causes of death and illness in the Third World are related to malnutrition (*millones de personas mueren cada año de hambre o de enfermedades producidas por la desnutrición*).

66. A. Humanitarian aid does not completely solve the problem of hunger in the Third World; rather, it merely provides a temporary solution (*estas organizaciones alivian el hambre endémica*).

67. C. The passage suggests that the first step to reduce world hunger is to increase the food production in the poorest areas (*aumentar la producción de alimentos en estas regiones pobres y luego asegurar una distribución equitativa*).

68. B. Richer nations can help by sending people to train the locals in new agricultural methods (*los países más privilegiados podrían ayudar enviando instructores técnicos para adiestrar a los agricultores locales en los modernos métodos de cultivo más idóneos para cada región*).

69. D. This passage concludes that the poorest nations will still be dependent upon the aid of the richer nations (*esas regiones del tercer mundo . . . seguirán viviendo a merced de la naturaleza y de la ayuda alimenticia de los países más afortunados*).

70. A. The introduction to this passage is based on the popular belief that the stork delivers babies to expectant mothers (*si de verdad fueran las cigüeñas las que "trajesen los bebés"*).

71. C. The stork spends a few months of the year in Africa (*la cigüeña pasa algunos meses del año invernando*).

72. A. The sun plays an important role in the nutrition of storks (*cuando el sol incandescente provoca . . . repentinos incendios, la cigüeña aguarda impasible a los ratones, los reptiles y los insectos que huyen aterrados del fuego*).

73. A. Africans call the stork *gran pájaro de las langostas,* which means "great bird of the locusts." They use this name because these insects are the main staple of the stork diet.

74. B. The stork is protected in Mali because it helps eliminate very dangerous insects such as locusts (*la langosta*).

75. D. Using pesticides to get rid of insects is very dangerous because, once the chemicals are absorbed into the ground, they will travel up the food chain and ultimately reach humans (*una vez absorbidos por el suelo los pesticidas entran en un círculo, envenenando primero la vegetación . . . y por último al hombre*).

76. A. *La campaña cigüeña* is used as a metaphor for the union of all human beings to protect the world (*unámonos todos, blancos y negros para la salvación del mundo*).

77. C. The name *cigüeña* is related to a magical symbol (*su nombre acuñado por los sumerios . . . alude a un símbolo mágico*).

78. D. The passage states that he found something wrong with every girl he met (*ninguna había conseguido enamorarle, pues les encontraba a todas mil defectos*).

79. A. According to the passage, the king loved to hunt (*su placer favorito era la caza*).

80. A. The passage states that Griselda was a shepherdess (*allí encontró a una pastora . . . le preguntó su nombre . . . ella contestó Griselda*).

81. A. You can deduce from the passage that their meeting was not planned; it was by chance.

82. C. According to the pasaje, Griselda had to obey the king unconditionally (*el rey le impuso como previa condición a su boda que tenía que obedecerle ciegamente*).

83. B. After each child's birth, the passage states that the king decided to kill the baby (*siento decirte que tengo que matar al niño que acaba de nacer*).

84. C. Because Griselda remembers the condition she agreed to before her marriage, she accepts her husband's decision (*la madre quedó horrorizada al oírlo, pero recordó la condición que ella había aceptado antes de su boda y, dominando su dolor . . .*).

85. A. You can infer from the passage that Griselda was a woman of her word (*la madre quedó desolada, pero sin que nadie le oyera un solo lamento*).

86. C. The words *tiro al blanco* appear in the passage (*cansado del tedioso tiro al blanco . . .*).

87. A. If you make an educated guess about the meaning of *guijarros,* you can deduce that a *resortera* is used to throw stones (*tirar piedras*).

88. B. The passage states that David soon found it was much more fun to aim at birds than bottles (*era mucho más divertido ejercer contra los pájaros*).

89. A. According to the passage, David's parents scolded him (*afearon su conducta en términos tan ásperos y convincentes que él reconoció su culpa*).

90. B. David learned his lesson and was later executed for releasing the enemy's messenger pigeon (*más tarde [fue] degradado y fusilado por dejar escapar viva una paloma mensajera del enemigo*).

Section II: Free Response Questions

Paragraph Fill-Ins

1. **llegar.** Use *al* + infinitive to denote the coexistence of two events.

2. **fijé.** Use the preterit to indicate that the action was completed in the past. The subject of the sentence is omitted, but the reflexive pronoun *me* tells you that the subject is in the first person singular.

3. **hacían.** Use the imperfect for descriptions in the past.

4. **mil.** Used as a numeral, *mil* does not show agreement when indicating a specific quantity.

5. **volviéndose.** Use the gerund to correspond with the "-ing" form in English in modal adverbial expressions. The reflexive pronoun *se,* included in the infinitive form given, remains the same because it is taking the place of *rincones.*

6. **tenebrosos.** This adjective is modifying *rincones,* a masculine plural noun. The previous adjective, *románticos,* gives you a clue.

7. **le.** The indirect object pronoun remains singular because it must agree with the indefinite *alguien.*

8. **callejuelas.** The word *maraña* (jungle, tangle) is a collective noun; therefore, the noun that is acting as a modifier must be plural.

9. **cortejado.** The past participle is used as an adjective to modify *sonido,* a masculine singular noun.

10. **acercando.** The gerund is used with *ir* to indicate "gradually" or "little by little."

Discrete Sentence Fill-Ins

11. **conozcas, conozca, conozcan.** Use the subjunctive after the expression *querer que.* Because no other clue is given, any of the Spanish second person forms may be correct.

12. **pagué, he pagado.** You can use either the preterit or the present perfect because the results of the action may or may not be seen in the present. The subject of the sentence is *yo.*

13. **empiece.** Use the subjunctive after an adverbial clause beginning with *cuando.*

14. **hubo.** Use the preterit to refer to an occurrence that was completed in the past. This is a case of the use of the impersonal verb *haber* (equivalent to "there is/there are"), which only takes the form of the third person singular.

15. **habrán florecido.** Use the future perfect to indicate that an event will be completed in the future before some other point in time in the future.

16. **se vistió.** Use the preterit to indicate that the action was completed in the past.

17. **diga, haya dicho.** The expression *no creer que* requires the present subjunctive or the present perfect subjunctive.

18. **yendo.** The use of the gerund is equivalent to the English phrase beginning with "when . . ."

19. **tengas.** Negative informal commands use the present subjunctive. The informal command is required because the speaker addresses the other person using her first name.

20. **pónganse.** Use the imperative form to indicate that a command is given. The informal command plural is required because the speaker sets up the tone of the conversation with the word *niños.*

Sample Answers for Essay Question

High-Scoring Essay

El siglo XX fue el testigo de muchos cambios, entre ellos la importancia de la tecnología y los avances tecnológicos. Este cambio, ciertamente afectó a las personas que buscan empleo, porque ahora para realizar algunos trabajos hay que saber trabajar con algunos de esos adelantos tecnológicos. A medida que se han ido descubriendo e inventando nuevos aparatos para la medicina, la comunicación y el transporte, los empleos requieren un adiestramiento especial para poder trabajar con estos instrumentos que antes no existían.

Antes del "boom" tecnológico, para realizar muchos trabajos solamente había que saber leer y escribir bien. Una secretaria solamente tenía que saber la mecanografía y la taquigrafía, para tomar dictados y redactar las cartas de su jefe. Los cajeros solamente tenían que saber un poco de matemáticas para trabajar con el dinero y usar una sencilla caja registradora. O sea, que con una educación básica se podía conseguir un buen empleo.

Ahora, para tener un buen trabajo, casi siempre es necesario tener una educación universitaria. En muchas compañías requieren que sus empleados sepan usar programas especializados de computadora. Una secretaria del siglo XXI tiene que saber utilizar los programas de computadora requeridos en su campo. Hoy en día, un cajero tiene una registradora que es una computadora y tiene que saber como darle la información para poder cobrar.

Como hemos visto con los dos ejemplos que he dado, conseguir un trabajo en el siglo XXI requiere muchos conocimientos relacionados con los avances de la tecnología.

Analysis of the High-Scoring Essay

In this essay, the reader finds a relevant and very well-developed treatment of the topic. The essay is well organized, and ease of expression is noticeable throughout. The writer makes good use of transitional words or phrases (*a medida que, antes de, o sea, ahora, hoy en día*). There is abundant evidence of the writer's control of complex grammatical structures (*este cambio . . . afectó a las personas que buscan . . . a medida que se han ido descubriendo . . .*). There is an ample usage of different verb forms and tenses, including the present, imperfect, preterit, and present perfect of the indicative, as well as present subjunctive and verb + infinitive. There is a wide range of vocabulary (*testigo, adelantos, adiestramiento, taquigrafía, redactar*). The writer shows very good control of spelling and other conventions of the written language. **Score: 9**

Medium-Scoring Essay

Es verdad que en esto tiempos el uso de la tecnología se ha convertido en algo muy importante. Es casi imposible a conseguir un buen empleo si no sabes algo de computadora.

Por ejemplo, ahora la gente que trabaja en la medicina tiene que usar unos aparatos que antes ni existían. Ahora se hace la cirugía con los rayos láser, que es más facil, pero el doctor tiene que saber como usar el instrumento.

No es solo en medicina que la tecnología ha avanzado. Cuando vas a un restaurante, notas los avances. Antes el camarero escribia la nota con todo lo que querias, y el cheque estaba escrito a mano. Ahora todo el orden se pone en la computadora y sale un recivo con los nombres de lo que comiste y el precio también. El problema es que el camarero tiene que saber usando la computadora para trabajar ahí.

Finalmente, yo creo que ahora la gente que quiere conseguir un trabajo tiene que saber también un poco de las cosas tecnicas.

Analysis of the Medium-Scoring Essay

In this essay, the reader observes a relatively good control of basic grammar structures, although there are some errors (*esto tiempo*). There is evidence that the writer does not have control of more complex patterns (*saber usando*). Although there is some variety of verbal tenses, including the present, the imperfect, and the present perfect, there is no evidence of the usage of the subjunctive or other modes. There are some redeeming features—such as the correct form of the past participle of *escribir,* which is irregular, to agree with the noun it modifies (*escrito*), and the use of more complex patterns, such as *tiene que saber como usar*—but in general, the essay maintains a basic grammatical usage. This essay shows a lack of control in the use of prepositions (*imposible a conseguir*). The range of vocabulary is limited. Spelling and accentuation are generally correct, although there are some errors in spelling (*recivo*), and there are some accent marks missing, especially in the forms of the imperfect tense. The essay is relevant to the topic, and the organization is adequate. **Score: 6**

Answer Sheet for Practice Test 2

(Remove this sheet and use it to mark your answers)

CUT HERE

PART A

1 Ⓐ Ⓑ Ⓒ Ⓓ
2 Ⓐ Ⓑ Ⓒ Ⓓ
3 Ⓐ Ⓑ Ⓒ Ⓓ
4 Ⓐ Ⓑ Ⓒ Ⓓ
5 Ⓐ Ⓑ Ⓒ Ⓓ
6 Ⓐ Ⓑ Ⓒ Ⓓ
7 Ⓐ Ⓑ Ⓒ Ⓓ
8 Ⓐ Ⓑ Ⓒ Ⓓ
9 Ⓐ Ⓑ Ⓒ Ⓓ
10 Ⓐ Ⓑ Ⓒ Ⓓ
11 Ⓐ Ⓑ Ⓒ Ⓓ
12 Ⓐ Ⓑ Ⓒ Ⓓ
13 Ⓐ Ⓑ Ⓒ Ⓓ
14 Ⓐ Ⓑ Ⓒ Ⓓ
15 Ⓐ Ⓑ Ⓒ Ⓓ
16 Ⓐ Ⓑ Ⓒ Ⓓ
17 Ⓐ Ⓑ Ⓒ Ⓓ
18 Ⓐ Ⓑ Ⓒ Ⓓ
19 Ⓐ Ⓑ Ⓒ Ⓓ
20 Ⓐ Ⓑ Ⓒ Ⓓ
21 Ⓐ Ⓑ Ⓒ Ⓓ
22 Ⓐ Ⓑ Ⓒ Ⓓ
23 Ⓐ Ⓑ Ⓒ Ⓓ
24 Ⓐ Ⓑ Ⓒ Ⓓ
25 Ⓐ Ⓑ Ⓒ Ⓓ
26 Ⓐ Ⓑ Ⓒ Ⓓ
27 Ⓐ Ⓑ Ⓒ Ⓓ
28 Ⓐ Ⓑ Ⓒ Ⓓ

PART B

29 Ⓐ Ⓑ Ⓒ Ⓓ
30 Ⓐ Ⓑ Ⓒ Ⓓ
31 Ⓐ Ⓑ Ⓒ Ⓓ
32 Ⓐ Ⓑ Ⓒ Ⓓ
33 Ⓐ Ⓑ Ⓒ Ⓓ
34 Ⓐ Ⓑ Ⓒ Ⓓ
35 Ⓐ Ⓑ Ⓒ Ⓓ
36 Ⓐ Ⓑ Ⓒ Ⓓ
37 Ⓐ Ⓑ Ⓒ Ⓓ
38 Ⓐ Ⓑ Ⓒ Ⓓ
39 Ⓐ Ⓑ Ⓒ Ⓓ
40 Ⓐ Ⓑ Ⓒ Ⓓ
41 Ⓐ Ⓑ Ⓒ Ⓓ
42 Ⓐ Ⓑ Ⓒ Ⓓ
43 Ⓐ Ⓑ Ⓒ Ⓓ
44 Ⓐ Ⓑ Ⓒ Ⓓ
45 Ⓐ Ⓑ Ⓒ Ⓓ
46 Ⓐ Ⓑ Ⓒ Ⓓ
47 Ⓐ Ⓑ Ⓒ Ⓓ
48 Ⓐ Ⓑ Ⓒ Ⓓ

PART C

49 Ⓐ Ⓑ Ⓒ Ⓓ
50 Ⓐ Ⓑ Ⓒ Ⓓ
51 Ⓐ Ⓑ Ⓒ Ⓓ
52 Ⓐ Ⓑ Ⓒ Ⓓ
53 Ⓐ Ⓑ Ⓒ Ⓓ
54 Ⓐ Ⓑ Ⓒ Ⓓ
55 Ⓐ Ⓑ Ⓒ Ⓓ
56 Ⓐ Ⓑ Ⓒ Ⓓ
57 Ⓐ Ⓑ Ⓒ Ⓓ
58 Ⓐ Ⓑ Ⓒ Ⓓ
59 Ⓐ Ⓑ Ⓒ Ⓓ
60 Ⓐ Ⓑ Ⓒ Ⓓ
61 Ⓐ Ⓑ Ⓒ Ⓓ
62 Ⓐ Ⓑ Ⓒ Ⓓ
63 Ⓐ Ⓑ Ⓒ Ⓓ

PART D

64 Ⓐ Ⓑ Ⓒ Ⓓ
65 Ⓐ Ⓑ Ⓒ Ⓓ
66 Ⓐ Ⓑ Ⓒ Ⓓ
67 Ⓐ Ⓑ Ⓒ Ⓓ
68 Ⓐ Ⓑ Ⓒ Ⓓ
69 Ⓐ Ⓑ Ⓒ Ⓓ
70 Ⓐ Ⓑ Ⓒ Ⓓ
71 Ⓐ Ⓑ Ⓒ Ⓓ
72 Ⓐ Ⓑ Ⓒ Ⓓ
73 Ⓐ Ⓑ Ⓒ Ⓓ
74 Ⓐ Ⓑ Ⓒ Ⓓ
75 Ⓐ Ⓑ Ⓒ Ⓓ
76 Ⓐ Ⓑ Ⓒ Ⓓ
77 Ⓐ Ⓑ Ⓒ Ⓓ
78 Ⓐ Ⓑ Ⓒ Ⓓ
79 Ⓐ Ⓑ Ⓒ Ⓓ
80 Ⓐ Ⓑ Ⓒ Ⓓ
81 Ⓐ Ⓑ Ⓒ Ⓓ
82 Ⓐ Ⓑ Ⓒ Ⓓ
83 Ⓐ Ⓑ Ⓒ Ⓓ
84 Ⓐ Ⓑ Ⓒ Ⓓ
85 Ⓐ Ⓑ Ⓒ Ⓓ
86 Ⓐ Ⓑ Ⓒ Ⓓ
87 Ⓐ Ⓑ Ⓒ Ⓓ
88 Ⓐ Ⓑ Ⓒ Ⓓ
89 Ⓐ Ⓑ Ⓒ Ⓓ
90 Ⓐ Ⓑ Ⓒ Ⓓ

Practice Test 2

Section I: Multiple Choice Questions

This section consists of four different parts: Part A, Part B, Part C, and Part D.

Total time: 1 hour and 30 minutes
Number of questions: 90
Percent of total grade: 50

Part A

Time: Approximately 30 minutes
The time for the questions below is paced by the tape.

You will hear a few dialogues. At the end of each, you will hear several questions about what you have just listened to. From the choices printed below, select the one that best responds to each question.

Ahora vas a oír algunos diálogos. Al final de cada uno escucharás unas preguntas sobre lo que has escuchado. De entre las opciones que aparecen impresas, escoge la que mejor responda a cada una de las preguntas.

Get ready to listen to the first dialogue.

Dialogue 1

PLAY TRACK 3 ON CD 2

1. A. Porque la familia estaba de vacaciones.
   B. Porque Enrique estaba tomando clases.
   C. Porque la familia tenía visitas.
   D. Porque Enrique no quería contestar tantas preguntas.

2. A. Uno.
   B. Dos.
   C. Tres.
   D. Cinco.

3. A. Es muy soñadora.
   B. Le gusta viajar mucho.
   C. Hace demasiadas preguntas.
   D. No conoce Italia.

4. A. Porque Dolores tiene que trabajar.
   B. Porque Dolores se va a Venecia.
   C. Porque Enrique tiene que ir a una clase.
   D. Porque Enrique tiene que almorzar con su familia.

Dialogue 2

PLAY TRACK 4 ON CD2

5. A. Está muy vieja.

   B. Está muy sucia.

   C. Está rota.

   D. Está seca.

6. A. Un accidente de automóvil.

   B. Una visita al rastro.

   C. La prisa al caminar.

   D. El tráfico de la Gran Vía.

7. A. Arreglar su carro.

   B. Beber un jugo de frutas.

   C. Comprar una chaqueta nueva.

   D. Pagar cinco euros.

Dialogue 3

PLAY TRACK 5 ON CD 2

8. A. A Sevilla.

   B. A un café.

   C. A la Ciudad Universitaria.

   D. A la estación de Ventas.

9. A. En autobús.

   B. En metro.

   C. Caminando.

   D. En taxi.

10. A. Tiene que recoger a su amigo.

    B. Se va con su amigo de viaje.

    C. Quiere salir antes de la huelga.

    D. Quiere tomar un café.

11. A. La compañía de teléfonos está en huelga.

    B. No hay un teléfono cerca.

    C. No tiene dinero.

    D. No sabe el número.

You will hear a few short narratives. At the end of each, you will hear several questions about what you have just listened to. From the choices printed below, select the one that best responds to each question.

Ahora vas a oír algunas narraciones cortas. Al final de cada una escucharás algunas preguntas sobre lo que has escuchado. De entre las opciones que aparecen impresas, escoge la que mejor responda a cada una de las preguntas.

Get ready to listen to the first narrative.

Narrative 1

PLAY TRACK 6 ON CD 2

12. **A.** Por catorce.

    B. Por sesenta.

    C. Por tres.

    D. Por ocho.

13. **A.** Fibras de colágeno.

    B. Las impurezas que penetran en la piel.

    C. Los depósitos de grasa.

    D. Agentes como el sol y el frío.

14. **A.** Para tratar arrugas.

    B. Para curar al ganado.

    C. Para preservar la piel.

    D. Para reducir la grasa.

Narrative 2

PLAY TRACK 7 ON CD 2

15. **A.** Porque no se mueven.

    B. Porque habitan en aguas poco profundas.

    C. Porque hay alrededor de tres mil tipos diferentes.

    D. Porque tienen muchas espinas.

16. **A.** Los canales.

    B. Las espinas.

    C. Los poros.

    D. El esqueleto.

17. **A.** Sirven para la limpieza.

    B. Cuando mueren de ellas crecen otros organismos submarinos.

    C. No necesitan oxígeno para vivir.

    D. No huyen de sus enemigos.

You will hear a longer selection. It is about five minutes in length. You may take notes, although you will not receive a grade for these notes. At the end of the selection, you will answer several questions about what you have just heard. Select the best answer for each question from the choices printed on the exam. Base your selections on the information you have heard.

Ahora vas a oír una selección más extensa. Su duración es de aproximadamente cinco minutos. Debes tomar apuntes en el espacio disponible en esta página, aunque los mismos no serán calificados. Al final de la selección, tendrás que contestar varias preguntas sobre lo que acabas de escuchar. De entre las opciones que aparecen en el examen, escoge la que mejor responda a cada una de las preguntas, teniendo en cuenta la información que has escuchado.

GO ON TO THE NEXT PAGE

Longer Narrative 1

PLAY TRACK 8 ON CD 2

18. ¿Qué puede ver un viajero en cualquier lugar de España?

    A. Manuscritos viejos.

    B. Campos de trigo.

    C. Fortalezas medievales.

    D. Crestas de sierras.

19. ¿A qué se debe el hecho de que en España haya tantos castillos?

    A. Al orgullo de los españoles.

    B. A la invasión árabe.

    C. A su herencia militar.

    D. A la aparición de las armas de fuego.

20. ¿Qué sucedió con muchos castillos después de que perdieron la importancia defensiva?

    A. Fueron olvidados.

    B. Fueron destruidos.

    C. El rey se los apropió.

    D. Fueron reconstruidos como museos.

21. ¿Cómo se originaron los castillos?

    A. Provienen de los poblados amurallados de los celtíberos.

    B. Los construyeron los romanos.

    C. Eran los campamentos de los visigodos.

    D. Fueron los baluartes de los árabes.

22. ¿Qué caracteriza a la sociedad española del siglo XIV?

    A. La fragmentación del poder.

    B. La unificación nacional.

    C. Un sistema centralista.

    D. Una nobleza cercana a la Corona.

23. ¿Qué provocó el abandono de los castillos en 1492?

    A. La presencia árabe.

    B. El protagonismo de las ciudades.

    C. El sistema centralista.

    D. La herencia de los títulos nobiliarios.

You will hear a longer selection. It is about five minutes in length. You may take notes, although you will not receive a grade for these notes. At the end of the selection, you will answer several questions about what you have just heard. Select the best answer for each question from the choices printed on the exam. Base your selections on the information you have heard.

Ahora vas a oír una selección más extensa. Su duración es de aproximadamente cinco minutos. Debes tomar apuntes en el espacio disponible en esta página, aunque los mismos no serán calificados. Al final de la selección, tendrás que contestar varias preguntas sobre lo que acabas de escuchar. De entre las opciones que aparecen en el examen, escoge la que mejor responda a cada una de las preguntas, teniendo en cuenta la información que has escuchado.

Longer Narrative 2

PLAY TRACK 9 ON CD 2

24. ¿Qué es Intimas Suculencias?

    A. Un platillo mexicano.

    B. El título de un libro.

    C. Una novela.

    D. El título de un álbum musical.

25. ¿Qué elemento cree Laura que está presente tanto en la cocina como en la literatura?

    A. El universo.

    B. El placer.

    C. La pasión.

    D. El amor.

26. ¿Cuál es para Laura una de las maravillas de la cocina?

    A. El laboratorio de alquimia.

    B. La ceremonia de unión con el universo.

    C. El misterio que ofrece cada día.

    D. La presencia del amor.

27. ¿De dónde le viene a Laura su afición por la cocina?

    A. De su familia.

    B. De su amiga Isabel.

    C. De su vocación literaria.

    D. De los problemas de comunicación.

28. Según Laura, ¿qué es lo importante de escribir?

    A. Gustar al público.

    B. Internarse en uno mismo.

    C. Crear imágenes.

    D. Provocar controversias.

29. ¿Qué cree Laura sobre el concepto de literatura femenina?

    A. Que no existe.

    B. Que hay que cambiarlo.

    C. Que no tiene que ver con el sexo.

    D. Que está relacionado con la cocina.

GO ON TO THE NEXT PAGE

Part B

Suggested time: 10 minutes

Cloze Passages

Each of the following passages contains numbered blanks, which indicate that words or groups of words are missing. There are four options to fill in each blank, but only one is correct.

In order to determine the general meaning of the passage, read quickly through it first. Read it again and select the option that best fills each blank according to the context of the complete passage.

Cada uno de los siguientes pasajes contiene espacios en blanco numerados para indicar que faltan palabras o grupos de palabras. Hay cuatro opciones para llenar cada espacio, pero solamente una es correcta.

Para poder determinar el sentido general del pasaje, léelo rápidamente; luego léelo de nuevo y selecciona la opción que mejor complete cada espacio de acuerdo con el contexto total del pasaje.

Manchas verdes, redondas, cuadradas, de blando, suave, sedoso césped. ¿No (30) yo coger todo este césped, acariciarlo con la mano, pasármelo suavemente por la cara? ¿(31) mi cara ardiente? Entre el césped, caminitos de arena; arena dorada, menuda, cernida, que (32) un leve ruidito, como un gemido, al ser pisada. Y esta arenita, ¿no puedo yo (33) también y hacerla escurrir (34) mis dedos? Sí; como hacía cuando (35) niño y estaba yo en la (36). ¿He sido yo niño (37) vez? En el cielo azul—azul en este momento—nubes redondas, blancas, de nácar, que caminan (38) . . . Entre el boscaje de los árboles, acá y allá, a cada momento, una tapia gris; (39) pierde el camino de arena entre los árboles; desaparece la tapia gris . . .

30. **A.** puedo

    B. puedes

    C. puedo

    D. pude

31. **A.** Estoy

    B. Está

    C. Estás

    D. Estaba

32. **A.** hace

    B. hago

    C. hacía

    D. hizo

33. **A.** cogerla

    B. ponerla

    C. recogerla

    D. poseerla

34. **A.** en

    B. desde

    C. entre

    D. hacia

35. **A.** fui

    B. era

    C. estaba

    D. estuve

36. **A.** playa

    B. selva

    C. montaña

    D. brisa

37. **A.** algún

    B. alguna

    C. alguno

    D. algunas

38. **A.** lento

    B. lenta

    C. lentos

    D. lentas

39. **A.** le

    B. lo

    C. la

    D. se

Era un (40) tarde ya cuando el funcionario (41) seguir de nuevo el vuelo de la mosca. La mosca, (42) su parte, como sabiéndose objeto de aquella observación, (43) esmeró en el programado desarrollo de sus acrobacias zumbando para sus adentros, toda vez que (44) que era una mosca doméstica común y corriente y que entre muchas posibilidades la del zumbido no era su mejor (45) de brillar, al contrario de lo que sucedía con sus evoluciones cada vez más amplias y elegantes en torno al funcionario, (46) viéndolas recordaba pálida pero insistentemente y como (47) a sí mismo lo que él (48) que evolucionar alrededor de otros funcionarios para llegar a su actual altura, sin (49) mucho ruido tampoco . . .

40. **A.** mucho

    B. muy

    C. poca

    D. poco

41. **A.** prosiguió

    B. decidió

    C. comenzó

    D. terminó

42. **A.** con

    B. para

    C. por

    D. sin

43. **A.** lo

    B. la

    C. le

    D. se

GO ON TO THE NEXT PAGE

44.
A. sabe
B. sabía
C. supo
D. supiera

45.
A. clase
B. tipo
C. camino
D. manera

46.
A. cual
B. cuyo
C. quien
D. quienes

47.
A. negándosela
B. negándoselo
C. negándosele
D. negándoseles

48.
A. ha tenido
B. haya tenido
C. había tenido
D. hubiera tenido

49.
A. hacer
B. oír
C. poner
D. tener

Part C

Suggested time: 10 minutes

Error Recognition

In the following sentences, select the underlined part of the sentence that needs to be changed in order to make the sentence grammatically correct.

En las oraciones que aparecen a continuación, escoge la parte subrayada que habría que cambiar para que la oración sea gramaticalmente correcta.

50. Esta es la <u>tercera</u> vez que tengo <u>a</u> hacer
         [A]   [B]
<u>este</u> informe para <u>mi</u> clase de química.
 [C]   [D]

51. Si todos <u>cooperaríamos</u> <u>en</u> la
           [A]   [B]
construcción del <u>nuevo</u> hospital, éste
              [C]
estará <u>funcionando</u> para la próxima
        [D]
primavera.

52. <u>En</u> mi opinión, <u>el</u> arte <u>ha</u> de estar libre
   [A]   [B]   [C]
de trabas <u>o</u> obstáculos.
        [D]

53. <u>Le</u> dije a mis alumnos que <u>trajeran</u> <u>sus</u>
  [A]   [B]   [C]
libros <u>al</u> aula hoy.
     [D]

54. Ni Ana <u>o</u> Inés <u>pudieron</u> resolver <u>el</u>
       [A]   [B]   [C]
problema que <u>les</u> dio el profesor.
         [D]

55. Si tú no <u>vas</u> al cine <u>esta</u> tarde, yo
        [A]   [B]
<u>también</u> <u>iré</u>.
  [C]   [D]

56. <u>Los</u> pilares de esas columnas <u>fueron</u>
  [A]   [B]
<u>construidas</u> <u>hace</u> muchos siglos.
  [C]   [D]

57. Aunque no <u>tengas</u> necesidad, debes
   [A]
   <u>buscarle</u> un trabajo <u>para que</u> te
   [B]   [C]
   <u>entretengas</u> un poco.
   [D]

58. No <u>es</u> cierto que Alberto <u>ha dicho</u> <u>que</u>
   [A]   [B]   [C]
   tú <u>estabas</u> enferma.
   [D]

59. Si <u>quieres</u> que te <u>dé</u> el dinero <u>por</u>
   [A]   [B]   [C]
   comprar el carro tienes que <u>decírmelo</u>.
   [D]

60. <u>Paseando</u> <u>para</u> la playa <u>encontramos</u>
   [A]   [B]   [C]
   caracoles <u>muy</u> raros.
   [D]

61. Antes de <u>mandando</u> la carta, <u>déjame</u>
   [A]   [B]
   <u>verla</u> <u>para</u> revisar los errores.
   [C]   [D]

62. Cuando Roly <u>fue</u> pequeño, <u>le</u> <u>gustaban</u>
   [A]   [B]   [C]
   <u>mucho</u> los chocolates.
   [D]

63. Anoche me <u>caí</u> y <u>me</u> rompí los vasos
   [A]   [B]
   que <u>llevaba</u> en <u>la</u> mano.
   [C]   [D]

64. <u>Para</u> ser <u>tan</u> pequeño, Rafaelito no <u>pudo</u>
   [A]   [B]   [C]
   ir <u>a</u> la escuela este año.
   [D]

Part D

Suggested time: 40 minutes

Reading Comprehension Passages

Read each of the following passages. After each passage, you will find a series of incomplete sentences or questions. From the four choices given, select the option that best completes the sentence or answers the question according to the passage.

Lee cada uno de los pasajes siguientes. Al final de cada pasaje encontrarás una serie de oraciones incompletas o preguntas. De las cuatro opciones que aparecen, escoge la que mejor completa cada oración o responda a cada pregunta de acuerdo con el fragmento leído.

La vida de Isabel cambió para siempre un 8 de enero, cuando en 1981 empezó a escribir una carta a su abuelo chileno desde el exilio venezolano. Esta se convirtió en una novela clásica de la literatura latinoamericana y mundial, escrita por las noches en la cocina de su casa en Caracas, después de trabajar durante el día de maestra, y de preparar la cena a su primer marido y a sus hijos Paula y Nicolás. *La casa de los espíritus* ha sido traducida a dos docenas de idiomas, desde el búlgaro y farsi hasta el mandarín y turco.

Gran parte del éxito de sus libros es la universalidad de sus personajes y las inquietudes que éstos viven, con las que se identifican tanto mujeres como hombres de todo el mundo. Sin embargo, publicar el manuscrito no fue fácil, en parte por el hecho de que Isabel es mujer, y, a principios de los años 80, no se publicaban novelas de escritoras en Latinoamérica. "Cuando ofrecí *La casa de los espíritus*—no me acuerdo a cuántas editoriales—ni siquiera quisieron leerla. Tuve suerte de que cayera en manos de Carmen

GO ON TO THE NEXT PAGE

Balcells porque, si no, estaría todavía en una bodega."

Isabel Allende comenzó su carrera como periodista de humor en Chile, y hasta tenía su propio programa de televisión. En una ocasión, el poeta Pablo Neruda se negó a ser entrevistado por Allende dada la reputación que ella tenía de añadir fantasía a la realidad, y le recomendó, que en lugar de al periodismo, se dedicara a la ficción, donde la imaginación era una virtud y no un defecto.

Su gran facilidad para contar historias viene de familia. Después del trabajo, siempre pasaba a tomar el té con el abuelo y a escuchar sus historias. "Mi abuelo fue una figura determinante en mi formación. Él forjó mi carácter a hierro y martillo. Era un vasco poderoso y maravilloso. A él le debo la disciplina, la fortaleza; pero creo que le debo la mayor parte de las historias que yo cuento porque era un gran contador de historias. Los cuentos de mi abuelo han entrado de alguna manera en todos mis libros."

Siempre ha empezado sus novelas un 8 de enero, sin otro tipo de planificación que una serie de notas en papeles con esbozos de historias que recoge por el mundo. "Creo que la inspiración siempre viene de una emoción profunda que ha estado conmigo por mucho tiempo, que se va fermentando dentro, hasta que está lista para salir transformada en otra cosa. A veces, la emoción parece no tener relación alguna con el libro que escribo; sin embargo, después que está escrito, me doy cuenta de lo que escribí y por qué lo escribí."

65. ¿Cómo comenzó la carrera artística de Isabel Allende?

    A. Con un exilio político.

    B. Con una novela clásica.

    C. Con una cena romántica.

    D. Con una carta familiar.

66. ¿A cuántos idiomas se ha traducido *La casa de los espíritus*?

    A. Solamente al búlgaro.

    B. A dos.

    C. A doce

    D. A veinticuatro

67. Según el pasaje, ¿en qué radica el éxito de las novelas de Allende?

    A. En sus temas clásicos.

    B. En sus fáciles manuscritos.

    C. En la universalidad de sus personajes.

    D. En la experiencia de la autora como maestra.

68. ¿Por qué fue difícil para Isabel Allende publicar su primera novela?

    A. Porque vivía en Venezuela.

    B. Debido a su condición de mujer.

    C. Porque no estaba en una bodega.

    D. Porque su abuelo tenía el manuscrito.

69. ¿Por qué se negó Neruda a ser entrevistado por Allende?

    A. Porque ella era una periodista pésima.

    B. Porque ella mezclaba la realidad con la fantasía.

    C. Porque a él no le gustaba salir en televisión.

    D. Porque Neruda no tenía ninguna imaginación.

70. Según el pasaje, ¿de dónde le viene a Allende su vocación de narradora?

    A. De las influencias de su abuelo.

    B. Del consejo de Neruda.

    C. De sus habilidades periodísticas.

    D. De su gran disciplina.

71. ¿Qué inspira las historias de Allende?

    A. El carácter de su abuelo.

    B. Una emoción interior.

    C. El amor a sus hijos.

    D. El recuerdo de su primer marido.

72. Isabel Allende normalmente comienza sus historias con

    A. notas en papeles.

    B. un esbozo bien planificado.

    C. historias de familia.

    D. cartas a su abuelo

En lo más intrincado de la Selva existió en tiempos lejanos un Búho que empezó a preocuparse por los demás.

En consecuencia se dio a meditar sobre las evidentes maldades que hacía el León con su poder; sobre la debilidad de la Hormiga, que era aplastada todos los días, tal vez cuando más ocupada se hallaba; sobre la risa de la Hiena, que nunca venía al caso; sobre la Paloma, que se queja del aire que la sostiene en su vuelo; sobre la Araña que atrapa a la Mosca y sobre la Mosca que con toda su inteligencia se deja atrapar por la Araña, y en fin, sobre todos los defectos que hacían desgraciada a la Humanidad, y se puso a pensar en la manera de remediarlos.

Pronto adquirió la costumbre de desvelarse y de salir a la calle a observar cómo se conducía la gente, y se fue llenando de conocimientos científicos y psicológicos que poco a poco iba ordenando en su pensamiento y en una pequeña libreta.

De modo que algunos años después se le desarrolló una gran facilidad para clasificar, y sabía a ciencia cierta cuándo el León iba a rugir y cuándo la Hiena se iba a reír, y lo que iba a hacer el Ratón del campo cuando visitara al de la ciudad, y lo que haría el perro que traía una torta en la boca cuando viera reflejado en el agua el rostro de un Perro que traía una torta en la boca, y el Cuervo cuando le decían que qué bonito cantaba.

Y así, concluía:

"Si el León no hiciera lo que hace sino lo que hace el Caballo, y el Caballo no hiciera lo que hace sino lo que hace el León; y si la Boa no hiciera lo que hace sino lo que hace el Ternero y el Ternero no hiciera lo que hace sino lo que hace la Boa, y así hasta el infinito, la Humanidad se salvaría, dado que todos vivirían en paz y la guerra volvería a ser como en los tiempos en que no había guerra."

Pero los otros animales no apreciaban los esfuerzos del Búho, por sabio que éste supusiera que lo suponían; antes bien pensaban que era tonto, no se daban cuenta de la profundidad de su pensamiento, y seguían comiéndose unos a otros, menos el Búho, que no era comido por nadie ni se comía nunca a nadie.

GO ON TO THE NEXT PAGE

73. ¿Qué ocupaba los pensamientos del Búho?

   A. Los tiempos antiguos.

   B. Los defectos de los otros animales.

   C. Las costumbres de las gentes.

   D. El conocimiento psicológico.

74. Según el pasaje, ¿qué defecto tenía la Hormiga?

   A. Su risa.

   B. Su maldad.

   C. Su debilidad.

   D. Su inteligencia.

75. ¿Qué decisión tomó el Búho?

   A. Remediar los problemas de la Humanidad.

   B. Desarrollar una habilidad de observación.

   C. Levantarse temprano.

   D. Obtener conocimientos científicos.

76. ¿Cómo obtuvo el Búho sus conocimientos?

   A. Estudiando mucho.

   B. Observando a la gente a su alrededor.

   C. Ordenando sus pensamientos.

   D. Criticando a los demás animales.

77. ¿Qué habilidad logró tener el Búho?

   A. Clasificar a los animales.

   B. Descubrir las maldades del León.

   C. Predecir el comportamiento ajeno.

   D. Hacer reír a la Hiena.

78. ¿A qué conclusión llegó el Búho?

   A. Que los animales tienen que cambiar su comportamiento.

   B. Que todos los animales eran sabios.

   C. Que las costumbres no se pueden cambiar.

   D. Que pronto habría otra guerra.

79. ¿Qué pensaban del Búho los otros animales?

   A. Que no tenía fuerzas.

   B. Que se comía a otros animales.

   C. Que tenía un pensamiento profundo.

   D. Que era tonto.

El último miércoles de cada agosto miles de amontonados cuerpos escasamente vestidos aguardan en inicio de la fiesta más representativa del carácter valenciano, la Tomatina. Durante meses, muchos han aguardado desesperadamente la llegada de la celebración que, por su colorido, recuerda las bacanales romanas. La muchedumbre está dispuesta a divertirse y olvidarse del mundo exterior.

Un total de 150 toneladas de jitomate maduro vuela por los aires como proyectil en la que es probablemente la guerra de comida más grande del mundo y, ciertamente, la más sucia. "Se ruega encarecidamente que antes de arrojar los tomates, se deshagan en la mano," advierten los organizadores, quizá a fin de evitar accidentes o para que las calles se conviertan más rápido en una piscina de puré.

La contienda da inicio a las once de la mañana en el pueblo de Buñol, muy cercano a la ciudad de Valencia, y a ella acuden decenas de miles de excéntricos, entre españoles de diferentes partes del país y extranjeros; lo sorprendente es que la sede del evento apenas alcanza los 9.000 habitantes. Los asistentes al convivio corean: "Tomate, tomate, queremos tomate", y entonces, desde camiones de carga, empiezan a repartirse las municiones. Cualquier cosa que se mueva es un blanco válido, hasta los testigos más neutros y pasivos. Los incesantes tomatazos vienen de todas partes; todo el mundo sabe que ésta es una guerra en la que no habrá vencedores, pues no hay quien no quede hecho una sopa colorada. De hecho, el objetivo principal de esta celebración es darle a Buñol un baño de sangre vegetal.

La Tomatina se celebró por primera ocasión después de terminada la Segunda Guerra Mundial, alrededor de 1945—el color escarlata de la festividad fue una paradoja. Sin duda, es una fiesta popular creada por y para el pueblo. Dicen que nació en los desfiles de "gigantes y cabezudos" de Buñol, que siempre terminaban a tomatazos. Como en sus inicios, la Tomatina carecía de reglas y de una organización formal, al gobierno le pareció un desorden excesivo y prohibió su festejo a principios de los años cincuenta. No obstante, los más decididos desafiaban a las autoridades y se lanzaban a la plaza del pueblo para continuar con la entonces joven tradición. La Guardia Civil se hizo presente en numerosas ocasiones realizando algunas detenciones. Los agresores eran dirigidos a la cárcel entre bromas y risas, para ser liberados poco tiempo después . . .

80. ¿Qué es la Tomatina?

A. Una celebración de la Segunda Guerra Mundial.

B. Una fiesta popular de Valencia.

C. Un festival agrícola para extranjeros.

D. Una manera de vender muchos tomates.

81. ¿Con qué se compara la Tomatina en el artículo?

A. Con una joven tradición española.

B. Con una guerra internacional.

C. Con unos festejos en homenaje a un dios antiguo.

D. Con un juego de encarcelamientos.

82. ¿Qué es lo primero que hay que hacer con los tomates durante la Tomatina?

A. Tirarlos.

B. Comérselos.

C. Deshacerlos.

D. Pisarlos.

83. ¿Quiénes participan en la Tomatina?

A. Solamente los habitantes de Buñol.

B. Nada más que extranjeros excéntricos.

C. Únicamente españoles de Valencia.

D. Gentes de toda España y del extranjero.

84. ¿Por qué no hay vencedores en esta "guerra"?

A. Porque todo sale sucio de tomates.

B. Porque la Guardia Civil se los lleva presos.

C. Porque los testigos los denuncian.

D. Porque todo el mundo toma sopa de tomate.

GO ON TO THE NEXT PAGE

Practice Test 2

Desde sus comienzos, las loterías o juegos de masas se implantaron por los Estados con el deseo claro de obtener unos ingresos que podrían considerarse como impuestos voluntarios. Más tarde, y sin abandonar, como es lógico, su papel generador de ingresos, los Estados más avanzados política y socialmente mantuvieron bajo su control una actividad que requiere, por su difusión, volumen y repercusión social una atención especial.

En España las loterías son muy antiguas, pues ya en el siglo XVI se celebraban, aunque de forma esporádica, con una autorización concreta y con un destino de beneficios también determinado.

Durante el siglo XVIII se fueron implantando en la mayor parte de Europa las loterías de Estado y España no iba a ser una excepción aunque, curiosamente, comenzó a funcionar en primer lugar en México, entonces perteneciente a la Corona de España.

Tanto en ese siglo como en los siguientes España no fue ajena a la polémica que suscitaba la existencia de las loterías. Los detractores basaron sus argumentos en los efectos nocivos que este juego podría tener en la población. Los defensores mantenían que un juego con las características propias de las loterías no presentaba riesgo de adicción o dependencia, y canalizaba ordenadamente la tendencia que tiene el ser humano a desafiar al destino a través de comportamientos dirigidos por el azar. Ahora bien, era preciso que la actividad estuviera perfectamente regulada y los beneficios generados se devolvieran a la sociedad para su contribución a la financiación de todas las obras y actividades que debía realizar el Estado.

La Lotería de Números o Loto fue instaurada durante el reinado de Carlos III, y sus sorteos se iniciaron en 1763. Posteriormente, en 1811, las Cortes de Cádiz establecieron otro tipo de lotería, una lotería de billetes que constituye lo que hoy conocemos como Lotería Nacional.

Al ciudadano español le atraían del sistema de la Lotería Nacional sus rasgos más característicos, como son: la determinación concreta de los premios sin que dependa del número de participantes así como la comodidad que representa la adquisición de un billete sin tener que aventurar ningún pronóstico. Todo ello contribuyó a su marcha ascendente y dio lugar a la mayor permanencia y regularidad que se conoce dentro de las loterías.

En 1946 se pone en marcha La Quiniela de fútbol, que pronto adquirirá una gran popularidad y supondrá de nuevo el inicio de la participación de los españoles en un juego en el que deberán señalar sus pronósticos u opciones preferidas.

El año 1985 representó un hito en los juegos del Estado. Por un lado se crea un organismo que va a gestionar la totalidad de los juegos existentes: Lotería Nacional y La Quiniela y, por otro, se restablece la Lotería de Números con el ya tradicional nombre usado durante el siglo XIX: Lotería Primitiva.

85. ¿Con qué fin se implantó la lotería?

- **A.** Para subir los impuestos.
- **B.** Para generar más ingresos.
- **C.** Para mejorar la política.
- **D.** Para llamar la atención de la sociedad.

86. ¿Qué caracterizaba a las loterías españolas del siglo XVI?

- **A.** Sus beneficios tenían un fin determinado.
- **B.** No necesitaban autorización.
- **C.** Tenían gran difusión.
- **D.** Se celebraban en eventos políticos.

87. ¿Cuándo se implantaron las loterías en Europa?

    A. En el siglo XVI.

    B. En el siglo XVIII.

    C. En el año 1811.

    D. En el año 1946.

88. Algunas personas estaban en contra de las loterías porque creían que éstas

    A. desafiaban al destino.

    B. eran perjudiciales para el pueblo.

    C. financiaban la adicción.

    D. contribuían a financiar al gobierno.

89. ¿Por qué les gustaba a los españoles la llamada Lotería Nacional?

    A. Porque el premio dependía de cuántos acertaban.

    B. Porque podían hacer sus propios pronósticos.

    A. Porque podían comprar billetes ya impresos.

    D. Porque no tenía mucho riesgo.

90. ¿Qué es la Lotería Primitiva?

    A. Una lotería de números del siglo XIX.

    B. La lotería que instauró Carlos III en 1763.

    C. La Lotería Nacional de España.

    D. Una lotería con autorización concreta del siglo XVI.

Practice Test 2

IF YOU FINISH BEFORE TIME IS CALLED, CHECK YOUR WORK ON THIS SECTION ONLY. DO NOT WORK ON ANY OTHER SECTION IN THE TEST.

Section II: Free Response

This section consists of two main parts, Part A and Part B, and each part contains more than one type of exercise.

Total time: 1 hour and 20 minutes

Percent of total grade: 50

Part A: Writing Skills

This part tests your writing skills in Spanish, and it consists of three different exercises: paragraph fill-ins, discrete sentence fill-ins, and an essay.

Time: 60 minutes

Paragraph Fill-Ins

Suggested time: 8 minutes

Read the following passage completely. Then read it a second time, and write on the line provided after each number the appropriate form of the word given in parentheses that will complete the fragment correctly, logically, and grammatically. Correct spelling and accent marks are necessary to receive credit. Only one word is allowed in each blank. In some instances, you may find that a change of the word in parentheses is not necessary, but you still need to write the word in the blank to receive credit.

Lee el siguiente pasaje. Luego vuélvelo a leer y escribe en la línea de la derecha, después de cada número, la forma apropiada de la palabra que está entre paréntesis, para completar el fragmento de forma correcta y lógica. La ortografía y los acentos deben ser correctos para recibir crédito. Solamente se permite una palabra para cada espacio. Es posible que la palabra sugerida no necesite ningún cambio; si es así, debes escribir la palabra en el espacio en blanco para recibir crédito.

Desde (1) escaparate, donde (2) distribui-
dos sin mucho orden como (3) centenar de libros de segunda mano, casi todos ellos
ediciones (4) en rústica, aunque también (5)
verse algún ejemplar encuadernado en tapa
dura o en tela y varios búhos de diferentes
materiales y tamaños. Lo que allí podía verse
era (6) pequeño local de forma alargada y
unos 40 metros cuadrados, (7) paredes estaban cubiertas por estanterías, que iban del
suelo al techo, (8) de libros. Había también
muchos ejemplares apilados en rimeros sobre
el suelo, que (9) una altura de sesenta o se-
tenta centímetros, pegados a la parte (10) de
las librerías.

1. _____ (aquel)

2. _____ (haber)

3. _____ (medio)

4. _____ (barato)

5. _____ (poder)

6. _____ (un)

7. _____ (cuyo)

8. _____ (atestado)

9. _____ (alcanzar)

10. _____ (bajo)

Discrete Sentence Fill-Ins

Suggested time: 7 minutes

*In the following set of sentences, one verb is missing. Write on the line after the number the
correct form and tense of the verb, taking into consideration the context of the sentence. In
some cases, you may have to use more than one word, but you need to use a tense of the verb
given in parentheses.*

*En el siguiente grupo de oraciones falta un verbo. Escribe en la línea después de cada número
la forma y el tiempo correctos del verbo, tomando en consideración el contexto de la oración.
En algunos casos vas a necesitar más de una palabra, pero es necesario que uses un tiempo
del verbo que aparece entre paréntesis.*

GO ON TO THE NEXT PAGE

11. Si hubieras estudiado más, (11) mejores notas.

11. _____(sacar)

12. A Laura no le parece bien que Pepito (12) tan cerca del agua.

12. _____(jugar)

13. Se me (13) la computadora y ahora no puedo terminar mi trabajo.

13. _____(descomponer)

14. Hasta que no (14) los intereses, la población no comprará casas nuevas.

14. _____(reducirse)

15. En cuanto(15) el niño, nos iremos a vivir a Segovia.

15. _____(nacer)

16. Cuando (16) pequeña, Hilda se cayó de la cuna cuatro veces.

16. _____(ser)

17. Si Adolfo supiera la verdad, la (17) inmediatamente.

17. _____(decir)

18. Por favor, Pilar, no (18) esos zapatos rosados tan feos.

18. _____(escoger)

19. (19) esos papeles, conseguirás borrar todas las pruebas.

19. _____(destruir)

20. Raulito, (20) temprano porque mañana tienes que madrugar.

20. _____(acostarse)

Essay

Suggested writing time: 45 minutes

> **NOTE:** During the AP Spanish Language Exam, you will be given a booklet in which to write the essay. For this practice test, use any lined paper.

Write a well-organized essay in Spanish of at least 200 words and about the topic given below. Your score will be based on organization, range and appropriateness of vocabulary, and grammatical accuracy. It is recommended that you use the first five minutes to organize your ideas.

Escribe un ensayo bien organizado, en español y de una extensión de al menos 200 palabras, sobre el tema que aparece a continuación. Tu calificación estará basada en la organización, la riqueza y la precisión del vocabulario y la corrección gramatical. Se te recomienda que utilices los primeros cinco minutos para organizar tus ideas.

La globalización ha sido uno de los elementos que ha caracterizado las relaciones internacionales en los últimos años. En un ensayo bien organizado, comenta cuáles crees tú que son las ventajas y las desventajas de un "mundo global," tanto a nivel económico, como cultural. Respalda tu opinión con ejemplos concretos.

Part B: Speaking Skills

The instructions for this section will be given to you by the Master CD. This section consists of two different exercises: a picture sequence story and directed response questions. Your voice will be recorded during this section of the exam. The instructions are mostly in English, but there are some questions in Spanish to which you must respond.

PLAY TRACK 10 ON CD 2

The six drawings on the next page represent a story. Use the pictures to tell the story, according to your interpretation.

Los seis dibujos que aparecen en la próxima página representan una historieta. Utiliza los dibujos para contar la historia, según tu propia interpretación.

GO ON TO THE NEXT PAGE

Directed Response

PLAY TRACK 11 ON CD 2

IF YOU FINISH BEFORE TIME IS CALLED, CHECK YOUR WORK ON THIS
SECTION ONLY. DO NOT WORK ON ANY OTHER SECTION IN THE TEST.

Practice Test 2 Scoring Worksheet

This worksheet is designed to help you calculate your score in this practice test following similar procedures to those used by the College Board. Try to be as objective as you can while evaluating the essay and the oral questions. In the case of the essay, you may compare the sample essays given to your own work to be able to determine your own score.

Section I: Multiple Choice Section

Part A: number correct (out of 29)_____ − ($\frac{1}{3}$ × **number wrong** _____) × 1.2414 = ☐

Part B: number correct (out of 20)_____ − ($\frac{1}{3}$ × **number wrong** _____) × .9000 = ☐

Part C: number correct (out of 15)_____ − ($\frac{1}{3}$ × **number wrong** _____) × .6000 = ☐

Part D: number correct (out of 26)_____ − ($\frac{1}{3}$ × **number wrong** _____) × 1.0385 = ☐

Total weighted section I score (add the 4 boxes): _____

Section II: Free Response Section

Fill-Ins: (out of 20)_____ × .6750 = ☐

Essay: (out of 9)_____ × .9474 = ☐

Picture Sequence: (out of 9)_____ × .5294 = ☐

Directed Responses: (out of 20)_____ × 1.1250 = ☐

Total weighted section II score (add the 4 boxes): _____

Final Score

weighted section I: _____ + weighted section II: _____ = final score: _____

Probable Final AP Score

Final Converted Score	Probable AP Score
180–134	5
133–114	4
113–86	3
85–63	2
62–0	1

Answer Key for Practice Test 2

Section I: Multiple-Choice Questions

Dialogue 1

1. A
2. D
3. C
4. C

Dialogue 2

5. B
6. C
7. C

Dialogue 3

8. C
9. A
10. B
11. D

Short Narrative 1

12. C
13. A
14. A

Short Narrative 2

15. A
16. C
17. B

Long Narrative 1

18. C
19. B
20. A
21. A
22. A
23. B

Long Narrative 2

24. B
25. D
26. C
27. A
28. B
29. C

Cloze Passages

30. A
31. B
32. A
33. A
34. C
35. B
36. A
37. B
38. D
39. D
40. D
41. B
42. C
43. D
44. B
45. D
46. C
47. B
48. C
49. A

Error Recognition

50. B
51. A

52. D
53. A
54. A
55. C
56. C
57. B
58. B
59. C
60. B
61. A
62. A
63. B
64. A

Reading Comprehension Passages

65. D
66. D
67. C
68. B
69. B
70. A
71. B
72. A
73. B
74. C
75. A
76. B
77. C
78. A
79. D
80. B
81. C
82. C

83. D

84. A

85. B

86. A

87. B

88. B

89. C

90. A

Section II: Free-Response Questions

Paragraph Fill-Ins

1. aquel

2. había

3. medio

4. baratas

5. podía

6. un

7. cuyas

8. atestadas

9. alcanzaban

10. baja

Discrete Sentence Fill-Ins

11. habrías sacado

12. juegue

13. descompuso, ha descompuesto

14. se reduzcan

15. nazca, haya nacido

16. era

17. diría

18. escojas

19. destruyendo

20. acuéstate

Essay Question

In the section "Answers and Explanations for Practice Test 2," you will find a guide to scoring essays together with essay samples, their scores, and analysis of each essay.

Answers and Explanations for Practice Test 2

Section I: Multiple Choice Questions

Dialogue 1

1. **A.** At the very beginning, Enrique states that the reason nobody answered the phone in his house is that the whole family spent two months in Europe (*pasamos dos meses en Europa*).

2. **D.** Even though Enrique only speaks about Italy, he tells Dolores that he was in five countries (*Estuve en cinco países*).

3. **C.** Because Dolores mentions she would love to visit Italy, and you can infer that she has not been there before, choice **D** is attractive—but it is incorrect. Choice **C** is justified not only by Enrique's statement *Haces muchas preguntas a la vez,* but also by Dolores's attitude at the beginning of the conversation.

4. **C.** The reason why the conversation is interrupted is that Enrique has a class at 3:00 (*tengo clase a las tres*). Even though the verb *to lunch* is mentioned (*almorzar*), it is Dolores who is inviting Enrique to lunch on Saturday.

Dialogue 2

5. **B.** In the beginning of the dialogue, the man states that he has to *lavar en seco esta chaqueta.* Also, because the conversation takes place at the dry cleaners, you can assume that the jacket is dirty (*sucia*).

6. **C.** Despite the car trouble he had, it was the way he walked that caused the red stains (*manchas rojas*).

7. **C.** The man decides to buy a new jacket at the flea market (*el rastro*) rather than pay ten euros for the dry cleaning.

Dialogue 3

8. **C.** Although answer **A** may be attractive, because he comments that they are leaving for Sevilla in a couple of hours, the student has already stated that he had to go meet his friend at *ciudad universitaria.*

9. **A.** The conversation is initiated by the student asking the lady if the bus that goes to Moncloa passes by that street. His question indicates that the bus is the means of transportation he would like to use to go where his friend is.

10. **B.** Even though choice **A** is attractive, because the student is going to meet his friend, it is not stated that he is picking him up (*recoger*). Through the complete conversation, you get the idea that the reason he is in a hurry is that they are going to go to Sevilla.

11. **D.** At the end of the dialogue, the student states that he has another problem: *no sé el número de teléfono de mi amigo*. Choices **A** and **C** are also good distracters: You may infer that the student doesn't have much money because he states that taking a cab is expensive.

Short Narrative 1

12. **C.** The narrative clearly states that the skin is made up of three layers (*tres capas*), and even mentions each of them. The other choices may be distracting because they all were used to describe *la piel*.

13. **A.** The narrative states that the skin layers are connected by *fibras de colágeno* and elastin. Answer **C** is a good distracter, because you may know from outside sources that there are fat deposits under the skin, although they do not connect the three layers.

14. **A.** The selection states that collagen is used nowadays, among other things, for the treatment of wrinkles (*arrugas*). Answer **B** may be distracting because the word *ganado* appeared previously to refer to the source of collagen.

Short Narrative 2

15. **A.** To correctly answer this question, you need to relate the word *inmóvil* with the verb *moverse*. The narrative states that the reason they were considered vegetables is that they do not move.

16. **C.** Although the words *espinas* and *esqueleto* are used to describe sponges, the narrative states that the main characteristic is the pores (*poros*).

17. **B.** This choice describes an ecological importance of sponges, whereas choices **C** and **D** describe characteristics of sponges. On the other hand, choice **A** describes an economical importance of sponges.

Longer Narrative 1

18. **C.** Even though choices **B** and **D** were also mentioned, they were used as descriptions of places where palaces may be found.

19. **B.** Although choice **C** may be tempting because it is also mentioned in the narrative, the number of castles in Spain is due to *la invasion árabe*.

20. **A.** Although the reconstruction of castles was also mentioned in the narrative, it states, *Cuando perdieron la importancia defensiva, cayeron en el olvido*.

21. **A.** Each choice mentions one of the ancient inhabitants of the Iberian Peninsula; however, it was due to the *celtíberos* that castles were built in Spain.

22. **A.** The narrative clearly states: *La fragmentación del poder, radicalizado durante el siglo XIV.*

23. **B.** The narrative clearly states: *El mayor protagonismo de las ciudades respecto al campo . . . provoca el abandono de muchas fortalezas.*

Longer Narrative 2

24. B. Even though you may confuse *suculencias* with its cognate *succulent* and think that *íntimas suculencias* refers to a Mexican dish, the narrative clearly states that it is the title of a book: *los textos recopilados bajo el título. . . .*

25. D. Although all the choices were used in the description of *cocina,* it is *amor* that appears in the narrative as an element of both cooking and literature.

26. C. The text states: *una de las maravillas de la cocina es . . . que siempre está el misterio.* Choice **A** is used to describe the cooking process and may be a tempting answer.

27. A. The interviewer directly asks Laura where her interest in cooking originates, and she answers: *de familia.*

28. B. Even though choice **C** was used to describe Laura's writing process, it doesn't explain what is actually important in the process: *Escribir te obliga a hacer un viaje interno.*

29. C. The narrative clearly states: *creo que sí hay una literatura femenina pero no tiene que ver con el sexo.*

Cloze Passage

30. A. The verb must agree with its subject, *yo* (first person singular).

31. B. The verb must agree with its subject, *mi cara* (third person singular).

32. A. It is the sand that makes a little noise; therefore, the verb must be in the third person singular form to maintain the agreement with the subject in person and number.

33. A. The verb must be the same as the one in the first question (*coger*) and the pronoun *la* refers to *la arena.*

34. C. It is necessary to understand the meaning of the verb *escurrir* (to drain, to drip) to be able to select the correct choice, *entre.* The sand will drip between the boys fingers.

35. B. Use the imperfect of the verb *ser* to describe people in the past.

36. A. Since the person is talking about the sand, it evokes memories of the beach.

37. B. Use the indefinite adjective *alguna* because it must agree with the noun *vez* (feminine, singular)

38. D. The adverb indicates the movement of the clouds (*nubes*); there must be agreement in gender and number.

39. D. Use the reflexive pronoun *se* in order to indicate that the action is done by and affects the subject.

40. D. Use the indefinite adjective *poco* before the word late (*tarde*) to signify a bit.

41. B. Use the verb *decidir* because the other choices require the prepositions *a* or *de.*

42. C. The preposition *por* is used in common expressions such as *por su parte.*

43. D. The reflexive pronoun *se* is used because it is part of the verb *esmerarse.*

44. B. The imperfect is used to indicate that the action is an ongoing action in the past.

45. D. Even though *camino* also means way, it is mostly used to indicate travel or journey, as opposed to *manera,* which indicates the manner in which something is done.

46. C. The relative pronoun *quien* is used as this clause's subject.

47. B. Use the neuter pronoun *lo* because the direct object of *negar* is implied, but not given.

48. C. The use of the pluperfect designates an event that happened before another that occurred further in the past.

49. A. The idiomatic expression requires the verb *hacer* with the word *ruido* (noise).

Error Recognition

50. B. *Tener que + infinitive* is the appropriate form to express "to have to."

51. A. The present tense of the indicative or the imperfect subjunctive should be used instead of the conditional.

52. D. The conjunction *o* changes to *u* when followed by a word beginning with the *o* sound.

53. A. The indirect object pronoun refers to *alumnos;* therefore, it should be plural.

54. A. This is a coordinating conjunction; *ni . . . ni* is used to mean "neither . . . nor."

55. C. This is a negative sentence; therefore, the negative adverb *tampoco* must be used instead of *también.*

56. C. The past participle is being used as an adjective and must show agreement in gender and number with the noun it modifies, which is *pilares.* The definite article *los* gives the clue.

57. B. The pronoun *le* must be changed to *te* to maintain the *tú* form in the sentence.

58. B. Use the subjunctive in a dependent clause following the expression of doubt *no es cierto que.*

59. C. Use the preposition *para* followed by the infinitive of a verb to refer to a figurative goal.

60. B. Use the preposition *por* to express motion through a place.

61. A. The expression *antes de* requires the use of the infinitive form rather than the gerund.

62. A. Use the imperfect to speak about physical or emotional characteristics in the past.

63. B. The action *rompí* refers to things (*los vasos*) not to a part of the body; therefore, the use of the reflexive pronoun *se* is incorrect in the context of this sentence.

64. A. Use the preposition *por* rather than *para* to designate the cause or the reason.

Reading Comprehension Passages

65. D. Isabel Allende begins her literary career writing a letter to her grandfather: *la vida de Isabel cambió para siempre un 8 de enero, cuando en 1981 empezó a escribir una carta a su abuelo chileno desde el exilio venezolano.*

66. D. *La casa de los espíritus* has been translated into 24 languages: *ha sido traducida a dos docenas de idiomas*.

67. C. The second paragraph of the passage states that Allende's success lies in the universality of her characters.

68. B. It was difficult for Allende to first publish her novel because she was rejected by publishers because she is a woman: *no se publicaban novelas de escritoras en Latinoamérica*.

69. B. The passage states: *En una ocasión, el poeta Pablo Neruda se negó a ser entrevistado por Allende dada la reputación que ella tenía de añadir fantasía a la realidad*.

70. A. Allende was greatly influenced by her grandfather, who used to tell her many stories that enhanced her narrative: *le debo la mayor parte de las historias que yo cuento porque era un gran contador de historias*.

71. B. The passage states: *creo que la inspiración siempre viene de una emoción profunda que ha estado conmigo por mucho tiempo*.

72. A. The passage states: *siempre ha empezado sus novelas un 8 de enero, sin otro tipo de planificación que una serie de notas en papeles con esbozos de historias que recoge por el mundo*.

73. B. The owl was more preoccupied with all the defects that the other animals had: *sobre todos los defectos que hacían desgraciada a la Humanidad*.

74. C. The passage states: *la debilidad de la Hormiga, que era aplastada todos los días*.

75. A. The passage states: *se puso a pensar en la manera de remediarlos*.

76. B. The owl gained his knowledge by observing those around him: *adquirió la costumbre de desvelarse y de salir a la calle a observar cómo se conducía la gente*.

77. C. The owl developed the ability to predict how others would behave: *se le desarrolló una gran facilidad para clasificar, y sabía a ciencia cierta cuándo el León iba a rugir. . . .*

78. B. The owl concluded that if the animals changed their behavior, the world would be a better place.

79. D. The passage states: *pero los otros animales no apreciaban los esfuerzos del Búho . . . antes bien pensaban que era tonto*.

80. B. *La tomatina* is a popular festival from Valencia: *la fiesta más representativa del carácter valenciano*.

81. C. *La tomatina* is described like a celebration of ancient gods: *por su colorido, recuerda las bacanales romanas*.

82. C. The first thing that the participants are asked to do is to soften the tomatoes: *se ruega encarecidamente que antes de arrojar los tomates, se deshagan en la mano*.

83. D. The passage states: *a ella acuden decenas de miles de excéntricos, entre españoles de diferentes partes del país y extranjeros*.

84. A. The passage states: *ésta es una Guerra en la que no habrá vencedores, pues no hay quien no quede hecho una sopa colorada*.

85. B. The passage states: *las loterías o juegos de masas se implantaron por los Estados con el deseo claro de obtener unos ingresos que podrían considerarse como impuestos voluntarios.*

86. A. The passage states: *en el siglo XVI se celebraban . . . con un destino de beneficios también determinado.*

87. B. The passage states: *durante el siglo XVIII se fueron implantando en la mayor parte de Europa las loterías de Estado.*

88. B. Some people were against the lottery because they thought that it would be detrimental to the population: *los detractores basaron sus argumentos en los efectos nocivos que este juego podría tener en la población.*

89. C. The Spanish liked the Lotería Nacional because they could purchase preprinted tickets: *la comodidad que representa la adquisición de un billete sin tener que aventurar ningún pronóstico.*

90. A. The passage states: *se restablece la Lotería de Números con el ya tradicional nombre usado durante el siglo XIX: Lotería Primitiva.*

Section II: Free Response Questions

Paragraph Fill-Ins

1. **aquel.** The demonstrative adjective must show gender and number agreement with the noun *escaparate*.

2. **había.** Use the imperfect tense for description in the past. This is a case of the use of the impersonal verb *haber,* equivalent to there is/there are, which only takes the form of the third-person singular.

3. **medio.** The adjective must show gender and number agreement with *centenar,* which is a collective, masculine, and singular noun.

4. **baratas.** This adjective is modifying the noun *ediciones*, which is feminine and plural.

5. **podía.** Use the imperfect tense for descriptions in the past. The third-person singular is required because this is a case of special construction with *se*.

6. **un.** The indefinite article remains masculine and singular to maintain the agreement with the noun and adjective it accompanies. Although the ending of the noun *local* does not facilitate the identification of the gender, the adjective *pequeño* gives the clue.

7. **cuyas.** The adjective must maintain the gender and number agreement with the noun *paredes*. Although the ending of the noun does not facilitate the identification of the gender, the adjective *cubiertas* gives the clue.

8. **atestadas.** The adjective must show agreement in gender and number with the noun that it modifies, in this case *estanterías*.

9. **alcanzaban.** Use the imperfect tense for descriptions in the past. The subject of the sentence is *rimeros;* therefore, the third-person plural form is required.

10. **baja.** The adjective must maintain the gender and number agreement with the noun *parte*. Although the ending of the noun does not facilitate the identification of the gender, the article *la* gives the clue.

Discrete Sentence Fill-Ins

11. **habrías sacado.** Use the conditional perfect to describe the result of another action.

12. **juegue.** Use the subjunctive when it is preceded by the expression *parecer que*.

13. **descompuso, ha descompuesto.** The preterit and the present perfect may alternate in this construction because the results can be seen in the present.

14. **se reduzcan.** Use the subjunctive after the expression *hasta que* to indicate that one event is posterior to another.

15. **nazca, haya nacido.** The present subjunctive indicates an expectation. The present perfect subjunctive is used to indicate that the action of the dependent clause happens before the action of the main clause.

16. **era.** Use the imperfect to indicate a continuous action in the past.

17. **diría.** Use the conditional after an if-clause that uses the present subjunctive.

18. **escojas.** Negative informal commands use the perfect subjunctive. The informal command is required because the speaker addresses the other person using her first name.

19. **destruyendo.** The use of the gerund is equivalent to the English phrase beginning with *by*. . . .

20. **acuéstate.** Use the command (imperative) form to indicate that a command is given. The informal command is required because the speaker addresses the other person using his first name.

Sample Answers for Essay Question

High-Scoring Essay

En los últimos años las compañías multinacionales han creado un sistema de cooperación entre ellas, causando el fenómeno de la globalización. Como resultado de este proceso, han surgido unas organizaciones compuestas por varios países que tienen como objetivo unas mejores relaciones entre las naciones en diferentes aspectos. Esto, por supuesto, tiene sus ventajas y desventajas.

Un ejemplo de este tipo de organización es la Unión Europea, que está formada por numerosos países de Europa. Una de las cosas que han hecho es tomar una moneda común: el euro. Esto es una ventaja para el turista porque así no tiene que cambiar su dinero a diferentes monedas que no conoce bien. También como resultado de este programa multinacional, ahora los ciudadanos de los países que pertenecen a la Unión Europea tienen un solo pasaporte y pueden cruzar las fronteras sin problemas. Esto es bueno porque hay más movilidad para esta gente. Es como si su país hubiese crecido. La globalización también ha sido útil en el campo de las ciencias. A través de la internet hay acceso a noticias e investigaciones en todos los campos científicos. Además hay ventajas en las comunicaciones, pues ahora se pueden ver por televisión eventos que ocurren en otros países y por la red se pueden leer las noticias internacionales.

A pesar de esto, hay personas que no están de acuerdo con la globalización. Una de las razones porque la gente no está de acuerdo es porque piensan que la riqueza mundial no está bien distribuida y piden que se haga una mejor distribución de ésta. Otras personas dicen que tanto desarrollo está perjudicando ecológicamente nuestro planeta. El desarrollo de nuevas compañías en lugares poco poblados perjudica a los animales y las plantas que viven en la zona. Las viviendas y las carreteras que hacen falta para que todo funcione bien, quitan el espacio a las especies que viven allí. También está el problema de la contaminación del aire y del agua.

En mi opinión, la globalización es algo bueno, solamente hay que tener cuidado de no hacer daño al planeta, para que todos podamos disfrutar de él.

Analysis of the High-Scoring Essay

The abundance of complex grammatical structures in the essay clearly demonstrates that the writer possesses excellence in written expression. The reader notices that there is an ease of expression throughout. The range of verb forms and tenses used is more than appropriate to deal with this specific topic: present, imperfect, gerund, future, and present perfect of the indicative, as well as the present and the past perfect subjunctive, passive voice, and verb + infinitive. The essay has very good organization, and the writer makes good use of transitional words or phrases (*como resultado, por supuesto, a pesar de*). The vocabulary used is of a very wide range (*riqueza, perjudicar, vivendas, contaminación*). The writer shows very good control of spelling and other conventions of the written language. **Score: 9**

Medium-Scoring Essay

La globalización tiene sus ventajas y desventajas. La globalización es un proceso economical que ayuda a los paises a ayudar uno a los otros.

La globalización hace que los paices vayan al capitalismo más rapidamente. Esta es una ventaja para los paices pobres, aunque la gente piensa que no es verdad. La gente piensa que los paices ricos exploitan a los pobres.

Otro punto importante de la globalización es la internet. Ahora con la internet una persona de un nación lejano puede a saber las cosas que esta pasando en un otro lugar. Hay muchos oportunidades para la gente aprender cosas de diferentes culturas, como las idiomas y costumbres extrañas. La internet no es buena para los carteros porque ellos tienen menos trabajo con el e-mail. Entonces los carteros piensan que la globalización tiene desventaja para ellos.

Yo creo además que la globalización no está buena para la ecología de Earth. Cuando hay muchas factorías, se usa el lugar para casas, caminos y otras cosas. Entonces los animales y las plantas no tienen más su enviromento y por ese razon mueren y se convierten en extinctos.

Para terminar, yo quiero decir que es posible que es mejor no hacer tanta globalización, para que no haya gente preocupada como los carteros y los animales.

Analysis of the Medium-Scoring Essay

In this essay, the reader observes a relatively good control of basic grammar structures, even though there are various errors of agreement (*muchos oportunidades, las idiomas*). The vocabulary seems to be adequate, but there is ample evidence of second language interference (*economical, exploitan, un otro lugar, earth, enviromento, se convierten en extinctos*). There is no evidence of the writer's control of more complex structures, since the only verb tense used extensively is the present of the indicative, and in cases where the subjunctive is required, the indicative is used (*hace que los paices van*). The essay also shows that the writer is not able to use correctly *ser* and *estar: la globalización no está buena para la ecología*. There is a lack of control in the use of verbal phrases with prepositions (*puede a saber*). There are some redeeming features like the correct use of the subjunctive in *para que no haya gente preocupada*. Spelling and accentuation are generally correct, although there are some errors in spelling (*paices*), and there are some accent marks missing. The essay is relevant to the topic and the organization is adequate. **Score: 5**

Answer Sheet for Practice Test 3

(Remove this sheet and use it to mark your answers)

CUT HERE

PART A	PART B	PART C	PART D

PART A
1 Ⓐ Ⓑ Ⓒ Ⓓ
2 Ⓐ Ⓑ Ⓒ Ⓓ
3 Ⓐ Ⓑ Ⓒ Ⓓ
4 Ⓐ Ⓑ Ⓒ Ⓓ
5 Ⓐ Ⓑ Ⓒ Ⓓ
6 Ⓐ Ⓑ Ⓒ Ⓓ
7 Ⓐ Ⓑ Ⓒ Ⓓ
8 Ⓐ Ⓑ Ⓒ Ⓓ
9 Ⓐ Ⓑ Ⓒ Ⓓ
10 Ⓐ Ⓑ Ⓒ Ⓓ
11 Ⓐ Ⓑ Ⓒ Ⓓ
12 Ⓐ Ⓑ Ⓒ Ⓓ
13 Ⓐ Ⓑ Ⓒ Ⓓ
14 Ⓐ Ⓑ Ⓒ Ⓓ
15 Ⓐ Ⓑ Ⓒ Ⓓ
16 Ⓐ Ⓑ Ⓒ Ⓓ
17 Ⓐ Ⓑ Ⓒ Ⓓ
18 Ⓐ Ⓑ Ⓒ Ⓓ
19 Ⓐ Ⓑ Ⓒ Ⓓ
20 Ⓐ Ⓑ Ⓒ Ⓓ
21 Ⓐ Ⓑ Ⓒ Ⓓ
22 Ⓐ Ⓑ Ⓒ Ⓓ
23 Ⓐ Ⓑ Ⓒ Ⓓ
24 Ⓐ Ⓑ Ⓒ Ⓓ
25 Ⓐ Ⓑ Ⓒ Ⓓ
26 Ⓐ Ⓑ Ⓒ Ⓓ
27 Ⓐ Ⓑ Ⓒ Ⓓ
28 Ⓐ Ⓑ Ⓒ Ⓓ

PART B
29 Ⓐ Ⓑ Ⓒ Ⓓ
30 Ⓐ Ⓑ Ⓒ Ⓓ
31 Ⓐ Ⓑ Ⓒ Ⓓ
32 Ⓐ Ⓑ Ⓒ Ⓓ
33 Ⓐ Ⓑ Ⓒ Ⓓ
34 Ⓐ Ⓑ Ⓒ Ⓓ
35 Ⓐ Ⓑ Ⓒ Ⓓ
36 Ⓐ Ⓑ Ⓒ Ⓓ
37 Ⓐ Ⓑ Ⓒ Ⓓ
38 Ⓐ Ⓑ Ⓒ Ⓓ
39 Ⓐ Ⓑ Ⓒ Ⓓ
40 Ⓐ Ⓑ Ⓒ Ⓓ
41 Ⓐ Ⓑ Ⓒ Ⓓ
42 Ⓐ Ⓑ Ⓒ Ⓓ
43 Ⓐ Ⓑ Ⓒ Ⓓ
44 Ⓐ Ⓑ Ⓒ Ⓓ
45 Ⓐ Ⓑ Ⓒ Ⓓ
46 Ⓐ Ⓑ Ⓒ Ⓓ
47 Ⓐ Ⓑ Ⓒ Ⓓ
48 Ⓐ Ⓑ Ⓒ Ⓓ

PART C
49 Ⓐ Ⓑ Ⓒ Ⓓ
50 Ⓐ Ⓑ Ⓒ Ⓓ
51 Ⓐ Ⓑ Ⓒ Ⓓ
52 Ⓐ Ⓑ Ⓒ Ⓓ
53 Ⓐ Ⓑ Ⓒ Ⓓ
54 Ⓐ Ⓑ Ⓒ Ⓓ
55 Ⓐ Ⓑ Ⓒ Ⓓ
56 Ⓐ Ⓑ Ⓒ Ⓓ
57 Ⓐ Ⓑ Ⓒ Ⓓ
58 Ⓐ Ⓑ Ⓒ Ⓓ
59 Ⓐ Ⓑ Ⓒ Ⓓ
60 Ⓐ Ⓑ Ⓒ Ⓓ
61 Ⓐ Ⓑ Ⓒ Ⓓ
62 Ⓐ Ⓑ Ⓒ Ⓓ
63 Ⓐ Ⓑ Ⓒ Ⓓ

PART D
64 Ⓐ Ⓑ Ⓒ Ⓓ
65 Ⓐ Ⓑ Ⓒ Ⓓ
66 Ⓐ Ⓑ Ⓒ Ⓓ
67 Ⓐ Ⓑ Ⓒ Ⓓ
68 Ⓐ Ⓑ Ⓒ Ⓓ
69 Ⓐ Ⓑ Ⓒ Ⓓ
70 Ⓐ Ⓑ Ⓒ Ⓓ
71 Ⓐ Ⓑ Ⓒ Ⓓ
72 Ⓐ Ⓑ Ⓒ Ⓓ
73 Ⓐ Ⓑ Ⓒ Ⓓ
74 Ⓐ Ⓑ Ⓒ Ⓓ
75 Ⓐ Ⓑ Ⓒ Ⓓ
76 Ⓐ Ⓑ Ⓒ Ⓓ
77 Ⓐ Ⓑ Ⓒ Ⓓ
78 Ⓐ Ⓑ Ⓒ Ⓓ
79 Ⓐ Ⓑ Ⓒ Ⓓ
80 Ⓐ Ⓑ Ⓒ Ⓓ
81 Ⓐ Ⓑ Ⓒ Ⓓ
82 Ⓐ Ⓑ Ⓒ Ⓓ
83 Ⓐ Ⓑ Ⓒ Ⓓ
84 Ⓐ Ⓑ Ⓒ Ⓓ
85 Ⓐ Ⓑ Ⓒ Ⓓ
86 Ⓐ Ⓑ Ⓒ Ⓓ
87 Ⓐ Ⓑ Ⓒ Ⓓ
88 Ⓐ Ⓑ Ⓒ Ⓓ
89 Ⓐ Ⓑ Ⓒ Ⓓ
90 Ⓐ Ⓑ Ⓒ Ⓓ

Section I: Multiple Choice Questions

This section consists of four different parts: Part A, Part B, Part C, and Part D.

Total time: 1 hour and 30 minutes

Number of questions: 90

Percent of total grade: 50

Part A

Time: Approximately 30 minutes

The time for the questions below is paced by the tape.

You will hear a few dialogues. At the end of each, you will hear several questions about what you have just listened to. From the choices printed below, select the one that best responds to each question.

Ahora vas a oír algunos diálogos. Al final de cada uno escucharás unas preguntas sobre lo que has escuchado. De entre las opciones que aparecen impresas, escoge la que mejor responda a cada una de las preguntas.

Get ready to listen to the first dialogue.

Dialogue 1
PLAY TRACK 12 ON CD 2

1. A. Porque quiere invitarla al cine.
    B. Porque quiere que vaya con él al teatro.
    C. Porque necesita que llame a Elena.
    D. Porque quiere conocer a Ernesto.

2. A. El próximo viernes.
    B. El sábado que viene.
    C. En el verano.
    D. Mañana por la tarde.

3. A. Tiene otro compromiso.
    B. Ernesto no la deja.
    C. Va a salir con Elena.
    D. Joaquín es muy celoso.

Dialogue 2
PLAY TRACK 13 ON CD 2

4. A. Ropa para su esposo.
    B. Una bolsa de viajes.
    C. Un frasco de crema.
    D. Una lata de café.

5. A. La señora no recuerda lo que tiene que comprar.

   B. La señora no puede describir a su esposo.

   C. El vendedor no puede ayudarle.

   D. La señora no sabe la talla de su esposo.

6. A. Que lleve una talla cualquiera.

   B. Que venga con su esposo.

   C. Que le describa al esposo.

   D. Que no compre nada.

Dialogue 3
PLAY TRACK 14 ON CD 2

7. A. Llenar un formulario.

   B. Tocar el piano.

   C. Mecanografiar dos cartas.

   D. Traer su currículum vitae.

8. A. Solamente dos horas al día.

   B. Más de cuatro horas al día.

   C. No más de veinte horas a la semana.

   D. Más de cuarenta horas a la semana.

9. A. Uno.

   B. Dos.

   C. Tres.

   D. Cuatro.

10. A. De que solamente haya trabajo a tiempo completo.

    B. De que no tenga ningún beneficio.

    C. De que tenga que traer tantos documentos.

    D. De que no pueda tocar el piano.

You will hear a few short narratives. At the end of each, you will hear several questions about what you have just listened to. From the choices printed below, select the one that best responds to each question.

Ahora vas a oír algunas narraciones cortas. Al final de cada una escucharás algunas preguntas sobre lo que has escuchado. De entre las opciones que aparecen impresas, escoge la que mejor responda a cada una de las preguntas.

Get ready to listen to the first narrative.

Narrative 1
PLAY TRACK 15 ON CD 2

11. A. Su larga cola.

    B. Su gran peso.

    C. Su pelo brillante.

    D. Sus ojos oblicuos.

12. A. Dorados.

    B. Verdes.

    C. Azules.

    D. Negros.

13. A. En 1860.

    B. En 1895.

    C. En 1950.

    D. En 1953.

Narrative 2

PLAY TRACK 16 ON CD 2

14. **A.** Es moderno.

    B. Es interactivo.

    C. Es sorprendente.

    D. Es futurista.

15. **A.** Una televisión a colores.

    B. Una tarjeta electrónica.

    C. Equipos de alta tecnología.

    D. Los controles de una cámara.

16. **A.** Una tarjeta electrónica.

    B. Una sala temática.

    C. El inicio del recorrido del museo.

    D. El laboratorio de audio.

17. **A.** Predecir un huracán.

    B. Simular un ultrasonido.

    C. Editar ondas de sonido.

    D. Convertirse en protagonista de una película.

You will hear a longer selection. It is about five minutes in length. You may take notes, although you will not receive a grade for these notes. At the end of the selection, you will answer several questions about what you have just heard. Select the best answer for each question from the choices printed on the exam. Base your selections on the information you have heard.

Ahora vas a oír una selección más extensa. Su duración es de aproximadamente cinco minutos. Debes tomar apuntes en el espacio disponible en esta página, aunque los mismos no serán calificados. Al final de la selección, tendrás que contestar varias preguntas sobre lo que acabas de escuchar. De entre las opciones que aparecen en el examen, escoge la que mejor responda a cada una de las preguntas, teniendo en cuenta la información que has escuchado.

Longer Narrative 1

PLAY TRACK 17 ON CD 2

18. ¿Qué efecto tienen las cuentas en la humanidad?

    A. Le causan fascinación.

    B. Le hacen gastar dinero.

    C. Le sirven de magia.

    D. Le provocan codicia.

19. ¿De qué se fabricaban las cuentas en las civilizaciones ancestrales?

    A. De vidrio y ágata.

    B. De arena y limón.

    C. De madera y conchas.

    D. De cobalto y cobre.

GO ON TO THE NEXT PAGE

20. ¿Qué consecuencia trajo el uso del vidrio para fabricar cuentas?

    A. Se usaron como dinero.

    B. Se usaron sustancias naturales.

    C. Se introdujo el color.

    D. Se controló su producción.

21. ¿Qué color producía el oro en el vidrio?

    A. Amarillo.

    B. Verde.

    C. Azul.

    D. Rojo.

22. ¿Qué podía sucederle a un fabricante de cuentas de Murano que abandonara la isla?

    A. Convertirse en rehén.

    B. Morir a manos de un asesino.

    C. Abandonar a sus familiares.

    D. Perder sus habilidades manuales.

23. ¿Qué es el cheurón?

    A. Una cuenta de Murano.

    B. Una piedra típica de Egipto.

    C. Una sustancia africana.

    D. Una cuenta de diferentes colores.

You will hear another selection. It is about five minutes in length. You may take notes, although you will not receive a grade for these notes. At the end of the selection, you will answer several questions about what you have just heard. Select the best answer for each question from the choices printed on the exam. Base your selections on the information you have heard.

Ahora vas a oír otra selección. Su duración es de aproximadamente cinco minutos. Debes tomar apuntes en el espacio disponible en esta página, aunque los mismos no serán calificados. Al final de la selección, tendrás que contestar varias preguntas sobre lo que acabas de escuchar. De entre las opciones que aparecen en el examen, escoge la que mejor responda a cada una de las preguntas, teniendo en cuenta la información que has escuchado.

Longer Narrative 2

PLAY TRACK 18 ON CD 2

24. ¿Cómo influenció la obra de Roth a Vargas Llosa?

    A. De manera muy específica.

    B. Ayudándolo a escribir en episodios.

    C. Enseñándole detalles sobre una época.

    D. Dándole la oportunidad de conocer a un tirano.

25. Según la entrevista, ¿por qué escogió Vargas Llosa a Trujillo para su novela?

    A. Porque era muy melodramático.

    B. Por su ambición de poder.

    C. Porque su dictadura fue la más autoritaria.

    D. Porque fue el Benefactor de la Patria.

26. Según la entrevista, ¿qué caracterizaba a Trujillo?

    A. Su origen aristocrático.

    B. Su formalismo teatral.

    C. Su tratamiento ficticio.

    D. Su manía de la limpieza.

27. ¿Cómo fue finalmente considerado el asesinato de Trujillo?

    A. Como magnicidio.

    B. Como ajusticiamiento.

    C. Como tiranicidio.

    D. Como gesta heroica.

28. ¿Cuál fue la gran tragedia de Trujillo?

    A. A su hijo mayor no le gustaba la política.

    B. No le gustaba ser moreno.

    C. Estaba demasiado familiarizado con la violencia.

    D. El pueblo siempre habló de ajusticiarlo.

Part B

Suggested time: 10 minutes

Cloze Passages

Each of the following passages contains numbered blanks, which indicate that words or groups of words are missing. There are four options to fill in each blank, but only one is correct.

In order to determine the general meaning of the passage, read quickly through it first. Read it again and select the option that best fills each blank according to the context of the complete passage.

Cada uno de los siguientes pasajes contiene espacios en blanco numerados para indicar que faltan palabras o grupos de palabras. Hay cuatro opciones para llenar cada espacio, pero solamente una es correcta.

Para poder determinar el sentido general del pasaje, léelo rápidamente; luego léelo de nuevo y selecciona la opción que mejor complete cada espacio de acuerdo con el contexto total del pasaje.

GO ON TO THE NEXT PAGE

La locomotora (29) un silbido autoritario y el tren (30) a rodar cachazudamente estremecién-dose con un sacudimiento lento y suave, como un desperezo; luego (31) su marcha, los coches pasaron veloces unos (32) otros, con sus ventanillas iluminadas, (33) las cuales se abocetaban perfiles borrosos de viajeros, y al fin el expreso desapareció en su vuelta del camino (34) esa tris-teza indefinible que deja tras sí (35) lo que huye . . . (36) lejos, sepultada en la inmensidad tene-brosa de la noche, quedaba la (37) con sus cuatro paredes renegridas por el (38) de las máquinas.

29. A. lanza

    B. lanzó

    C. lanzaba

    D. ha lanzado

30. A. echó

    B. terminó

    C. salió

    D. dejó

31. A. aceleró

    B. aminoró

    C. atrasó

    D. arrebató

32. A. tras

    B. detrás

    C. delante

    D. enfrente

33. A. de

    B. hasta

    C. por

    D. sin

34. A. derramar

    B. derramando

    C. derramado

    D. derramó

35. A. toda

    B. todo

    C. todas

    D. todos

36. A. allá

    B. aquí

    C. ahí

    D. acá

37. A. emoción

    B. estación

    C. ilusión

    D. sensación

38. A. humo

    B. humor

    C. rumor

    D. zumo

El amor, que como una sombra me (39) desde tiempo atrás en las novelas y en los libros de gramática ((40) allí como podía, en los ejemplos de versificación), me anunciaba que ahora iba a (41) en la vida real, pues si por casualidad yo veía una flor me (42) pensativo no sé por cuánto tiempo (43) que algún ruido me hacía volver en (44); si llovía, peor, porque (45) no pensaba en nada sino que sólo me (46) triste, sin saber por qué, viendo (47) la lluvia a través de los vidrios; y en las tardes de sol, el simple vuelo de una mosca me inquietaba (48) y mi imaginación se remontaba quién sabe a dónde . . .

39. A. persigue
B. persiguió
C. perseguía
D. persiga

40. A. metida
B. metido
C. metidas
D. metidos

41. A. llamar
B. llegar
C. llenar
D. llevar

42. A. quedo
B. quedé
C. quedaba
D. quedaría

43. A. de
B. desde
C. hacia
D. hasta

44. A. me
B. mí
C. ti
D. sí

45. A. entonces
B. antes
C. cuando
D. en cuanto

46. A. puse
B. ponía
C. he puesto
D. había puesto

47. A. caber
B. caer
C. callar
D. cavar

48. A. lentamente
B. extrañamente
C. raramente
D. copiosamente

GO ON TO THE NEXT PAGE

Part C

Suggested time: 10 minutes

Error Recognition

In the following sentences, select the underlined part of the sentence that needs to be changed in order to make the sentence grammatically correct.

En las oraciones que aparecen a continuación, escoge la parte subrayada que habría que cambiar para que la oración sea gramaticalmente correcta.

49. Los alumnos no <u>regresarían</u> a la escuela
[A]
<u>hasta que</u> <u>pasen</u> todos los meses <u>de</u>
[B]   [C]   [D]
verano.

50. Si <u>hubieras depositado</u> el dinero <u>entre</u>
[A]   [B]
el banco, <u>habría estado</u> <u>más</u> seguro.
[C]   [D]

51. En Madrid <u>hay</u> <u>tantos</u> catedrales <u>como</u>
[A] [B]   [C]
museos <u>y</u> teatros.
[D]

52. Aunque Rita es <u>tan inteligente que</u>
[A]
Aurora, <u>la</u> última <u>saca</u> <u>mucho</u> mejores
[B]   [C]   [D]
calificaciones.

53. Me <u>dijo</u> Luis que anoche <u>hubieron</u>
[A]   [B]
<u>varios</u> accidentes <u>en</u> la autopista.
[C]   [D]

54. <u>Por</u> más que <u>llores</u> no <u>se</u> saldrás con la
[A]   [B]   [C]
<u>tuya</u>, Lolita.
[D]

55. Isabel <u>tuvo</u> que hacer <u>veintiuno</u>
[A]   [B]
informes <u>para</u> la compañía <u>de</u> seguros.
[C]   [D]

56. <u>Por</u> facturar <u>el</u> equipaje <u>deberías</u> haberle
[A]   [B]   [C]
<u>puesto</u> un candado a cada maleta.
[D]

57. Si no <u>te</u> <u>sentía</u> bien, <u>¿por qué</u> viniste a
[A] [B]   [C]
la escuela <u>esta</u> tarde?
[D]

58. No son ésos <u>mis</u> zapatos, <u>pero los</u> que
[A]   [B]   [C]
<u>están</u> allá en el rincón.
[D]

59. No sé <u>la</u> razón por la que <u>pasas</u> <u>tantos</u>
[A]   [B] [C]
rato <u>viendo</u> la televisión.
[D]

60. Por <u>lo</u> que <u>veo</u>, Joaquín no está <u>sacar</u>
[A]   [B]   [C]
buenas notas <u>este</u> semestre.
[D]

61. Rebeca <u>vivía</u> en el <u>primero</u> piso de ese
[A]   [B]
apartamento <u>cuando</u> <u>era</u> pequeña.
[C]   [D]

62. Quizás <u>tengas</u> razón, pero no <u>creo</u> que
[A]   [B]
Xavier <u>y</u> Higinio <u>sean</u> gemelos.
[C]   [D]

63. Hoy <u>en</u> día, los jóvenes <u>parezcan</u> que no
[A]   [B]
tienen <u>ningún</u> interés <u>por</u> los estudios.
[C]   [D]

Part D

Suggested time: 40 minutes

Reading Comprehension Passages

Read each of the following passages. After each passage, you will find a series of incomplete sentences or questions. From the four choices given, select the option that best completes the sentence or answers the question according to the passage.

Lee cada uno de los pasajes siguientes. Al final de cada pasaje encontrarás una serie de oraciones incompletas o preguntas. De las cuatro opciones que aparecen, escoge la que mejor completa cada oración o responda a cada pregunta de acuerdo con el fragmento leído.

Durante siglos, el aceite de oliva ha sido la principal fuente de grasa de los países mediterráneos. Antiguas civilizaciones usaban el aceite de oliva no sólo como alimento, sino también como maquillaje, perfume, jabón y champú. Desde luego, también era empleado como medicina para aliviar dolores musculares e infecciones del oído. Hoy en día, la ciencia trata de descifrar el fundamento científico de tantos usos no tan desencaminados.

El imperio romano dio el impulso definitivo a la producción de aceite de oliva. El creciente consumo y la falta de abastecimiento en su propia tierra obligó a los romanos a extender los cultivos en los campos del sur de la península ibérica, lo que hoy es la región de Andalucía, en España. El aceite se transportaba a Roma en ánforas de barro de 50 litros, con un sello que indicaba el nombre del transportista y la fecha de elaboración.

Para producir un litro de aceite de oliva son necesarios entre 4 y 5 kg de aceitunas. Un olivo empieza a producir aceitunas entre los cinco y diez años de edad y alcanza la madurez hacia los veinte años. Entre los 100 y 150 años, su producción empieza a declinar. El color de la aceituna no está ligado a la variedad, sino a la etapa de maduración. Las aceitunas son verdes al principio y se vuelven negras al madurar.

El proceso empieza con la recolección de la aceituna en su punto óptimo. La recogida se puede hacer a mano (el "ordeño"), golpeando el árbol con unas varas flexibles ("vareo") para que las aceitunas caigan sobre unas lonas preparadas en el suelo o por medios mecánicos de vibración.

Las aceitunas recolectadas se llevan al molino, donde, una vez escogidas y limpias, se trituran, incluido el hueso, hasta que se forme una pasta. Esta pasta se lleva a las prensas que extraen una mezcla de aceite y agua. Por decantación, el aceite sube a la superficie mientras el agua se queda abajo. Métodos más modernos, por centrifugación, logran la separación del agua y el aceite.

El aceite de oliva está compuesto en un 77% de grasa monoinsaturada que, según los investigadores, puede reducir el riesgo de ataques de corazón, disminuyendo el nivel del colesterol "malo" (LDL) en la sangre, mientras que mantiene o incrementa los niveles de colesterol "bueno" (HDL). Por otro lado, a causa de su contenido de ácido oleico, estudios apuntan a que el aceite de oliva se digiere mucho mejor que cualquier otra grasa alimenticia, ejerce un ligero efecto laxante y

GO ON TO THE NEXT PAGE

tonifica y estimula el páncreas. Todo ello afecta positivamente al aparato digestivo.

Además, el aceite de oliva contiene antioxidantes, en particular vitaminas A y E, que ayudan a proteger el cuerpo contra el proceso de envejecimiento y que contribuyen a la prevención del cáncer y de enfermedades del corazón. Recientes estudios indican que la sustitución de otros aceites y grasas por aceites ricos en grasa monoinsaturada—como el aceite de oliva—pueden reducir el riesgo de cáncer de seno. Y más y más estudios de universidades proclaman que el aceite de oliva es beneficioso para la memoria y actúa contra la arteriosclerosis, la presión sanguínea alta, la calcificación ósea, la diabetes y hasta la depresión.

64. Según este pasaje, ¿cómo era usado antiguamente el aceite de oliva?

    A. Solamente para remedios médicos.

    B. Exclusivamente como fuente de grasa para cocinar.

    C. Extensamente en múltiples usos.

    D. Únicamente en productos de perfumería.

65. ¿Por qué llega la producción de aceite de oliva a España?

    A. Porque ya los romanos no tenían tierra para cultivar olivos.

    B. Porque los romanos no lo consumían mucho.

    C. Porque los olivos crecían bien en Andalucía.

    D. Porque los españoles lo usaban como medicina.

66. ¿Cuántos años, aproximadamente, se puede aprovechar la producción de un olivo?

    A. Entre 5 y 10 años.

    B. Unos 20 años más o menos.

    C. Menos de 100 años.

    D. Alrededor de 145 años.

67. ¿De qué depende el color de las aceitunas?

    A. Del tipo de olivo.

    B. De la edad del olivo.

    C. De la maduración de la aceituna.

    D. Del método de recolección.

68. ¿Cómo se recogen las aceitunas?

    A. Por tres métodos diferentes.

    B. Usando solamente unas varas.

    C. Sin usar las manos.

    D. Con el uso exclusivo de máquinas.

69. ¿Qué se consigue con la centrifugación?

    A. Recoger más aceitunas.

    B. Triturar el hueso de la aceituna.

    C. Separar el agua del aceite.

    D. Formar una pasta decantada.

70. ¿Qué efecto tiene el consumo de aceite de oliva en el sistema digestivo?

    A. Incrementa el nivel de colesterol.

    B. Sirve de laxante.

    C. Protege contra el envejecimiento.

    D. Actúa contra la depresión.

71. La presencia de antioxidantes en el aceite de oliva hace que éste

    A. ayude a la prevención del cáncer.

    B. aumente el nivel de colesterol.

    C. controle la presión sanguínea.

    D. estimule el páncreas.

La vida da vueltas y nos lleva por caminos inesperados. Para algunos, la vocación se despierta muy pronto, y para otros más tarde. Para Priscilla Bianchi, natural de Guatemala, tuvieron que pasar cuarenta años antes de que descubriese su verdadera vocación. Socióloga industrial, ha viajado extensamente por Latinoamérica y el Caribe impartiendo cursos para grandes compañías multinacionales. Llevaba una vida muy intensa y agitada, pero ya empezaba a preguntarse: ¿Es esto lo que quiero seguir haciendo el resto de mi vida?"

Siempre le ha gustado la costura, hasta el punto de que recuerda haber jugado con una máquina de coser a los cuatro años de edad. Ya de jovencita le gustaba hacer punto y *crochet* y, además, pintaba óleos y acuarelas pero el *quilting* (escultura textil) fue para ella una gran revelación como expresión artística, ya que podía combinar todas sus habilidades manuales y creativas. Todo comenzó un día, en uno de sus viajes a Estados Unidos, cuando compró un libro de *quilting*. Al regresar a Guatemala, se puso a la máquina de coser para tratar de hacer uno. Ansiosamente trataba de terminar el primero porque ya estaba deseosa de empezar el segundo.

El *quilting*—sin nombre equivalente en español—se originó en Europa hace varios siglos y llegó a su máxima expresión en Estados Unidos cuando los colonizadores europeos, especialmente los ingleses, llegaron a las costas norteamericanas. Con hilo y aguja, las mujeres empalmaban pequeños trozos de tela y elaboraban así tejidos más grandes. Combinando colores y dibujos, conseguían textiles de original belleza. Los edredones eran la forma más común del *quilting*.

Hace unos veinticinco años hubo un renacimiento del *quilting* en Estados Unidos, esta vez como elemento decorativo, para colgar los trabajos en las paredes como si fuesen tapices. Es un arte casi desconocido en Latinoamérica.

Bianchi aprendió todas las técnicas de costura y construcción en Estados Unidos, llevándose además telas a Guatemala. Con el tiempo fue experimentando con telas guatemaltecas, ricas en colores y dibujos. Hoy en día, sus piezas se alternan entre los dos tipos de tejidos pues no parece que en su país haya mucho interés por la tela típica; por el contrario, sus *quiltings* logran mucha aceptación en el extranjero. Una vez se confirma el famoso dicho de que nadie es profeta en su tierra.

72. ¿Cuándo descubrió Bianchi su vocación?

    A. Cuando tenía cuatro años..

    B. Cuando vivía en Guatemala.

    C. Alrededor de los 40 años de edad.

    D. Mientras estudiaba sociología industrial.

GO ON TO THE NEXT PAGE

73. ¿Qué le gustaba hacer a Priscilla cuando era pequeña?

    A. Coser.

    B. Jugar.

    C. Pintar.

    D. Hacer *crochet.*

74. ¿Qué oportunidad le brinda a Priscilla el arte del *quilting*?

    A. Viajar extensamente.

    B. Utilizar todos sus talentos artísticos.

    C. Permanecer en Guatemala.

    D. Llevar una vida intensa.

75. ¿Cómo se inició Priscilla en el arte del *quilting*?

    A. Pintando acuarelas.

    B. Jugando con una máquina de coser.

    C. Comprando un libro.

    D. Tejiendo a *crochet.*

76. ¿Dónde se originó el *quilting*?

    A. En el Caribe.

    B. En Guatemala.

    C. En los Estados Unidos.

    D. En Europa.

77. ¿Cómo renació el uso del *quilting* en los Estados Unidos recientemente?

    A. Como edredones.

    B. Como óleos.

    C. Como tapices.

    D. Como acuarelas.

78. ¿Qué caracteriza a los tejidos guatemaltecos?

    A. Su construcción elaborada.

    B. Su belleza artística.

    C. Su tamaño excepcional.

    D. Su gran colorido.

79. Del pasaje puede deducirse que el dicho "nadie es profeta en su tierra" quiere decir

    A. que en Guatemala no hay profetas.

    B. que nadie triunfa en su país de origen.

    C. que ya nadie cree en los profetas.

    D. que con los tapices se hacían profecías.

Aunque los primeros españoles que ven amanecer son los isleños de Menorca—y en esta vieja península de Hispania sale el sol por Cataluña—se ha dado en llamar Levante a las tres provincias de Castellón, Valencia y Alicante, acompañadas a veces por Murcia. Y si hay algo que las distingue del resto del país es su pasión por llenar la oscuridad de la noche con estruendo luminoso de los cohetes, las tracas y la quema de las fallas y las hogueras. Como si no tuvieran luz de sobra—o para permanecer siempre iluminados—los levantinos veneran la pólvora y el fuego.

Todo en la tierra valenciana tiene un aire de exceso y desmesura. Absolutamente todo—del barroco a la barraca—sugiere la abundancia y la demasía: desde la fertilidad de sus huertos y jardines hasta el sol de sus playas encendidas; desde el innato sentido musical de gente y su carácter apasionado hasta la luz cegadora de su cielo. Semejante exuberancia culmina en gozo de la destrucción por el fuego, en ese espectáculo nihilista de llamas, ceniza y humo que brindan las hogueras.

La tradición levantina de plantar en las plazas unos muñecotes de cartón y de cera para reírse con ellos y luego quemarlos se inició, al parecer, en el siglo XVI. En un principio se trataba de un recurso del que los carpinteros se valían para poner orden en sus talleres año con año. Recogían las maderas y trebejos inservibles, los sacaban a la calle y los quemaban amontonados. Dicha labor de limpieza solía coincidir con el comienzo de un ciclo—primavera y verano, principalmente—y en los pueblos se ajustaba a las cosechas.

La quema maderera se convirtió pronto en un entrañable rito vecinal, en el que destacan tres fechas: los días de San José, de San Antonio y de San Juan. De hecho, así se mantenía—aunque ya cristianizada—la antigua tradición de celebrar con una fiesta de fuego el equinoccio de primavera y el solsticio de verano.

El significado real de la hoguera se traduce en el Levante cuando en el montón de leña aparece en la picota el ninot como un condenado del medioevo para el escarnio del público. En estas estatuas caricaturizadas se descubre la tendencia innata de los valencianos a la mordacidad. Y se esculpen muñecos con el rostro de personajes conocidos o de tipos despreciables. Todo lo criticable se expone y se planta en esta picota popular, condenado al fuego: la injusticia, la cursilería, las modas, los acontecimientos recientes y tantas cosas más.

80. ¿Qué es el Levante?

    A. La península donde está España.

    B. La isla de Menorca.

    C. Un grupo de provincias españolas.

    D. La región de Cataluña.

81. ¿Qué caracteriza la zona del Levante?

    A. Su gran oscuridad.

    B. Su pasión por el fuego.

    C. Su devoción religiosa.

    D. Su espíritu crítico.

82. En el segundo párrafo, la característica de la zona levantina que más se destaca es

    A. la abundancia.

    B. la oscuridad.

    C. la alegría.

    D. la mordacidad.

GO ON TO THE NEXT PAGE

83. ¿Cuál es el origen de la tradición levantina de quemar muñecos de cartón?

    A. La costumbre de reírse de la gente.

    B. La celebración del cambio de estación.

    C. La limpieza de los talleres de los carpinteros.

    D. La necesidad de recoger las cosechas.

84. De la lectura se infiere que un "ninot" es

    A. un santo católico.

    B. un dios pagano.

    C. un muñeco de cartón.

    D. un personaje importante.

El polémico filólogo mexicano residente en Estados Unidos Ilan Stavans, convencido de que "la pureza de la lengua es una abstracción" y de que "sólo las lenguas muertas no cambian," ha comenzado la primera traducción de *El Quijote* al *spanglish,* la jerga que mezcla español e inglés y que hablan buena parte de los hispanoamericanos que viven en Estados Unidos y Puerto Rico. A partir de ahora, la novela más conocida de Cervantes también puede empezar así: "In un placete de la Mancha of which nombre no quiero remembrearme . . ."

Stavans, catedrático de Filología y Estudios Culturales en el Amherst College de Massachusetts, donde creó hace dos años la primera cátedra de *spanglish,* sostiene que utilizan este dialecto, salpicado de anglicismos y de palabras adaptadas en forma *sui generis* directamente del inglés, más de 25 millones de personas a ambos lados de la frontera entre México y Estados Unidos.

Stavans, todo un pionero del estudio de este dialecto que ya publicó hace un año y medio el primer diccionario de *spanglish* con más de 6.000 voces, ha explicado al diario *La Razón* que este trabajo es "un desafío a los puristas y un acto de legitimación de un dialecto que va camino de convertirse en un nuevo idioma."

Aunque el *spanglish* no es un idioma, "está en un momento interesante," según Stavans, al volverse común el uso de algunas palabras que, al pasar de la oralidad a la literatura, plantean una ortografía y un orden sintáctico.

"La espontaneidad ha empezado a dar paso a una convención," asegura el investigador.

"Somos testigos y partícipes de la creación de una nueva cultura que es una realidad y no puede ser ninguneada," afirma el doctor en Letras Hispánicas por la Universidad de Columbia. Pero Stavans tiene otros argumentos en su defensa del *spanglish.*

Por ejemplo: "Si más de 35 millones de hispanohablantes que viven en EE UU, la única comunidad de emigrantes con dos canales de televisión y cientos de emisoras de radio, deciden usar 'rufa' (del inglés *roof*) en lugar de techo, ¿es quijotesco tratar de convencerlos de lo contrario? La lengua es como un río y hay que navegar por él en lugar de mirar desde la orilla."

A este filólogo le gusta soñar con el *spanglish* convertido en un idioma muy imaginativo y alegre ("algo parecido al *jazz*"), algo con lo que no está de acuerdo el director de la Real Academia Española (RAE), Víctor García de la Concha. En un curso de la Universidad Complutense de El Escorial, señaló: "De lo que estoy absolutamente seguro es de que eso que se llama 'spanglish' no es una lengua."

A su juicio, "afirmar que lo es, lingüísticamente, es una falsedad." Para el director de la RAE, el español que se habla en Estados Unidos es un típico caso de lengua en contacto. "Lo que se está produciendo es la alternancia de códigos, que consiste en que un hispano que no domina el inglés está utilizando un esquema sintáctico del español con palabras inglesas."

85. ¿Qué hizo Stavans en Amherst College?

A. Estudió filología.

B. Enseñó Estudios Culturales.

C. Fundó la primera cátedra *spanglish.*

D. Utilizó anglicismos en sus clases.

86. ¿Qué pretende Stavans con su obra?

A. Convertir el *spanglish* en un idioma oficial.

B. Hacer que se considere el *spanglish* como un verdadero dialecto.

C. Convencer a los puristas para que usen el *spanglish* en sus clases.

D. Ridiculizar el español de los Estados Unidos.

87. Según el fragmento, el *spanglish* está sufriendo

A. una evolución.

B. un orden.

C. un retraso.

D. una purificación.

88. La expresión "La lengua es como un río . . . mirar desde la orilla," significa que

A. no se puede aprender una lengua.

B. hay que aceptar los cambios que sufre una lengua.

C. dos lenguas no pueden convivir en un territorio.

D. una lengua siempre influye a la otra cuando están en contacto.

89. La opinión de García de la Concha rechaza

A. el parecido del *spanglish* con el *jazz.*

B. la pureza de las lenguas imaginativas.

C. la categorización del *spanglish* como lengua.

D. la idea de la traducción de Stavans.

90. ¿Qué es para García de la Concha el *spanglish?*

A. Un esquema sintáctico del español.

B. Un caso de una lengua en contacto con otra.

C. Un dialecto inferior al español.

D. Una alternancia de códigos.

IF YOU FINISH BEFORE TIME IS CALLED, CHECK YOUR WORK ON THIS SECTION ONLY. DO NOT WORK ON ANY OTHER SECTION IN THE TEST.

STOP

Section II: Free Response

This section consists of two main parts, Part A and Part B, and each part contains more than one type of exercise.

Total time: 1 hour and 20 minutes

Percent of total grade: 50

Part A: Writing Skills

This part tests your writing skills in Spanish, and it consists of three different exercises: paragraph fill-ins, discrete sentence fill-ins, and an essay.

Time: 60 minutes

Paragraph Fill-Ins

Suggested time: 8 minutes

Read the following passage completely. Then read it a second time, and write on the line provided after each number the appropriate form of the word given in parentheses that will complete the fragment correctly, logically, and grammatically. Correct spelling and accent marks are necessary to receive credit. Only one word is allowed in each blank. In some instances, you may find that a change of the word in parentheses is not necessary, but you still need to write the word in the blank to receive credit.

Lee el siguiente pasaje. Luego vuélvelo a leer y escribe en la línea de la derecha, después de cada número, la forma apropiada de la palabra que está entre paréntesis, para completar el fragmento de forma correcta y lógica. La ortografía y los acentos deben ser correctos para recibir crédito. Solamente se permite una palabra para cada espacio. Es posible que la palabra sugerida no necesite ningún cambio; si es así, debes escribir la palabra en el espacio en blanco para recibir crédito.

Comenzó a estar triste a la edad de siete años. Debido a su carácter huraño no (1) mantener relaciones con otros chicos de su edad. Rápidamente (2) degeneraban en riñas. Su exceso de sensibilidad no toleraba bromas. (3) palabra un (4) disonante hacía sufrir indeciblemente a esta criatura taciturna. Erdosain se recordaba a sí mismo como un chiquillo hosco, enfurruñado que piensa con terror a la hora de ir a la escuela. En la escuela (5) chicos brutales con los que tenía que trompearse de vez en cuando. Por (6) parte, los niños (7) educados (8) su trato silvestre y se espantaban de (9) precocidades suyas, observándolo con cierto desprecio (10) encubierto.

1. _____(poder)

2. _____(éste)

3. _____(Cualquier)

4. _____(poco)

5. _____(haber)

6. _____(otro)

7. _____(bien)

8. _____(rehuir)

9. _____(cierto)

10. _____(mal)

Discrete Sentence Fill-Ins

Suggested time: 7 minutes

In the following set of sentences, one verb is missing. Write on the line after the number the correct form and tense of the verb, taking into consideration the context of the sentence. In some cases, you may have to use more than one word, but you need to use a tense of the verb given in parentheses.

En el siguiente grupo de oraciones falta un verbo. Escribe en la línea después de cada número la forma y el tiempo correctos del verbo, tomando en consideración el contexto de la oración. En algunos casos vas a necesitar más de una palabra, pero es necesario que uses un tiempo del verbo que aparece entre paréntesis.

GO ON TO THE NEXT PAGE

11. Cuando (11) al perro, ten cuidado no lo pises, porque te puede morder.

11. _____(acercarse)

12. Yo no (12) a qué hora llegará Leonardo de la universidad

12. _____(saber)

13. Antes, todos los veranos nosotros (13) a la casa de nuestros abuelos a pasar las vacaciones.

13. _____(ir)

14. No (14) tantos problemas si fueras un poco más responsable.

14. _____(tener)

15. No creyó que (15) posible hacer tantos gastos.

15. _____(ser)

16. Para las cuatro de la tarde, ya yo (16) este trabajo.

16. _____(terminar)

17. Graciela me pidió que no te (17) la verdad.

17. _____(decir)

18. (18) se aprende mucho.

18. _____(Leer)

19. Andrés, (19) cuidado con el gato, no te vaya a arañar.

19. _____(tener)

20. Teresa, (20) de ahí inmediatamente.

20. _____(levantarse)

Essay

Suggested writing time: 45 minutes

> **NOTE:** During the AP Spanish Language Exam, you will be given a booklet in which to write the essay. For this practice test, use any lined paper.

Write a well-organized essay in Spanish of at least 200 words and about the topic given below. Your score will be based on organization, range and appropriateness of vocabulary, and grammatical accuracy. It is recommended that you use the first five minutes to organize your ideas.

Escribe un ensayo bien organizado, en español y de una extensión de al menos 200 palabras, sobre el tema que aparece a continuación. Tu calificación estará basada en la organización, la riqueza y la precisión del vocabulario y la corrección gramatical. Se te recomienda que utilices los primeros cinco minutos para organizar tus ideas.

Has encontrado un amigo por correspondencia que reside en Europa. Él quiere venir a los Estados Unidos a estudiar su carrera universitaria y quiere que le expliques cómo es el sistema universitario en este país. Escríbele una carta donde le comentes con detalles cómo funciona el sistema universitario en los Estados Unidos.

Part B: Speaking Skills

The instructions for this section will be given to you by the Master CD. This section consists of two different exercises: a picture sequence story and directed response questions. Your voice will be recorded during this section of the exam. The instructions are mostly in English, but there are some questions in Spanish to which you must respond.

PLAY TRACK 19 ON CD 2

The six drawings on the next page represent a story. Use the pictures to tell the story, according to your interpretation.

Los seis dibujos que aparecen en la próxima página representan una historieta. Utiliza los dibujos para contar la historia, según tu propia interpretación.

Directed Response

PLAY TRACK 20 ON CD 2

IF YOU FINISH BEFORE TIME IS CALLED, CHECK YOUR WORK ON THIS
SECTION ONLY. DO NOT WORK ON ANY OTHER SECTION IN THE TEST.

225

Practice Test 3 Scoring Worksheet

This worksheet is designed to help you calculate your score in this practice test following similar procedures to those used by the College Board. Try to be as objective as you can while evaluating the essay and the oral questions. In the case of the essay, you may compare the sample essays given to your own work to be able to determine your own score.

Section I: Multiple Choice Section

Part A: number correct (out of 28)_____ – ($\frac{1}{3}$ × **number wrong** _____) × 1.2857 = ☐

Part B: number correct (out of 20)_____ – ($\frac{1}{3}$ × **number wrong** _____) × .9000 = ☐

Part C: number correct (out of 15)_____ – ($\frac{1}{3}$ × **number wrong** _____) × .6000 = ☐

Part D: number correct (out of 27)_____– ($\frac{1}{3}$ × **number wrong** _____) × 1.0000 = ☐

Total weighted section I score (add the 4 boxes): _____

Section II: Free Response Section

Fill-Ins: (out of 20)_____ × .6750 = ☐

Essay: (out of 9)_____ × .9474 = ☐

Picture Sequence: (out of 9)_____ × .5294 = ☐

Directed Responses: (out of 20)_____ × 1.1250 = ☐

Total weighted section II score (add the 4 boxes): _____

Final Score

weighted section I: _____ + **weighted section II:** _____ = **final score:** _____

Probable Final AP Score

Final Converted Score	Probable AP Score
180–134	5
133–114	4
113–86	3
85–63	2
62–0	1

Answer Key for Practice Test 3

Section I: Multiple-Choice Questions

Dialogue 1
1. B
2. A
3. A

Dialogue 2
4. A
5. D
6. C

Dialogue 3
7. A
8. C
9. C
10. C

Short Narrative 1
11. A
12. B
13. C

Short Narrative 2
14. B
15. B
16. C
17. A

Long Narrative 1
18. A
19. C
20. C
21. D
22. B
23. D

Long Narrative 2

24. B
25. C
26. D
27. D
28. A

Cloze Passages

29. B
30. A
31. A
32. A
33. C
34. B
35. B
36. A
37. B
38. A
39. C
40. B
41. B
42. C
43. D
44. B
45. A
46. B
47. B
48. B

Error Recognition

49. A
50. B
51. B

52. A
53. B
54. C
55. B
56. A
57. B
58. B
59. C
60. C
61. B
62. C
63. B

Reading Comprehension Passages

64. C
65. A
66. D
67. C
68. A
69. C
70. B
71. A
72. C
73. A
74. B
75. C
76. D
77. C
78. D
79. B
80. C
81. B
82. A

83. C	**87.** A
84. C	**88.** B
85. C	**89.** C
86. B	**90.** B

Section II: Free-Response Questions

Paragraph Fill-Ins

1. podía
2. éstas
3. cualquier
4. poco
5. había
6. otra
7. bien
8. rehuían
9. ciertas
10. mal

Discrete Sentence Fill-Ins

11. te acerques
12. sé
13. íbamos
14. tendrías
15. fuera, fuese
16. habré terminado
17. dijera, dijese
18. leyendo
19. ten
20. levántate

Essay Question

In the section "Answers and Explanations for Practice Test 3," you will find a guide to score essays together with essay samples, their scores, and analysis of each essay.

Answers and Explanations for Practice Test 3

Section I: Multiple Choice Questions

Dialogue 1

1. **B.** The reason Paco is glad to see Sofía is that he wants her to go to the theater. Choice **C** is attractive because Sofía volunteers to call Elena so that she could accompany them to the theater, but this answer is incorrect because Paco never asks Sofía to call Elena.

2. **A.** The opening night (*el estreno*) for the play is on Friday. Choice **B** is attractive because that is Sofía's suggestion.

3. **A.** Even though the reason Sofía can't go to the theater on Friday has to do with Ernesto, Choice **B** is not correct; she does not say that he won't let her go. The expression *tener un compromiso* means to have a previous commitment.

Dialogue 2

4. **A.** In the beginning of the dialogue, the lady tells the salesperson that she has to buy clothes for her husband, who is going on a business trip.

5. **D.** Although Choice **B** may be an attractive choice because the lady's descriptions are vague, toward the middle of the dialogue she states that she doesn't know her husband's size.

6. **C.** When the lady says that she doesn't know her husband's size, he says, "*descríbame a su esposo.*"

Dialogue 3

7. **A.** *Formulario* and *solicitud* are synonyms that mean *application* (*tendrá que empezar por llenar una solicitud*).

8. **C.** The young lady is asking for a part-time job (*empleo a medio tiempo*) and states that she can work no more than 20 hours a week.

9. **C.** When she is naming her skills, she says that she speaks English, Spanish, and French (*hablo inglés, español y francés*).

10. **C.** The word *increíble* at the end of the dialogue is the clue to the correct answer. She cannot believe that so much documentation is required for a waitress job.

Short Narrative 1

11. **A.** Although the remaining choices are used to describe the Maine coon, the narrative states that its most attractive feature is its long tail (*cola larga*).

12. B. Despite the use of the remaining colors in the narrative to describe the hair of the Maine coon, this animal's eyes are green (*verdes*).

13. C. To select the correct answer, you must relate the cognate *desaparecer* (disappear) with the cognate *extinguirse* (extinction). The knowledge of numbers in order to pinpoint years is also of great importance.

Short Narrative 2

14. B. Even though each choice may be used to describe the museum, only *interactivo* refers to the nature of the museum (*museo tecnológico de carácter interactivo*).

15. B. Although the narrative states that a visitor is able to engage in a series of activities once inside the museum, an electronic card is the only item he or she is given.

16. C. Here, you must relate words that belong to the same family. The narrative states that *El Puente de la Comunicación* initiates (*inicia*) a route in the museum. The correct answer contains the word *inicio* (beginning).

17. A. Although visitors can engage in all the activities listed, the only choice related to the environment (*ambiente*) is predicting a hurricane (*predecir un huracán*).

Longer Narrative 1

18. A. The narrative clearly states that humans have been fascinated by them for a long time (*estos pequeños objetos coloridos han fascinado a la humanidad por mucho tiempo*).

19. C. Although all the choices were mentioned in the narrative, *madera y conchas* were the materials used to create *cuentas*.

20. C. The narrative states that the use of glass allowed the introduction of color (*la magia de los colores se conseguía al introducir en los cúmulos de vidrio varias sustancias producidas de manera natural*).

21. D. Although you may be tempted to select Choice **A** for the color produced by gold, the narrative states that the addition of gold resulted in a red color (*una esencia de oro producía el intenso rojo carmesí*).

22. B. The narrative states that, in order to prevent their secrets from being revealed, assassins were sent after deserters (*también enviaban asesinos detrás de los desertores*).

23. D. Although all the choices were mentioned in relation to the *cheurón*, only this answer gives an actual description of it.

Longer Narrative 2

24. B. The narrative clearly states that Roth's novel helped him write his own novel (*me ayudó . . . a describir ese proceso populoso de descomposición, condensándolo en episodios clave*).

25. C. In order to answer this question, you must comprehend that *la manifestación más extrema del autoritarismo militar* is an explanation of the nature of Trujillo's dictatorship.

26. D. Although *la aristocracia* was previously mentioned in the interview, it doesn't refer to Trujillo's character (*tenía la manía de la limpieza*).

27. D. Despite the fact that each choice was mentioned in the narrative, the description of Trujillo's assassination was characterized as a *gesta heroica*.

28. A. The narrative clearly states that the fact that his son had no interest in politics was the great tragedy in his life (*pero a Ramfis no le interesaba la política . . . esa fue la gran tragedia de su vida*).

Cloze Passages

29. B. The preterit is used to indicate that the action is completed in the past.

30. A. Use the verb *echar* to indicate the movement of the train. (The verb *echar* is equivalent to *to begin.*)

31. A. The train moves slowly at first and then accelerates (*aceleró*).

32. A. The preposition *tras* is used to indicate *after.*

33. C. The preposition *por* is used to indicate *through.*

34. B. Use the gerund (*derramando*) as an adverb of *manner.*

35. B. *Todo* must show gender and number agreement with the pronoun *lo.*

36. A. *Allá* is used to indicate the furthest distance.

37. B. By recognizing that *locomotora* means train (or locomotive, a cognate), you can deduce that the word *estación* indicates the train station that is left behind.

38. A. In order to answer this question, you must understand the word *renegridas* (related to the color *negro,* or black) to mean *blackened;* therefore, the smoke, or *humo,* is what made the walls this way.

39. C. Use the imperfect tense to indicate an ongoing action in the past.

40. B. The past participle *metido* refers to *el amor;* therefore, there must be gender and number agreement.

41. B. The verb *llegar* is used to refer to the arrival of *el amor.*

42. C. Use the imperfect tense to indicate an ongoing action in the past.

43. D. The preposition *hasta* is used to indicate a break in the passage of time.

44. B. *Volver en* + a pronoun is an idiomatic expression that means *to recover conciousness.* The pronoun must agree with the subject.

45. A. *Entonces* is used to mean *then.*

46. B. Use the imperfect to indicate ongoing action in the past.

47. B. *Caer* is used because it is the only verb that refers to the rain (*la lluvia*) falling.

48. B. The adverb *extrañamente* is used because, although the flight of a fly should not worry anyone, in this passage it does. *Raramente* may be an attractive choice because *raro* and *extraño* are synonyms, but the word *raramente* is a time expression equivalent to *rarely.*

Error Recognition

49. A. Use the future rather than the conditional to indicate fact and not probability.

50. B. Because of the meaning, the preposition *entre* is incorrect within the context of the sentence. To make the sentence correct, use the preposition *en*.

51. B. *Tantos* is an adjective modifying the noun *catedrales,* which is a feminine, plural noun. *Tantas* should be used for proper gender and number agreement between the adjective and the noun.

52. A. The pattern to express the comparison of equality is *tan* + adjective + *como*.

53. B. This is a case of the use of the impersonal verb *haber* (equivalent to *there is/there are*), which only takes the form of the third person singular. To make the sentence correct, *hubo* must be used instead of *hubieron*.

54. C. The reflexive pronoun must agree with the subject of the sentence (*tú*), which—even though it is omitted—is hinted at by the verb *llores*.

55. B. The ordinal adjective drops the final *-o* when written before a masculine, singular noun.

56. A. Use the preposition *para* rather than *por* before the infinitive of a verb to express purpose or intention.

57. B. The verb should show agreement with the subject of the sentence (*tú*), which—even though it is omitted—is hinted at by the reflexive pronoun *te*.

58. B. The conjunction *sino* should be used instead of *pero* after a negative clause.

59. C. *Tantos* is an adjective modifying the noun *rato,* which is a masculine, singular noun. *Tanto* should be used for proper gender and number agreement between the adjective and the noun.

60. C. Here, the present progressive is used to indicate that an action is in progress. This tense is made up of the present forms of the auxiliary verb *estar* and the gerund of the main verb.

61. B. The ordinal adjective drops the final *-o* when written before a masculine, singular noun.

62. C. The conjunction *y* changes to *e* when it is followed by the *i* sound.

63. B. The phrase *parecer que* is an idiomatic expression.

Reading Comprehension Passages

64. C. The passage discusses the multiple uses of olive oil. (*antiguas civilizaciones usaban el aceite de oliva no sólo como alimento, sino también como maquillaje, perfume, jabón y champú*)

65. A. The production of olive oil reached Spain because the Romans did not have enough land to plant trees (*el creciente consumo y la falta de abastecimiento en su propia tierra obligó a los romanos a extender los cultivos en los campos del sur de la península ibérica*).

66. D. The passage states that the productivity of olive trees begins to decline between the ages of 100 and 150 years (*entre los 100 y 150 años su producción empieza a declinar*).

67. C. The passage states that an olive's color changes as it ripens (*el color de la aceituna no está ligado a la variedad, sino a la etapa de maduración*).

68. A. The passage discusses three methods of harvesting olives (*la recogida se puede hacer a mano, golpeando el árbol con unas varas flexibles o por medios mecánicos de vibración*).

69. C. The passage states that the water and oil are separated by modern methods (*métodos más modernos, por centrifugación, logran la separación del agua y el aceite*).

70. B. Consuming olive oil has several benefits, but the digestive benefit mentioned is its laxative properties (*ejerce un ligero efecto laxante*).

71. A. The presence of antioxidants in olive oil helps prevent cancer, as stated in the last paragraph of the passage.

72. C. Priscilla Bianchi discovered her true calling when she was 40 years old (*tuvieron que pasar 40 años antes de que descubriese su verdadera vocación*).

73. A. Priscilla liked to sew when she was little (*siempre le ha gustado la costura, hasta el punto que recuerda haber jugado con una máquina de coser a los cuatro años de edad*).

74. B. The passage states that quilting allows Priscilla to use her artistic abilities (*el* quilting *fue para ella una gran revelación como expresión artística, ya que podía combinar todas sus habilidades manuales y creativas*).

75. C. Priscilla started quilting when she bought a book on the subject on one of her trips to the United States (*en uno de sus viajes a los Estados Unidos . . . compró un libro de* quilting).

76. D. The passage states that the art of quilting originated in Europe (*el* quilting *se originó en Europa hace varios siglos*).

77. C. Twenty-five years ago, there was a resurgence of quilting as a decorative element (*para colgar los trabajos en las paredes como si fuesen tapices*).

78. D. The last paragraph states that Guatemalan fabrics are rich in colors and drawings (*ricas en colores y dibujos*).

79. B. The saying *nadie es profeta en su tierra* refers to the fact that Bianchi has had more success with her quilts in foreign countries than in her own country.

80. C. The passage states that Levante is a group of provinces in Spain (*se ha dado en llamar Levante a las tres provincias de Castellón, Valencia y Alicante, acompañadas a veces por Murcia*).

81. B. The passage states that Levante is characterized by a passion for fire (*si hay algo que las distingue del resto del país es su pasión por llenar la oscuridad de la noche con estruendo de los cohetes, las tracas y la quema de las fallas y la hogueras*).

82. A. The second paragraph describes this zone as one of excess (*todo en la tierra valenciana tiene un aire de exceso y desmesura*).

83. C. The passage states that the tradition originated with carpenters (*la tradición levantina de plantar en las plazas unos muñecotes de cartón . . . en un principio se trataba de un recurso del que los carpinteros se valían para poner orden en sus talleres*).

84. C. It can be inferred from the passage that *ninot* is the name given to these cardboard dolls.

85. C. The passage states that Stavans created the first Spanglish curriculum (*Stavans, catedrático de Filología y Estudios Culturales en el Amherst College de Massachusetts, donde creó hace dos años la cátedra de* spanglish).

86. B. Stavans wants linguists to consider Spanglish a true dialect (*este trabajo es "un desafío a los puristas y un acto de legitimación de un dialecto que va camino de convertirse en un nuevo idioma"*).

87. A. According to the passage, Spanglish is undergoing an evolution (*la espontaneidad ha empezado a dar paso a una convención*).

88. B. The statement *la lengua es como un río* . . . refers to the fact that language is not stagnant and that it is always undergoing changes that have to be acknowledged and accepted.

89. C. García de la Concha rejects categorizing Spanglish as a language (*afirmar que lo es, lingüísticamente, es una falsedad*).

90. B. García de la Concha considers Spanglish to be a direct result of two languages in contact (*el español que se habla en los Estados Unidos es un típico caso de lengua en contacto*).

Section II: Free Response Questions

Paragraph Fill-Ins

1. podía. Use the imperfect tense rather than the preterit to talk about continuous or habitual actions in the past. The third person singular is the correct form because, even though it is omitted, you can tell that the subject of the sentence is either *él* or *ella,* which is hinted at by the possessive adjective *su.*

2. éstas. The demonstrative pronoun is replacing the noun *relaciones,* which is feminine and plural.

3. cualquier The adjective remains the same, because it is invariable. The word *cualquiera* is a pronoun.

4. poco. Here, the word *poco* is an adverb; therefore, it remains invariable.

5. había. Use the imperfect tense for description in the past. This is a case of the use of impersonal verb *haber* (equivalent to *there is/there are*), which only takes the form of the third person singular.

6. otra. The adjective must maintain gender and number agreement with the noun it modifies, *parte.*

7. bien. *Bien* is an adverb; therefore, it remains unchanged.

8. rehuían. Use the imperfect tense rather than the preterit to talk about continuous or habitual actions in the past. The third person singular is the correct form because the subject of the sentence is *los niños bien educados.*

9. **ciertas.** The adjective must maintain gender and number agreement with the noun it modifies, *ideas.*

10. **mal.** In this case, *mal* is used as an adverb; therefore, it remains unchanged.

Discrete Sentence Fill-Ins

11. **te acerques.** Use the subjunctive after an adverb clause beginning with *cuando*. The second person singular is required, as hinted at by the verb *ten.*

12. **sé.** Use the present to indicate not knowing when an event takes place.

13. **íbamos.** Use the imperfect to indicate that the action occurred habitually in the past. The required form of the verb is the first person plural because the subject is *nosotros.*

14. **tendrías.** Use the conditional in the main clause when the if clause uses the present subjunctive. The required form of the verb is the second person singular because the subject, as hinted at by the verb *fueras,* is *tú.*

15. **fuera, fuese.** Use the subjunctive after *no creer que* when the verb in the main clause is in the preterit.

16. **habré terminado.** Use the future perfect to indicate that an event will be completed before a certain point in time in the future.

17. **dijera, dijese.** Use the subjunctive after the expression *pedir que* when the verb in the main clause is in the preterit. The required form of the verb is the first person singular because the subject, as hinted at by the object pronoun *me,* is *yo.*

18. **leyendo.** The use of the gerund is equivalent to an English phrase beginning with *when* (in this case, *when reading*).

19. **ten.** Use the imperative to indicate that a command is given. The informal command is required because the speaker addresses the other person using his first name.

20. **levántate.** Use the imperative to indicate that a command is given. The informal command is required because the speaker addresses the other person using her first name.

Sample Answers for Essay Question

High-Scoring Essay

Querido Juan:

¿Cómo estás? Espero que cuando recibas esta carta te encuentres bien. Me dio gran alegría saber que quieres venir a estudiar en los Estados Unidos. Por lo que me explicas en tu carta, estás interesado en saber algunas cosas sobre el sistema universitario de nuestro país.

Pues bien, te cuento que cuando terminamos la escuela secundaria, tenemos que tomar por lo menos dos examenes: el SAT y el ACT. Estos examenes son importantes porque las calificaciones que recibas se tienen en cuenta para admitirte a la universidad. Después que tomes los examenes tienes que mandar los resultados a todas las universidades que a ti te gustaría ir. Se me olvidaba decirte que tienes que llenar una solicitud para que te admitan a la universidad. Cuando mandes la solicitud, debes incluir todas tus calificaciones de la escuela secundaria. Y no te olvides mandar un cheque. Cuando la universidad recibe los documentos, hace una evaluación y te mandan una carta para avisarte de su decisión. Si te admiten, entonces ya puedes hablar con un consejero para que te ayude a seleccionar los cursos que necesites.

Como tú eres estudiante extranjero me parece que tienes que tomar un examen para demostrar tus conocimientos de inglés. Casi todas las universidades tienen un portal en la internet, así que puedes obtener más información si la necesitas. Espero que esta información te sea de utilidad.

Un abrazo,

Tu amiga, Sarita

Analysis of the High-Scoring Essay

This essay clearly demonstrates excellence in written expression. The writer shows control of the elements needed in the organization of a letter, and the content of the text is relevant to the topic. There is abundant evidence of the writer's control of complex grammatical structures (for example, *espero que cuando recibas . . .*, *las calificaciones que recibas se tienen en cuenta . . .*). The range of verb forms and tenses used (present, preterit, and imperfect of both the indicative and present subjunctive; commands; verb + *infinitive*) is more than appropriate to deal with this specific topic. The writer demonstrates great control of the use of *ser* versus *estar*. Prepositions are used correctly, and there is very good use of transitional words or phrases (such as *por lo que, pues bien, después que*). There is also ample evidence of a wide vocabulary (*encontrarse, solicitud, avisar, portal*). The writer shows very good control of spelling and other conventions of the written language. **Score: 9**

Medium-Scoring Essay

Querida Susy:

Estoy contenta de recibiendo tu carta. Me gusto mucho la idea que vas a venir aquí para estudiar en la Universidad. Creo que en Madrid es un pocito diferente aquí, así que voy a explicar un poco las cosas para ver si te ayudan.

Cuando eres un senior (que es el ultimo año, 12) tienes que tomar el SAT. Este es un examen de ingles y matemática. Si tus notas son buenas, entonces puedes empezar a llenar las aplicaciones para las universidades que tu quieres. Si no pasaste el examen puedes tomarlo otra vez. Por ser admitido a muchas universidades tienes que tener como 1200 puntos en el SAT. También son importantes las notas de la escuela secundaria, así que tienes que mandar ese documento.

Yo creo que como eres extranjera tienes que tomar un examen de inglés. Hay mucho información que no sé. Es mejor ir a la red para ver las páginas de las universidades que te gustan. Si todo está bien con tus papeles, entonces un conselor te habla y te dice las clases para tu carrera y también los requirimientos para esa universidad.

Espero que esto sea suficiente para ti. Si necesitas más cosas, escribe otra vez. Un beso.

Aurora

Analysis of the Medium-Scoring Essay

This essay shows some control of basic grammar structures, although there are some errors (*contenta de recibiendo*). The phrase *por ser admitido* shows that the writer lacks control of the uses of *por* versus *para;* on the other hand, the phrase shows good usage of the passive voice. There are some redeeming features, such as the correct use of the present subjunctive in *espero que esto sea suficiente . . . ,* but in general, the paper maintains a basic grammatical usage. The vocabulary is limited, and there is an evident interference from English (*senior, aplicaciones, conselor, requirimientos*). There is good organization, and the letter structure is appropriate. Spelling and accentuation are generally correct, although there are some errors in spelling (*pocito*). This essay shows that the writer possesses more than a basic command of the language. **Score: 6**

PART V

APPENDICES

These appendices cover information that will help you score well on the AP Spanish Language exam.

The following are included:

- **A grammar review:** The basics on Spanish grammar are compiled in this handy review.

- **A glossary:** The glossary will help you understand any Spanish word or phrase used in this book.

Additional information that will help you prepare for the test can be found on the Web at www.cliffsnotes.com/extras.

Grammar Review

In this section of the book, you will find most of the solutions to your grammatical concerns. This section also provides you with more practice for those patterns of Spanish grammar that are most difficult to master. As you know, to succeed in the AP Spanish Language Exam, you must have control of both basic and complex grammatical structures, including verb sequences and prepositions.

To facilitate your learning or review process, this section is organized by objective. The objectives cover the areas where students find the most difficulties regarding the usage of the written language. For each objective, you will find the rules to master the specific pattern and exercises with which to practice your newly sharpened skills.

This section may be helpful in two ways:

- It may clarify or help you to learn any grammatical issue.

- It may help you to understand the mistakes you may have made in the different practice portions of this book.

> Remember to access more helpful information, including lists of classified vocabulary and lists of idioms, at www.cliffsnotes.com/extras. This Web site also has the complete script for the CDs.

Syllabication

Objective 1: To Learn How to Divide Spanish Words into Syllables

Knowing how to divide words into syllables is an important step on the road to being able to follow the rules of accentuation. These are the rules for syllabication in Spanish:

- A consonant between two vowels will form syllable with the second vowel. Examples:

  - *li-bro*

  - *lá-piz*

  - *u-ña*

- Two consonants between two vowels will split unless they belong to what is called a consonantic group. These groups are: *bl, cl, fl, gl, pl, br, cr, dr, fr, gr, pr,* and *tr.* The groups *ch, ll,* and *rr* are considered one sound; therefore, they also stay in the same syllable. Examples:

  - *car-ta*

  - *lás-ti-ma*

  - *blu-sa*

- Three consonants between two vowels group together as follows: Two consonants will form a syllable with the first vowel, and the third consonant will form a syllable with the second vowel. The consonantic groups mentioned above are the exception to this rule. Examples:

  - *subs-ti-tuir*

  - *trans-pi-ra-ción*

  - *abs-ten-ción*

- Four consonants between two vowels will split in two groups of two. Examples:

  - *cons-truc-ción*

  - *subs-tra-er*

- Two strong vowels (*a, e,* or *o*) next to each other will form different syllables. Examples:

  - *a-é-re-o*

  - *to-a-lla*

  - *te-a-tro*

- Two weak vowels (*i* or *u*) together or a combination of a weak and strong vowel will form a syllable called a diphthong. If the diphthong is broken with a written accent, the vowels split into two syllables. Examples:

  - *ciu-dad*

  - *cui-da-do*

  - *pei-ne*

Práctica

Divide the following words into syllables:

1. apropiar   _____

2. transgredir   _____

3. callejuela   _____

4. librería   _____

5. baúl   _____

Rules for Word Stress in Spanish

Objective 2: To Master the Rules of Accentuation in Spanish

In Spanish, there are only two rules in regard to the stress of the words. If either of those two rules is broken, a written accent is necessary to indicate where the word is stressed.

- If the last letter of a word is a vowel, an *n*, or an *s*, the word should be stressed on the next to the last syllable. Examples:
  - **li-***bro*
  - **me-***sa*
  - *men-***ti-***ra*
- If the last letter of a word is any consonant except *n* or *s*, the word should be stressed on the last syllable. Examples:
  - *tam-***bor**
  - *es-cri-***bir**
  - *ne-ce-si-***dad**

Words that do not follow those rules will carry a written accent.

Spanish words can also carry a written accent for other reasons, regardless of the ending of the word:

- To distinguish between two words that are identical in spelling, but have a different meaning or function within a sentence. Examples:
  - *el* = the; *él* = he, him
  - *de* = of, from; *dé* = give (formal command of *dar*)
  - *tu* = your; *tú* = you
- The word is the result of a combination of a verb form and one or more pronouns. Examples:
  - *siéntate* = sit down
  - *póngaselo* = put it on
  - *dámelo* = give it to me
- There is a diphthong (two weak vowels together or one weak vowel and one strong vowel in the same syllable) that needs to be broken. The written accent is placed on the weak vowel to stress it. The weak vowels are *i* and *u*. Examples:
  - *co-***mí-***a*
  - *in-si-***nú-***o*
  - *Ma-***rí-***a*

243

Práctica

In the following words, underline the stressed syllable:

1. azúcar

2. bisturí

3. calle

4. bosque

5. caracol

In the following words, write the accent when necessary:

1. mortal

2. cascabel

3. corazon

4. angel

5. andaluz

Articles

Objective 3: To Use Definite Articles Correctly

There are four definite articles in Spanish, and their usage depends on the gender and number of the nouns they accompany. Remember that, in Spanish, you must maintain the agreement in gender and number between the noun and all its modifiers, such as articles and adjectives. In Spanish, all nouns are either masculine or feminine. Most nouns ending in -*a* are feminine and most nouns ending in -*o* are masculine. You will find more information about nouns and genders as you read on. As in English, nouns in Spanish are either singular or plural. Later in this section, you will learn to identify the gender and number of nouns in Spanish.

	Masculine	*Feminine*
Singular	*el*	*la*
Plural	*los*	*las*

The use of the definite article in Spanish is different from its use in English. There are some instances in which the definite article is used in both languages. There are other instances in which the definite article is used in English and omitted in Spanish, or the other way around. There are still other instances in which the definite article is omitted in both languages. The following are some rules for the use and omission of the definite article in Spanish.

The definite article is used:

- With abstract nouns and with nouns that refer to a class or group in general.
    - **Los** *niños nacen para ser felices.*
    - **El** *café es el producto principal de Colombia.*
- In place of the possessive adjective to refer to parts of the body and items one wears.
- In front of titles of treatment to refer indirectly to a person, with the exception of *Don, Doña, Santa,* and *Santo.*
    - **La** *doctora Jiménez me recomendó una buena dieta.*
    - **El** *señor Ramírez es ingeniero eléctrico.*
- With days of the week.
- With the names of all meals.
- With the names of languages.
- With nouns that are known to the speaker.
    - *Dame* **el** *libro que me trajo Roberto.*
    - **La** *casa de Juan está pintada de amarillo.*
- With the cardinal numbers to refer to time.
    - *Son* **las** *nueve.*
    - *Eran* **las** *tres cuando Pedro llegó.*
- With modified expressions of time.
    - *Llegué de Madrid* **la** *semana pasada.*
    - **El** *mes que viene terminarán la casa.*

The definite article is omitted:

- When you are talking about a quantity.
    - *Había niños de todos tamaños en la escuela.*
    - *Nunca tomo café.*
- When you are addressing someone directly, using a title of treatment.
    - *Señora García, déjeme ver sus documentos.*
    - *Señorita Alonso, su ropa ya está lista.*

- With days of the week when they immediately follow the verb *ser*.
  - *Ayer fue domingo.*
  - *No sabía que hoy es viernes.*

- With the names of languages when they immediately follow *de, en,* and *hablar.* Sometimes, the definite article is also omitted after the verbs *escribir, aprender, leer, estudiar,* and *enseñar.*
  - *En español, los verbos son muy difíciles.*
  - *Es preciso que aprendas japonés para trabajar en esa compañía.*

- With the names of king and popes.

- Before nouns in apposition.
  - *París, capital de Francia, es conocida como la ciudad luz.*
  - *Cervantes, autor del Quijote, fue un hombre de armas.*

Práctica

In the space provided, write the correct form of the definite article.

Fill in the blanks with the correct form of the definite article, if necessary.

1. Estos son _____ libros de que te hablé.

2. Luis tiene _____ sonrisa muy bonita.

3. _____ hambre es un problema mundial.

4. Me puse _____ guantes porque hacía mucho frío.

5. _____ Sra. González, póngase de pie.

Objective 4: To Use Indefinite Articles Correctly

There are four indefinite articles in Spanish, and their usage depends on the gender and number of the nouns they accompany.

	Masculine	Feminine
Singular	un	una
Plural	unos	unas

In general, the indefinite article is used in Spanish in the same instances it is used in English. There are, however, instances in which the indefinite article is used in English, but it is omitted in Spanish.

The indefinite article is omitted:

- When speaking about professions, nationalities, and religious and political affiliations, unless the noun is being modified.
  - *Mi padre es ingeniero.*
  - *Javier es **un** buen estudiante.*
  - *Raimundo es **un** cristiano viejo.*
- In the equivalent Spanish expressions for *a hundred* (*cien*), *a thousand* (*mil*), *another* (*otro*), *a certain* (*cierto*), and *What a...!* (*¡Qué . . .!*).
  - *Había mil personas en la celebración.*
  - *¡Qué partido te perdiste anoche!*

Práctica

In the space provided, write the correct form of the indefinite article.

Fill in the blanks with the correct form of the indefinite article, if necessary.

1. Me lo contó _____ cierta persona.

2. Luis y Rosa van a hacer _____ viaje a Portugal.

3. En el pueblecito vivían solamente _____ mil personas.

4. El padre de Roberto es _____ excelente abogado.

5. _____ mujer vino a verte ayer.

Nouns

Objective 5: To Identify the Gender of Nouns

In Spanish, all nouns are either masculine or feminine. The following are some general rules to help you identify the gender of nouns.

- Generally, nouns ending in *-a* are feminine in gender. The most common exception to this rule is *día,* which is masculine.

- Generally, nouns ending in -o are masculine in gender. The most common exception to this rule is *mano*, which is feminine.

- All nouns that refer to males (human and animals) are masculine in gender, regardless of their endings.

- All nouns that refer to females (human and animals) are feminine in gender, regardless of their endings.

- Nouns ending in -e, -i, and -u, could be either masculine or feminine. The same is true for words ending in consonants. The only way to learn the gender of a word like this is to memorize it when you see the word for the first time. Otherwise, you may have to figure out the gender from the context in which the word appears.

- Nouns ending in -ad, -ie, -umbre, -ud, -ción, and -sión are feminine in gender.

- Most nouns ending in -aje are masculine in gender.

- Most compound nouns, whose first element is a verb, are masculine in gender.

  - *el abrelatas*

  - *el portamonedas*

  - *el salvavidas*

- Some Spanish nouns are of Greek origin, ending in -ma, -ta, and sometimes -pa. They are all masculine.

  - *el programa*

  - *el planeta*

  - *el mapa*

- Some nouns use the same ending to refer to males and females. The only way to identify the gender of such a noun is to look at any modifiers of the noun.

  - *el espía*

  - *esa cantante*

  - *una turista*

- Some nouns form their feminine gender in an irregular way.

  - *el actor, la actriz*

  - *el emperador, la emperatriz*

  - *el gallo, la gallina*

- Some nouns change meaning depending on gender.

  - *el puerto* = the port

  - *la puerta* = the door

  - *el capital* = capital (money)

  - *la capital* = capital city

  - *el libro* = book

  - *la libra* = the pound

- Some nouns that refer to animals add the words *macho* (male) or *hembra* (female) to identify the sex of the animal.

Práctica

In the space provided, write **F** if you think the noun is feminine and **M** if you think the noun is masculine.

1. _____ sacapuntas

2. _____ noche

3. _____ ilusión

4. _____ escritora

5. _____ teorema

Objective 6: To Correctly Form the Plural of Nouns

Grammatically, the word *number* refers to singular and plural. In Spanish, there are several ways to form the plural of a noun. These are some rules that will help you form the plural of Spanish nouns. They will also help you recognize whether a noun is singular or plural.

To form the plural in Spanish, you may do one of the following:

- For words ending with a non-stressed vowel, add an *-s*.
  - *libro/libros*
  - *mesa/mesas*
  - *tarde/tardes*
- For words ending with a stressed vowel, add *-es*. There are some exceptions to this rule (*café, bebé, sofá, mamá, papá*). The plural of these nouns are formed according to the rule above (see last item in list directly below).
  - *ají/ajíes*
  - *bambú/bambúes*
  - *alhelí/alhelíes*
  - *café/cafés*
- For words ending in a consonant, except for *x* or *z,* add *-es.*
  - *mamey/mameyes*
  - *tambor/tambores*
  - *corazón/corazones*

- For words ending in a *z*, change the *z* to *c* and add *-es*.
  - *luz/luces*
  - *voz/voces*
  - *avestruz/avestruces*
- Some words ending in an *s* (following a non-stressed vowel) or an *x* have only one form.
  - *el análisis/los análisis*
  - *la tesis/las tesis*
  - *el ónix/los ónix*

Práctica

Form the plural of the following nouns:

1. mes   /   _____

2. colibrí   _____

3. canción   _____

4. ley   _____

5. autobús   _____

Adjectives

Objective 7: To Correctly Use Adjectives in Order to Maintain Gender-Number Agreement with the Noun

In Spanish, as in English, adjectives are used to modify a noun. In English, the adjective is invariable; that is, it does not change. In Spanish, most adjectives change to agree in gender and number with the nouns they modify. The following rules must be followed when changing adjectives.

- Adjectives ending in *-o* and *-or* change in both gender and number. Exceptions to this rule are the comparative adjectives (*mayor, menor, mejor,* and *peor*), which change only in number.
  - *bajo/baja/bajos/bajas*
  - *destructor/destructora/destructores/destructoras*

- Adjectives of nationality change in both gender and number.
  - *español/española/españoles/españolas*
  - *francés/francesa/franceses/francesas*
- All other adjectives change only in number, not in gender.
  - *grande/grandes*
  - *azul/azules*

Práctica

Give the correct form of the adjective in parentheses according to the noun it modifies. In some cases, a change may not be necessary.

1. alimento (natural)   _____

2. estrategias (educativo)   _____

3. situaciones (difícil)   _____

4. blusas (gris)   _____

5. emperadores (ruso)   _____

Objective 8: To Place Adjectives Correctly

Unlike in English, in Spanish the adjective generally follows the noun it modifies. This holds true for adjectives that describe and somehow differentiate a noun from the rest of its class.

- *el libro viejo*
- *el gato negro*
- *los automóviles caros*

On the other hand, adjectives that limit or restrict the noun they modify normally precede the noun.

- *varios lectores*
- *algunas clases*
- *cualquier día*

When a descriptive adjective is placed before the noun, the emphasis changes. Generally, descriptive nouns that precede a noun refer to a quality that is inherent to the noun. Adjectives preceding nouns appear frequently in poems and literary passages.

- *la fría nieve*

- *el duro mármol*

There are some cases when the adjective totally changes the meaning of a phrase depending on its position with regard to the noun it modifies.

- *el viejo amigo* = the longtime friend

- *el amigo viejo* = the elderly friend

The above rules are also followed when using more than one adjective for a single noun.

- *una mujer joven y feliz*

- *algunos ejercicios difíciles*

Práctica

Write the adjectives given in parentheses in the correct place.

1. (viejo) Es un _____ amigo _____. Lo conozco hace años.

2. (algún) _____ día _____ volveré a la ciudad.

3. (cualquier) _____ cosa _____ sobre Egipto me interesa.

4. (blanca) La _____ nieve _____ caía sobre los árboles.

5. (roja) De la herida salía la _____ sangre _____.

Pronouns

Objective 9: To Use the Correct Form of Personal Pronouns in Order to Maintain the Agreement with the Noun They Refer To

One of the most difficult aspects of Spanish grammar for students of Spanish as a second language to master is the use of personal pronouns. As in English, personal pronouns take different forms according to two aspects: One is the person they substitute for within a sentence; the other is the function they perform in the sentence. In the following tables, you will find all Spanish personal pronouns grouped by function.

Subject Pronouns

	Singular	Plural
First Person	yo	nosotros, nosotras
Second Person	tú, usted	ustedes, vosotros, vosotras
Third Person	él, ella	ellos, ellas

Direct Object Pronouns

	Singular	Plural
First Person	me	nos
Second Person	te, lo, la	los, las, os
Third Person	lo,la	los, las

Indirect Object Pronouns

	Singular	Plural
First Person	me	nos
Second Person	te, le	les, os
Third Person	le	les

Pronouns Used as Objects of Prepositions

	Singular	Plural
First Person	mí, conmigo	nosotros, nosotras
Second Person	ti, usted, contigo	ustedes, vosotros, vosotras
Third Person	sí, consigo	sí, consigo

Reflexive Pronouns

	Singular	Plural
First Person	me	nos
Second Person	te, se	se, os
Third Person	se	se

One difficulty you face when using object pronouns in Spanish is determining their position within the sentence. Subject pronouns take the place of the subject in a sentence, no matter where it is located. Subject pronouns are frequently omitted in Spanish because the verb endings indicate the subject of the verb.

- *Anoche* **Pedro** *llegó tarde.*
- *Anoche* **él** *llegó tarde.*

Direct, indirect, and reflexive pronouns are placed, contrary to English, before the verb. If you have more than one object pronoun in the same sentence, the direct object is always placed closer to the verb.

- *Yo* **me** *lavo* **el pelo** *todos los días*

- *Yo* **me lo** *lavo todos los días.*

- *Ana* **te** *escribió* **una carta.**

- *Ana* **te la** *escribió.*

When *le* or *les* must precede *lo, la, los,* or *las,* they change to *se* to avoid *cacophony,* that is, the unpleasant repetition of sounds.

- *Yo* **le** *di* **el dinero** *a Rosa.*

- *Yo* **se lo** *di.*

With some forms of the verbs, object pronouns are used after the verb to form a single word. This occurs with the imperative, the infinitive, and the gerund. Notice how the pronouns are attached to these verb forms.

- *Juanito,* **ponte** *los pantalones.*

- *Juanito,* **póntelos.**

- *Tienes que comprar* **un disco.**

- *Tienes que* **comprarlo.**

- **Le** *estaba diciendo* **la verdad** *a Tina.*

- *Estaba* **diciéndosela.**

Pronouns used as objects of a preposition are generally placed after the preposition.

- *Las flores son para* **mí.**

- *Ellos se fueron sin* **ti.**

- *Ya no confías en* **mí.**

Práctica

Rewrite each sentence using the pronouns that substitute for the underlined words.

1. María no vio el camión que venía por la calle.

2. Tú pediste <u>el dinero</u> a <u>tu padre</u> para ir al cine

_____

3. Vas a tener que comprar <u>un libro nuevo</u>.

_____

4. Estaba diciendo <u>la verdad</u> a <u>Marcela</u>, cuando <u>Ulises</u> llegó.

_____

5. No hagas <u>los ejercicios</u> hasta que <u>Rita</u> no te lo diga.

_____

Verbs

Objective 10: To Conjugate Regular Verbs Correctly to Maintain the Agreement with the Subject of the Sentence in All Tenses

The infinitives of Spanish verbs end in *-ar, -er,* or *-ir.* These three groups are called *conjugations.* Knowing the ending of the infinitive of a verb is convenient because other important issues depend on this fact. As you probably know, in Spanish, there is a different verb ending for each mode, tense, person, and number. This makes Spanish verb usage difficult to master. The first step to succeeding in this task is to understand the mechanics behind the process and to memorize the endings for each conjugation.

Each verb can be separated into two elements: the stem and the ending. For the verb *amar,* the stem is *am* and the ending is *-ar.* It is important to know this because, as you will see later, verbs in Spanish are also classified according to the different changes they take. Normally, when you conjugate a verb (that is, you change it according to mode, tense, person, and number), what you do is change the ending. Each conjugation has a specific set of endings.

Spanish verbs belong to different types according to the changes they undergo. Most verbs are *regular verbs.* What this means is that they follow the rules of conjugation following a model. If you know a verb is regular, you can go ahead and conjugate it according to the pattern given. The stem does not undergo any change, and the only thing you need to know is what ending you need for any specific context. There are other verbs that are called *stem-changing verbs.* These verbs, besides taking the changes in endings necessary for conjugation, undergo changes in the stem. These changes are vowel changes. In Objective 12, those types of verbs are addressed in detail. The third group of verbs is the *irregular verbs.* As the name indicates, these verbs undergo changes that are not predictable or classified. They may change in both the stem and the ending. They may even look totally different from the infinitive in their conjugated forms. In Objective 13, the most common irregular verbs are addressed.

In the following tables, you can find a summary of all regular verb endings for all tenses for the three conjugations.

Simple Tenses

Indicative Mode—Present Tense		
Verb	**Stem**	**Endings**
amar	am-	-o, -as, -a, -amos, -áis, -an
comer	com-	-o, -es, -e, -emos, -éis, -en
vivir	viv-	-o, -es, -e, -imos, -ís, -en

Indicative Mode—Preterit Tense		
Verb	**Stem**	**Endings**
amar	am-	-é, -aste, -ó, -amos, -asteis, -aron
comer	com-	-í, -iste, -ió, -imos, -isteis, -ieron
vivir	viv-	-í, -iste, -ió, -imos, -isteis, -ieron

Indicative Mode—Imperfect Tense		
Verb	**Stem**	**Endings**
amar	am-	-aba, -abas, -aba, -ábamos, -abais, -aban
comer	com-	-ía, -ías, -ía, -íamos, -íais, -ían
vivir	viv-	-ía, -ías, -ía, -íamos, -íais, -ían

Indicative Mode—Future Tense	
Verb	**Endings**
amar	-é, -ás, -á, -emos, -éis, -án
comer	-é, -ás, -á, -emos, -éis, -án
vivir	-é, -ás, -á, -emos, -éis, -án

Note: All three conjugations take the same set of endings. The endings attach directly to the end of the verb (amaré, amarás, and so on).

Indicative Mode—Conditional Tense	
Verb	**Endings**
amar	-ía, -ías, -ía, -íamos, -íais, -ían
comer	-ía, -ías, -ía, -íamos, -íais, -ían
vivir	-ía, -ías, -ía, -íamos, -íais, -ían

Note: All three conjugations take the same set of endings. The endings attach directly to the end of the verb (amaría, amarías, and so on).

Subjunctive-Mode—Present Tense		
Verb	**Stem**	**Endings**
amar	am-	-e, -es, -e, -emos, -éis, -en
comer	com-	-a, -as, -a, -amos, -áis, -an
vivir	viv-	-a, -as, -a, -amos, -áis, -an

Subjunctive Mode—Imperfect Tense		
Verb	**Stem**	**Endings**
amar	am-	-ara, -aras, -ara, -áramos, -arais, -aran or -ase, -ases, -ase, -ásemos, -aseis, -asen
comer	com-	-iera, -ieras, -iera, -iéramos, -ierais, -ieran or -iese, -ieses, -iese, -iésemos, -ieseis, -iesen
vivir	viv-	-iera, -ieras, -iera, -iéramos, -ierais, -ieran or -iese, -ieses, -iese, -iésemos, -ieseis, -iesen

Compound Tenses

The compound tenses are formed using the various simple tenses of the verb *haber* and the past participle of the main verb.

Past Participle		
Verb	**Stem**	**Endings**
amar	am-	-ado
comer	com-	-ido
vivir	viv-	-ido

Indicative Mode—Present Perfect Tense

Verb	Forms of Haber	Past Participle
amar	he, has, ha, hemos, habéis, han	amado
comer	he, has, ha, hemos, habéis, han	comido
vivir	he, has, ha, hemos, habéis, han	vivido

Indicative Mode—Pluperfect Tense

Verb	Forms of Haber	Past Participle
amar	había, habías, había, habíamos, habíais, habían	amado
comer	había, habías, había, habíamos, habíais, habían	comido
vivir	había, habías, había, habíamos, habíais, habían	vivido

Indicative Mode—Preterit Perfect Tense

Verb	Forms of Haber	Past Participle
amar	hube, hubiste, hubo, hubimos, hubisteis, hubieron	amado
comer	hube, hubiste, hubo, hubimos, hubisteis, hubieron	comido
vivir	hube, hubiste, hubo, hubimos, hubisteis, hubieron	vivido

Indicative Mode—Future Perfect Tense

Verb	Forms of Haber	Past Participle
amar	habré, habrás, habrá, habremos, habréis, habrán	amado
comer	habré, habrás, habrá, habremos, habréis, habrán	comido
vivir	habré, habrás, habrá, habremos, habréis, habrán	vivido

Indicative Mode—Conditional Perfect Tense

Verb	Forms of Haber	Past Participle
amar	habría, habrías, habría, habríamos, habríais, habrían	amado
comer	habría, habrías, habría, habríamos, habríais, habrían	comido
vivir	habría, habrías, habría, habríamos, habríais, habrían	vivido

Subjunctive Mode—Present Perfect Tense

Verb	Forms of Haber	Past Participle
amar	haya, hayas, haya, hayamos, hayáis, hayan	amado
comer	haya, hayas, haya, hayamos, hayáis, hayan	comido
vivir	haya, hayas, haya, hayamos, hayáis, hayan	vivido

Subjunctive Mode—Pluperfect Tense		
Verb	**Forms of Haber**	**Past Participle**
amar	hubiera, hubieras, hubiera, hubiéramos, hubierais, hubieran or hubiese, hubieses, hubiese, hubiésemos, hubieseis, hubiesen	amado
comer	hubiera, hubieras, hubiera, hubiéramos, hubierais, hubieran or hubiese, hubieses, hubiese, hubiésemos, hubieseis, hubiesen	comido
vivir	hubiera, hubieras, hubiera, hubiéramos, hubierais, hubieran or hubiese, hubieses, hubiese, hubiésemos, hubieseis, hubiesen	vivido

Objective 11: To Correctly Conjugate Stem-Changing Verbs

Stem-changing verbs are verbs that undergo some type of change in their stems. Stem-changing verbs ending in *-ar* or *-er* change the stem vowel in the present tense in two ways: *e* to *ie* or *o* to *ue*. The changes occur in all persons except *nosotros* and *vosotros*. Below are some of the most common stem-changing verbs of this type.

Verb	**Stem Change**	**Conjugations**
acertar	e to i	acierto, aciertas, acierta, acertamos, acertáis, aciertan
contar	o to ue	cuento, cuentas, cuenta, contamos, contáis, cuentan
servir	e to i	sirvo, sirves, sirve, servimos, servís, sirven

Verbs changing *e* to *ie:*

acertar	encender
apretar	encerrar
ascender	entender
atravesar	gobernar
cerrar	pensar
comenzar	perder
confesar	quebrar
defender	querer
descender	recomendar
despertar	sentarse
empezar	

Verbs changing *o* to *ue*:

acordarse	mostrar
acostarse	mover
almorzar	poder
conmover	probar
contar	recordar
costar	resolver
demostrar	soler
devolver	tronar
doler	volar
encontrar	volver
envolver	

Stem-changing verbs ending in *-ir* change the stem vowel in the present tense in three ways: *e* to *ie*, *o* to *ue*, or *e* to *i*. The changes occur in all persons except *nosotros* and *vosotros*. These verbs also undergo a stem change in the preterit tense: The stem vowel changes either from *e* to *i* or from *o* to *u*. The change occurs in only the third person singular and third person plural forms. Below are some of the most common stem-changing verbs of this type.

Verbs changing *e* to *ie*:

advertir	mentir
consentir	preferir
convertir	referir
divertirse	sentir
hervir	

Verbs changing *o* to *ue*:

dormir	morir

Verbs changing *e* to *i*:

despedirse	reñir
gemir	repetir
impedir	seguir
medir	servir
pedir	sonreír
reír	vestirse

Read the following examples of changes in the present tense:

> **Prefiero** *el helado de chocolate.*

> *Nunca* **miente***, siempre dice la verdad*
> *Si* **duermes** *poco, estarás cansado.*

> **Pides** *la comida pero no la comes.*

However, no stem changes in the following examples:

> *Nos despedimos ya.*
> *Si* **repetimos** *la canción, te cansas.*

Notice the changes in the third person singular and plural of the preterit forms:

> *El agua* **hirvió** *rápidamente.*
> *Los chicos* **prefirieron** *el helado de vainilla.*
> **Repitió** *la frase cinco veces.*
> *Los camareros* **sirvieron** *el postre.*

Objective 12: To Correctly Conjugate the Most Common Irregular Verbs

Irregular verbs present a problem for students of Spanish as a second language. Not only do they not follow the pattern of regular verb conjugations, nor are they irregular in all tenses and persons, and their irregularities may vary from one tense to another. Many irregular verbs are high-frequency words, that is, words frequently used as part of most Spanish speakers' daily vocabulary. The probability of finding these verbs in reading and cloze passages is rather high. You will probably need to include some of these verbs and their irregular forms in your composition, in your answers to the free response questions, and in your description of the sequence of pictures. The following is a list of the most commonly used irregular verbs and the irregularities they present.

Note: Remember that this list shows only the irregular aspects of these verb conjugations.

Andar	
Tense	*Conjugations*
Preterit	*anduve, anduviste, anduvo, anduvimos, anduvisteis, anduvieron*
Imperfect subjunctive	*anduviera, anduvieras, anduviera, anduviéramos, anduvierais, anduvieran* or *anduviese, anduvieses, anduviese, anduviésemos, anduvieseis, anduviesen*

Caber	
Tense	*Conjugations*
Present indicative	*quepo, cabes, cabe, cabemos, cabéis, caben*
Preterite	*cupe, cupiste, cupo, cupimos, cupisteis, cupieron*
Future	*cabré, cabrás, cabrá, cabremos, cabréis, cabrán*
Conditional	*cabría, cabrías, cabría, cabríamos, cabríais, cabrían*
Present subjunctive	*quepa, quepas, quepa, quepamos, quepáis, quepan*
Imperfect subjunctive	*cupiera, cupieras, cupiera, cupiéramos, cupierais, cupieran* or *cupiese, cupieses, cupiese, cupiésemos, cupieseis, cupiesen*

Caer	
Tense	*Conjugations*
Present indicative	*caigo, caes, cae, caemos, caéis, caen*
Preterit	*caí, caíste, cayó, caímos, caísteis, cayeron*
Present subjunctive	*caiga, caigas, caiga, caigamos, caigáis, caigan*
Imperfect subjunctive	*cayera, cayeras, cayera, cayéramos, cayerais, cayeran* or *cayese, cayeses, cayese, cayésemos, cayeseis, cayesen*
Gerund	*cayendo*
Past participle	*caído*

Conducir	
Tense	*Conjugations*
Present indicative	*conduzco, conduces, conduce, conducimos, conducís, conducen*
Preterit	*conduje, condujiste, condujo, condujimos, condujisteis, condujeron*
Present subjunctive	*conduzca, conduzcas, conduzca, conduzcamos, conduzcáis, conduzcan*
Imperfect subjunctive	*condujera, condujeras, condujera, condujéramos, condujerais, condujeran* or *condujese, condujeses, condujese, condujésemos, condujeseis, condujesen*

Dar	
Tense	*Conjugations*
Present indicative	*doy, das, da, damos, dais, dan*
Preterit	*di, diste, dio, dimos, disteis, dieron*
Present subjunctive	*dé, des, dé, demos, deis, den*
Imperfect subjunctive	*diera, dieras, diera, diéramos, dierais, dieran* or *diese, dieses, diese, diésemos, dieseis, diesen*

Decir	
Tense	*Conjugations*
Present indicative	*digo, dices, dice, decimos, decís, dicen*
Preterit	*dije, dijiste, dijo, dijimos, dijisteis, dijeron*
Future	*diré, dirás, dirá, diremos, diréis, dirán*
Conditional	*diría, dirías, diría, diríamos, diríais, dirían*
Present subjunctive	*diga, digas, diga, digamos, digáis, digan*
Imperfect subjunctive	*dijera, dijeras, dijera, dijéramos, dijerais, dijeran* or *dijese, dijeses, dijese, dijésemos, dijeseis, dijesen*
Gerund	*diciendo*
Past participle	*dicho*
Command	*di (tu)*

Estar	
Tense	*Conjugations*
Present indicative	*estoy, estás, está, estamos, estáis, están*
Preterit	*estuve, estuviste, estuvo, estuvimos, estuvisteis, estuvieron*
Present subjunctive	*esté, estés, esté, estemos, estéis, estén*
Imperfect subjunctive	*estuviera, estuvieras, estuviera, estuviéramos, estuvieseis, estuvieran* or *estuviese, estuvieses, estuviese, estuviésemos, estuvieseis, estuviesen*

Haber	
Tense	**Conjugations**
Present indicative	he, has, ha, hemos, habéis, han
Preterit	hube, hubiste, hubo, hubimos, hubisteis, hubieron
Future	habrá, habrás, habrá, habremos, habréis, habrán
Conditional	habría, habrías, habría, habríamos, habríais, habrían
Present subjunctive	haya, hayas, haya, hayamos, hayáis, hayan
Imperfect subjunctive	hubiera, hubieras, hubiera, hubiéramos, hubierais, hubieran or hubiese, hubieses, hubiese, hubiésemos, hubieseis, hubiesen

Hacer	
Tense	**Conjugations**
Present indicative	hago, haces, hace, hacemos, hacéis, hacen
Preterit	hice, hiciste, hizo, hicimos, hicisteis, hicieron
Future	haré, harás, hará, haremos, haréis, harán
Conditional	haría, harías, haría, haríamos, haríais, harían
Present subjunctive	haga, hagas, haga, hagamos, hagáis, hagan
Imperfect subjunctive	hiciera, hicieras, hiciera, hiciéramos, hicierais, hicieran or hiciese, hicieses, hiciese, hiciésemos, hicieseis, hiciesen
Past participle	hecho
Command	haz (tú)

Ir	
Tense	**Conjugations**
Present indicative	voy, vas, va, vamos, vais, van
Imperfect indicative	iba, ibas, iba, íbamos, ibais, iban
Preterit	fui, fuiste, fue, fuimos, fuisteis, fueron
Present subjunctive	vaya, vayas, vaya, vayamos, vayáis, vayan
Imperfect subjunctive	fuera, fueras, fuera, fuéramos, fuerais, fueran or fuese, fueses, fuese, fuésemos, fueseis, fuesen
Gerund	yendo
Command	ve (tú)

Oír

Tense	Conjugations
Present indicative	*oigo, oyes oye, oímos, oís, oyen*
Preterit	*oí, oíste, oyó, oímos, oísteis, oyeron*
Present subjunctive	*oiga, oigas, oiga, oigamos, oigáis, oigan*
Imperfect subjunctive	*oyera, oyeras, oyera, oyéramos, oyerais, oyeran* or *oyese, oyeses, oyese, oyésemos, oyeseis, oyesen*
Gerund	*oyendo*

Poder

Tense	Conjugations
Present indicative	*puedo, puedes, puede, podemos, podéis, pueden*
Preterit	*pude, pudiste, pudo, pudimos, pudisteis, pudieron*
Future	*podré, podrás, podrá, podremos, podréis, podrán*
Conditional	*podría, podrías, podría, podríamos, podríais, podrían*
Present subjunctive	*pueda, puedas, pueda, podamos, podáis, puedan*
Imperfect subjunctive	*pudiera, pudieras, pudiera, pudiéramos, pudierais, pudieran* or *pudiese, pudieses, pudiese, pudiésemos, pudieseis, pudiesen*
Gerund	*pudiendo*

Poner

Tense	Conjugations
Present indicative	*pongo, pones, pone, ponemos, ponéis, ponen*
Preterit	*puse, pusiste, puso, pusimos, pusisteis, pusieron*
Future	*pondré, pondrás, pondrá, pondremos, pondréis, pondrán*
Conditional	*pondría, pondrías, pondría, pondríamos, pondríais, pondrían*
Present subjunctive	*ponga, pongas, ponga, pongamos, pongáis, pongan*
Imperfect subjunctive	*pusiera, pusieras, pusiera, pusiéramos, pusierais, pusieran* or *pusiese, pusieses, pusiese, pusiésemos, pusieseis, pusiesen*
Past participle	*puesto*
Command	*pon (tú)*

Querer	
Tense	**Conjugations**
Present indicative	quiero, quieres, quiere, queremos, queréis, quieren
Preterit	quise, quisiste, quiso, quisimos, quisisteis, quisieron
Future	querré, querrás, querrá, querremos, querréis, querrán
Conditional	querría, querrías, querría, querríamos, querríais, querrían
Present subjunctive	quiera, quieras, quiera, queramos, queráis, quieran
Imperfect subjunctive	quisiera, quisieras, quisiera, quisiéramos, quisierais, quisieran or quisiese, quisieses, quisiese, quisiésemos, quisieseis, quisiesen

Saber	
Tense	**Conjugations**
Present indicative	sé, sabes, sabe, sabemos, sabéis, saben
Preterit	supe, supiste, supo, supimos, supisteis, supieron
Future	sabré, sabrás, sabrá, sabremos, sabréis, sabrán
Conditional	sabría, sabrías, sabría, sabríamos, sabríais, sabrían
Present subjunctive	sepa, sepas, sepa, sepamos, sepáis, sepan
Imperfect subjunctive	supiera, supieras, supiera, supiéramos, supierais, supieran or supiese, supieses, supiese, supiésemos, supieseis, supiesen

Salir	
Tense	**Conjugations**
Present indicative	salgo, sales, sale, salimos, salís, salen
Future	saldré, saldrás, saldrá, saldremos, saldréis, saldrán
Conditional	saldría, saldrías, saldría, saldríamos, saldríais, saldrían
Present subjunctive	salga, salgas, salga, salgamos, salgáis, salgan
Command	sal (tú)

Ser	
Tense	**Conjugations**
Present indicative	*soy, eres, es, somos, sois, son*
Imperfect indicative	*era, eras, era, éramos, erais, eran*
Preterit	*fui, fuiste, fue, fuimos, fuisteis, fueron*
Present subjunctive	*sea, seas, sea, seamos, seáis, sean*
Imperfect subjunctive	*fuera, fueras, fuera, fuéramos, fuerais, fueran* or *fuese, fueses, fuese, fuésemos, fueseis, fuesen*
Command	*sé (tú)*

Tener	
Tense	**Conjugations**
Present indicative	*tengo, tienes, tiene, tenemos, tenéis, tienen*
Preterit	*tuve, tuviste, tuvo, tuvimos, tuvisteis, tuvieron*
Future	*tendré, tendrás, tendrá, tendremos, tendréis, tendrán*
Conditional	*tendría, tendrías, tendría, tendríamos, tendríais, tendrían*
Present subjunctive	*tenga, tengas, tenga, tengamos, tengáis, tengan*
Imperfect subjunctive	*tuviera, tuvieras, tuviera, tuviéramos, tuvierais, tuvieran* or *tuviese, tuvieses, tuviese, tuviésemos, tuvieseis, tuviesen*
Command	*ten (tú)*

Traer	
Tense	**Conjugations**
Present indicative	*traigo, traes, trae, traemos, traéis, traen*
Preterit	*traje, trajiste, trajo, trajimos, trajisteis, trajeron*
Present subjunctive	*traiga, traigas, traiga, traigamos, traigáis, traigan*
Imperfect subjunctive	*trajera, trajeras, trajera, trajéramos, trajerais, trajeran* or *trajese, trajeses, trajese, trajésemos, trajeseis, trajesen*
Gerund	*trayendo*
Past participle	*traído*

Valer	
Tense	**Conjugations**
Present indicative	*valgo, vales, vale, valemos, valéis, valen*
Future	*valdré, valdrás, valdrá, valdremos, valdréis, valdrán*
Conditional	*valdría, valdrías, valdría, valdríamos, valdríais, valdrían*
Present subjunctive	*valga, valgas, valga, valgamos, valgáis, valgan*

Venir	
Tense	**Conjugations**
Present indicative	*vengo, vienes, viene, venimos, venís, vienen*
Preterit	*vine, viniste, vino, vinimos, vinisteis, vinieron*
Future	*vendré, vendrás, vendrá, vendremos, vendréis, vendrán*
Conditional	*vendría, vendrías, vendría, vendríamos, vendríais, vendrían*
Present subjunctive	*venga, vengas, venga, vengamos, vengáis, vengan*
Imperfect subjunctive	*viniera, vinieras, viniera, viniéramos, vinierais, vinieran* or *viniese, vinieses, viniese, viniésemos, vinieseis, viniesen*
Gerund	*viniendo*
Command	*ven (tú)*

Ver	
Tense	**Conjugations**
Present indicative	*veo, ves, ve, vemos, veis, ven*
Imperfect indicative	*veía, veías, veía, veíamos, veíais, veían*
Preterit	*vi, viste, vio, vimos, visteis, vieron*
Present subjunctive	*vea, veas, vea, veamos, veáis, vean*
Past participle	*visto*

Objective 13: To Correctly Use the Preterit Tense Versus the Imperfect Tense According to the Context

Using the preterit and the imperfect in context is a difficult task for students of Spanish as a second language. Although both tenses carry the idea of the past, they are not interchangeable. The following rules will help you master the usage of the preterit versus the imperfect in context.

The preterit is used:

- To report completed actions or states of being in the past.

    - *Anoche comí un pollo delicioso.*

- In sequence of events that took place in the past.

    - *Roberto se levantó, se vistió y salió rápidamente para la escuela.*

The following words and phrases are normally associated with the preterit: *ayer, anteayer, anoche, una vez, dos veces, el año pasado, el lunes pasado,* and *de repente.* In a given context, these expressions of time will help you identify the need to use the preterit, because they tend to express a specific time in the past when an action took place.

The imperfect is used:

- To talk about ongoing or habitual actions in the past without reference to the ending point.

    - *Todos los veranos íbamos a casa de los abuelos.*

- For descriptions in the past.

    - *La noche estaba lluviosa.*

- To describe physical, mental, and emotional states in the past.

    - *El niño estaba muy triste.*

    - *Margarita era una niña muy inteligente.*

- To express time in the past.

    - *Eran las doce cuando Pablo llegó.*

- To express ideas equivalent to the English *was* + -*ing, were* + -*ing,* and *used to.*

    - *Me gustaban los chocolates.* (I used to like chocolate.)

    - *María estaba cantando tangos.* (María was singing tangos.).

The following words and phrases are normally associated with the imperfect: *todos los días, todos los lunes, siempre, frecuentemente,* and *mientras.* Notice that these expressions of time tend to underscore the duration of the action expressed by the verb. These expressions will help you identify the need to write a form of the imperfect tense in your answers.

Práctica

Fill in the blanks with the correct form of the preterit or the imperfect of the verb in parentheses.

1. Cuando Manuel (llegar) _____ ya yo había terminado de hacer la comida.

2. Hoy Amalia (estar) _____ muy enferma.

3. Cuando Julio llegó al aeropuerto (llover) _____ a cántaros.

4. Cuando (ser) _____ pequeños, mis hermanos y yo (jugar) _____ a la pelota.

5. (Ser) _____ las nueve de la noche cuando cerraron las puertas del teatro.

Objective 14: To Correctly Use the Subjunctive Mode

One of the most difficult aspects of verbal usage in Spanish is to know when to use the subjunctive mode, in most instances as opposed to using the indicative mode. This mode is used very much in Spanish. It is the mode used to express speculation, wishes, doubt, and any other thought that is not a fact. Below most of the uses of the subjunctive are listed.

The subjunctive is used:

- In certain dependant clauses.
- After *tal vez* and *quizás*.
- After nonexistent and/or indefinite antecedents.
- After certain conjunctions.
- After *aunque*.
- After conjunctions of time.

In Dependent Clauses

The subjunctive is used in dependent clauses as follows:

OJALÁ . . . (que) . . . SUBJUNCTIVE

Ojalá is a word that comes from the Arabic language; it implies meanings such as *I hope, I wish,* and so on. It is always followed by a verb in the subjunctive:

Ojalá *que* **vengas** *a la fiesta mañana.*

EXPRESSIONS OF WILLING . . . (que) . . . SUBJUNCTIVE

Among the verbs found in expressions of willing are *decir, desear, insistir (en), mandar, pedir, permitir, preferir, prohibir, querer,* and *recomendar.* When conveying information, however, *decir* is not considered an expression of willing. In expressions of willing, if there is no change of subject, the infinitive, rather than the subjunctive, is used in the dependent clause.

Yo **prefiero** *que Juan* **venga.**
Yo **prefiero ir.**

EXPRESSIONS OF EMOTION . . . (que) . . . SUBJUNCTIVE

Among the verbs found in expressions of emotion are *alegrarse (de), esperar, gustar, sentir, sorprender, temer,* and *tener miedo (de).* The infinitive, not the subjunctive, is used after expressions of emotion when there is no change of subject.

> **Siento** *que* **llegues** *tarde.*
>
> **Siento llegar** *tarde.*

EXPRESSIONS OF DOUBT . . . (que) . . . SUBJUNCTIVE

Among the expressions of doubt are *no creer, dudar, no estar seguro,* and *negar.* With the opposite expression, the indicative, rather than the subjunctive, is used.

> **No creo** *que Rolando* **sea** *tan inteligente.*
>
> **Estoy segura** *que Fernando no tiene dinero.*

IMPERSONAL EXPRESSIONS OF WILLING, EMOTION, OR DOUBT . . . (que) . . . SUBJUNCTIVE

Some of the most commonly used impersonal expressions of willing are *es necesario, es importante, es urgente, es preferible,* and *es preciso.*

Some of the most commonly used impersonal expressions of emotion are *es terrible, es ridículo, es mejor (bueno, malo, and so on), es increíble, es extraño, qué extraño, es lástima,* and *qué lástima.*

Among the most commonly used impersonal expressions of doubt are *es posible, es imposible, es probable, es improbable, no es verdad, no es cierto,* and *no es seguro.*

> **Es necesario** *que* **comas** *más verduras.*
>
> **Es increíble** *que los niños* **hablen** *dos idiomas correctamente.*
>
> **No es cierto** *que Maruja* **cante** *bien.*

After *Tal Vez* and *Quizás*

If you wish to imply doubt, use *tal vez* or *quizás* followed by the subjunctive in a single-clause sentence.

> **Tal vez sea** *amigo de Reinaldo.*
>
> **Quizás** *María* **regrese** *mañana.*

After Nonexistent and/or Indefinite Antecedents

An adjective clause is a dependent clause that modifies a noun or a pronoun. The noun or pronoun that precedes the adjective clause, and it is modified by it, is called the *antecedent* of the clause. In Spanish, when the antecedent of an adjective clause refers to someone or something that does not exist, the subjunctive must be used in the adjective clause.

Nonexistent antecedent: *No hay nada aquí que me* **interese.**

Existent antecedent: *Hay algo aquí que me* **interesa.**

Similarly, when the existence of the antecedent is indefinite or uncertain, the subjunctive is used.

Indefinite antecedent: *Necesitamos a un portero que lo* **arregle** *todo.*

Definite antecedent: *Tenemos un portero que lo* **arregla** *todo.*

After Certain Conjunctions

The subjunctive is always used when the dependent clause is introduced by the following conjunctions: *a menos que, antes (de) que, con tal que, en caso de que, para que,* and *sin que.* When there is no change in subject, prepositions are used together with the infinitive of the verb.

Estoy aquí para que **aprendan.**

Estoy aquí para **aprender.**

After *Aunque*

The subjunctive is used after the conjunction *aunque* to imply doubt or uncertainty. Where there is no doubt or uncertainty, *aunque* is followed by the indicative.

No me gusta **aunque sea** *amigo de Rita.*

No me gusta **aunque es** *amigo de Rita.*

After Conjunctions of Time

In a dependent clause after a conjunction of time, the subjunctive is used to express a future action or a state of being that has not yet occurred. The events in dependent clauses are not real events. Conjunctions of time include *después (de) que, cuando, en cuanto, hasta que,* and *tan pronto como. Antes de que* always requires the subjunctive. The subjunctive is used with conjunctions of time even when there is no change in subject in the dependent clause. The indicative is used after conjunctions of time to describe a habitual action in the past.

Iré **después que coma.**

Tan pronto *te* **vayas,** *llamaré a Ramón.*

Antes de que hagas *la tarea, llama a Marta.*

Todos los días, **cuando como,** *tomo una siesta.*

Práctica

Fill in the blanks with the correct form of the present indicative or the present subjunctive, according to the context.

1. Se lo digo una vez para que no me (molestar) _____ más.

2. Es increíble que una persona educada (decir) _____ esas cosas.

3. Te presto el dinero con tal que me lo (devolver) _____ la semana que viene.

4. Ojalá me (sacar) _____ la lotería esta semana.

5. Aunque tú (querer) _____ ayudarme, no tienes tiempo para hacerlo.

Objective 15: To Correctly Use Commands

There are two types of direct commands in Spanish: the informal command (*tú, vosotros*) and the formal command (*usted, ustedes*).

The form of the singular informal command (*tú*) is generally the third person singular form of the present indicative. Some singular informal command forms are irregular. Refer to **Objective 12** for the irregular forms of informal singular commands of the most commonly used verbs.

> *Pepito,* **trabaja** *duro para que te paguen bien.*
> *Ana,* **haz** *la tarea antes de que vengan tus padres.*

The form of the plural informal command (*vosotros*) is formed by changing the final *-r* of the infinitive form to a *d*. In Latin America, this form is very seldom used.

> *Niños,* **mirad** *que juguete tan bonito.*
> *Chicas,* **poned** *los vasos encima de la mesa.*

For both forms of formal commands, the form of the present subjunctive is used.

> *Doña Tecla,* **tenga** *usted paciencia con su nieto.*
> *Queridos amigos,* **escriban** *cuando lleguen a Madrid.*

For the four negative informal and formal commands, the form of the present subjunctive is used.

> *Juan,* **no tengas** *miedo del perro, es muy manso.*
> *Chicos,* **no hagáis** *los ejercicios pares, solamente los impares.*
> *Señor González,* **no traiga** *animales a la fiesta, por favor.*
> *Niñas,* **no esperen** *a que las saquen a bailar.*

Objective 16: To Correctly Use the Future and the Conditional Tenses

The future is used in Spanish to:

- Express future time:

    Llegaremos *mañana a la ciudad.*

- Express wonderment or probability in the present time. In many instances, it is equivalent to *I wonder, probably,* and similar expressions:

    Margarita **tendrá** *alrededor de veinte años.*

The conditional is used in Spanish as in English:

No **diría** *una mentira.* (I would not tell a lie.)

It is also used to express wonderment or probability in the past:

Margarita **tendría** *alrededor de veinte años cuando se casó.*

Práctica

Fill in the blanks with the correct form of the future or the conditional of the verb given in parentheses, according to the context.

1. Arturo y Luis (salir) _____ mañana para Ecuador.

2. Ellos dijeron que (escribir) _____ pero no lo han hecho.

3. ¿Qué hora (ser) _____ cuando llegó Rafael anoche?

4. Me (gustar) _____ vivir en una casa en la montaña.

5. ¿Cuántos años (tener) _____ ese bebé que está llorando?

Objective 17: To Correctly Form and Use the Impersonal Forms of Verbs

There are three impersonal verb forms in Spanish: the infinitive, the gerund, and the past participle. Each of them is used in different patterns. Sometimes, the impersonal forms are used in the same way they are used in English; at other times, they are used differently. This causes learners of Spanish to make mistakes.

The infinitive is used:

- As a noun in a sentence. It may be followed by a conjugated verb, and it may function as the subject of the sentence. English equivalents usually use the *-ing* form of the verb.

  - **Fumar** *es nocivo para la salud.* (Smoking is bad for your health.)

- As the object of a conjugated verb.

  - *No sabe* **cantar.** (He/She does not know how to sing.)

  - *Te sentí* **llorar.** (I heard you crying.)

- As the object of a preposition. English equivalents usually use the *-ing* form of the verb.

  - *Después de* **salir,** *cerró la puerta.* (After leaving, he closed the door.)

The gerund is formed in Spanish by adding the endings *-ando* or *-iendo* to the stem of the verb. Some gerunds are irregular. Refer to Objective 12 for the irregular gerunds of the most commonly used verbs.

The gerund is used:

- With the progressive forms of the verb. This pattern requires an auxiliary verb. The most commonly used is *estar,* but others such as *andar, seguir, ir, venir,* and *continuar* are also used. The auxiliary verb may be in any tense.

  - *Los alumnos están* **aprendiendo** *mucho.*

  - *Continúa* **lloviendo** *desde ayer.*

  - *Ya le dije a Pepín que no siguiera* **gritando** *por que me duele la cabeza.*

- To modify a verb in a sentence.

  - *Rosalía salió* **corriendo** *cuando supo que su papá había llegado.*

  - **Hablando** *español, no tendrás problema en Argentina.*

The past participle is formed in Spanish by adding the endings *-ado* or *-ido* to the stem of the verb. Some past participles are irregular. Refer to Objective 12 for the irregular past participle of the most commonly used verbs. Some verbs have two different past participles: One is used as an adjective and the other is used with an auxiliary verb in the perfect tenses.

No **han imprimido** *los libros todavía.*
La revista está **impresa** *en Perú.*

The past participle is used:

- With the verb *haber* to form the perfect tenses of the verb.

  - *Los alumnos* **han aprendido** *mucho.*

  - *No* **había llovido** *mucho este verano.*

- With the verb *ser* to form the passive voice. In this case, the past participle must agree in gender and number with the noun it refers to.

    - *La casa **fue destruída** por el incendio.*

    - *Los heridos **serán rescatados** por los bomberos.*

- As an adjective. In this case, it could be used either with the verb *estar* or after a noun. The past participle must agree in gender and number with the noun it refers to.

    - *La ropa ya **está lavada.***

    - *Traigo la cabeza **rota.***

    - *Los muebles llegaron **desarmados.***

Práctica

Fill in the blanks with the infinitive, the gerund, or the past participle of the verb in parentheses, according to the context.

1. Sin (leer) _____ la carta, no podrás contestarla.

2. ¿Sigues (ir) _____ a las clases de flamenco?

3. Todavía Pedrito no ha (terminar) _____ los problemas de matemática.

4. (Hablar) _____ más de dos idiomas es muy conveniente.

5. Cuando yo llegué, Maura estaba (fregar) _____ los platos.

Objective 18: To Correctly Use *Ser* and *Estar*

Two verbs in Spanish are equivalent to the English verb *to be*. These verbs are *ser* and *estar;* they are used to express different ideas and in different situations. The following rules will help you decide whether to use *ser* or *estar* within a given context.

Ser

Ser is used:

- To express fundamental qualities of a person, animal, or thing.

    - *La sangre **es** roja.*

    - *La tierra **es** redonda.*

- To express nationality and origin.

  - *Tomás* **es** *mexicano.*

  - *Estas bolsas* **son** *del Brasil.*

- To express ownership.

  - *Los libros nuevos* **son** *de Daniel.*

  - *Esta falda* **es** *de Cecilia.*

- To refer to the material something is made of.

  - *Ese vaso* **es** *de vidrio.*

  - *El vestido que compré* **es** *de seda.*

- To express profession or occupation.

  - *Carlos* **es** *abogado.*

  - *Magdalena* **es** *agente de viajes.*

- To express destination or use.

  - *Las flores* **son** *para mi mamá.*

  - *Estas frutas* **son** *para merendar hoy.*

- To express the location of an event.

  - *El juego de pelota* **es** *en Tampa.*

  - *¿Dónde* **es** *la fiesta de Laura?*

- To express a religious or a political affiliation.

  - *Ramón* **es** *católico.*

  - *Anastasio* **es** *demócrata.*

- To express time.

  - **Son** *las cinco.*

  - **Eran** *las tres cuando Patricio llegó.*

Estar

Estar is used:

- To express location.

  - *El vaso* **está** *sobre la mesa.*

  - *Joaquín* **está** *en Alemania.*

- To form the progressive tenses of a verb.

  - *Rosaura* **está** *cantando.*

  - *Ellos* **estuvieron** *mirando la televisión hasta muy tarde anoche.*

- To describe temporary physical, mental, or spiritual conditions.
  - *Las tiendas* **están** *cerradas hoy.*
  - *Tú* **estás** *muy contenta con tu carro nuevo.*

Both *ser* and *estar* are used in fixed expressions that do not belong in any of the categories discussed above. To master these expressions, you must memorize them. For example:

- *Está muerto.* (He is dead)
- *Están muertos de cansancio.* (They are dead tired.)

Práctica

Fill in the blanks with the correct present tense form of *ser* or *estar,* according to the context.

1. Rocío _____ sevillana, pero ahora _____ en Madrid.

2. El pobre Paco _____ loco de remate.

3. Las flores que traje _____ para Leonor.

4. Raúl, ¿dónde _____ mis pantalones de pana?

5. Aunque _____ muy inteligente, no sabes la respuesta del problema.

Prepositions

Objective 19: To Correctly Use the Prepositions *Por* and *Para*

Because *por* and *para* have essentially the same meaning in English, their usage presents difficulty for learners of Spanish. The following are some basic rules to help you use *por* and *para* correctly.

Por

Por is used as an equivalent of the following English words:

- by, by means of
  Ella habla mucho **por** *teléfono.*

- through, along

    Quiero dar una vuelta **por** *el parque.*

    Ellos caminaron **por** *la playa.*

- during

    Por *la noche, siempre leo el periódico.*

- because of

    Estaba triste **por** *la muerte de su perrito.*

- for, when it means

    • in exchange for

    ¿Cuánto pagaste **por** *este jarrón?*

    • for the sake of, on behalf of

    No me gusta ir al cine, si lo hago es **por** *ti.*

- ir order to get, in search of

    Al ver que Rosita tenía fiebre, su padre fue **por** *el médico.*

- for a period of time

    No sé como no te cansas, has estado hablando **por** *tres horas seguidas.*

Por is also used to introduce the agent in a passive voice sentence.

América fue descubierta **por** *Cristóbal Colón.*

Finally, *por* is used in a number of fixed expressions:

por Dios	*por lo menos*
por ejemplo	*por lo visto*
por eso	*por lo común*
por favor	*por primera vez*
por fin	*por si acaso*
por lo general	*por supuesto*

Para

Para is used as an equivalent of the following English expressions:

- in order + infinitive

    Los chicos fueron a la biblioteca **para** *estudiar.*

- for, when it means

  - destined for, to be given to

    Las flores son **para** *Eulalia.*

  - by (specific time)

    El trabajo tiene que estar listo **para** *mañana.*

  - toward, in the direction of

    Después de la boda, los noviòs salieron **para** *París.*

  - to be used for

    Emilia me regaló unas tazas **para** *té.*

  - compared with, in relation to

    Para *Raúl, las computadoras son fáciles de manejar.*

  - in the employ of

    Los chicos trabajan **para** *el director del banco.*

Sometimes, either preposition may be used, but the meaning of the sentence will change. For example:

> *Viajó por Madrid* = He traveled in Madrid.
> *Viajó para Madrid* = He traveled to Madrid.

Práctica

Fill in the blanks with *por* or *para*.

1. No tengo dinero _____ el almuerzo.

2. Ellos estaban muy asustados _____ la tormenta.

3. _____ que la carta llegue rápido, tendrás que enviarla _____ avión.

4. Te lo digo _____ que lo sepas.

5. Durante su viaje pasarán _____ Ginebra.

Answers for Prácticas

Objective 1

1. a-pro-piar
2. trans-gre-dir
3. ca-lle-jue-la
4. li-bre-rí-a
5. ba-úl

Objective 2

First set:

1. az**ú**car
2. bistur**í**
3. **ca**lle
4. **bos**que
5. cara**col**

Second set:

1. mortal
2. cascabel
3. corazón
4. ángel
5. andaluz

Objective 3

1. los
2. la
3. El
4. los
5. no article needed

Objective 4

1. no article needed
2. un
3. no article needed
4. no article needed
5. Una

Objective 5

1. M
2. F
3. F
4. F
5. M

Objective 6

1. meses
2. colibríes
3. canciones
4. leyes
5. autobuses

Objective 7

1. natural
2. educativas
3. difíciles
4. grises
5. rusos

Objective 8

1. viejo amigo
2. Algún día
3. Cualquier cosa
4. blanca nieve
5. roja sangre

Objective 9

1. Ella no lo vio que venía por la calle.
2. Tú se lo pediste para ir al cine.
3. Vas a tener que comprarlo.
4. Estaba diciéndosela cuando él llegó.
5. No los hagas hasta que ella no te lo diga.

Objective 13

1. llegó
2. estaba
3. llovía
4. éramos, jugábamos
5. Eran

Objective 14

1. moleste
2. diga
3. devuelvas
4. saque
5. quieras

Objective 16

1. saldrán
2. escribirían
3. sería
4. gustaría
5. tendrá

Objective 17

1. leer
2. yendo
3. terminado
4. Hablar
5. fregando

Objective 18

1. es, está
2. está
3. son
4. están
5. eres

Objective 19

1. para
2. por
3. Para, por
4. para
5. por

Spanish-English Vocabulary

This Spanish-English vocabulary list contains all the words that appear in the different parts of this book, including the listening and oral parts, except for the following types of words:

- Cognates
- Conjugated verb forms
- Diminutive and augmentatives
- Feminine and plural forms of nouns and adjectives
- Proper nouns
- Adverbs ending in -*mente*
- Words that are included in the classified vocabulary lists

Words beginning with *ch* and *ll* are found under C and L respectively.

A

abajo below, down
abandonar to abandon, to give up
abandono abandonment, neglect
abarcar to take in
abastecer to supply
abastecimiento supplies
abocetar to sketch
abordar to board
aborrecer to hate, to abhor
abrasarse to burn, to scorch
abril April
abrir to open
ábside apse
absorbido absorbed
abstracción abstraction; introspection
abundancia abundance
aburrirse to get bored
acariciar to caress
acelerar to accelerate
aceptación acceptance; approval
aceptar to accept
acerca de about, concerning, regarding

acercamiento rapprochement
acercar to bring close
acertar to get right
acervo heap, pile
aclarar to clear; to clear up
acogedor cozy
acogida reception, acceptance
acompañado accompanied
acompañar to go with; to accompany
acontecimiento event, happening
acordar to decide; to agree upon
acostarse to go to bed
acostumbrarse to get used to
acreditar to credit
acrobacia acrobatics
actividad activity
acto act, action
acudir to respond
acuñado coined, minted
adaptado adapted
adecuado adequate; appropriate
adelantarse to advance
adelante ahead

adelanto advancement

además moreover; in addition

adepto follower

adicción addiction

adiestrar to train

admiración admiration

adorno ornament

adquisición adquisition

adulto adult

advertir to warn, to advise

afear to make ugly

afición liking, taste, fondness

afilado sharp

afín akin, kindred

afirmar to affirm, to assert; to declare

aforrado lined

afortunado fortunate

afrancesado fond of French customs

afuera out, outside

agitado agitated, excited

agobiar to overwhelm

agosto August

agradecer to be thankful for

agregado aggregate

agregar to add

agresor aggressor

agrícola agricultural

aguardado expected

aguardar to wait for

ahí there

ahora now

ahorrar to save

aire air

ajeno belonging to another

ajustar to adjust; to adapt

ajusticiamiento execution

ajusticiar to execute (a criminal)

alabar to praise

alambrada wire fence

alargado elongated

alarmarse to become alarmed

albergar to provide shelter

albores the beginnings

alcance reach; range

alcanzar to reach; to get

aleación alloy

alegre happy

alegría happiness

alemán German

alga seaweed

algo something; somewhat, rather

algún some, any

alimentar to feed, to nourish

alimenticio nutritional

alimento food

aliviar to alleviate

alivio relief

allí there

alma soul

almacén warehouse

almacenar to stack

alquimia alchemy

alrededor around

altar altar

alternancia alternation

alto high

altura height

aludir to allude

alumbrado lit

amable lovable; pleasant

amanecer to dawn; to wake up

amarillo yellow

ambición ambition; drive

ambicioso ambitious

ambiental environmental

ambiente environment

ámbito boundary

ambos both

amenaza threat
amigo friend
aminorar to diminish
amistad friendship
amontonado accumulated
amontonar to crowd together
amor love
amorío minor love affair
amplio ample, extensive, comprehensive
amueblado furnished
amurallado fortified with walls
analizar analize
ánfora amphora
anglicismo Anglicism
angustia anguish
anhelo desire
anidar to nest
animar encourage
ánimo spirit
anoche last night
anochecer to arrive at nightfall
antaño long ago
antepasado ancestor
antes before
antiguo ancient; antique
anunciar to announce
añadir to add
año year
aparato apparatus, device
aparecer to appear, to show up
aparentar to pretend; to look, to appear
aparición appearance
apasionado passionate
apasionante exhilarating
apasionar to impassion
apelativo surname
apenas hardly, scarcely
apilado piled up
aplastado crushed

aplicar to apply; to use
apoderado empowered; authorized
apoyo support
aprender to learn
apropiar to appropriate, to seize
aprovechar to take advantage of
apto fit, capable
apuesto handsome, good-looking
apuntar to write down; to point to
aquí here
árabe Arab
arañar to scratch
arco arc; arch
ardiente burning; ardent, passionate
arena arena; sand
arenoso sandy, gritty
argumento argument
armado armed
arrebatar to snatch away
arrecife reef
arreglar to fix
arrepentirse to repent
arribar to arrive
arrojar to fling, to throw; to yield
arrojo daring, boldness
arrugar to wrinkle
artesanía craftsmanship
artífice artist; artisan
ascendido promoted
asedio harassment
asegurar to assure
asentamiento settlement
así such; so, thus, in this manner
asistente assistant, attendant
asistir to attend, to be present at
asombrarse to be amazed, to be astonished
asombro amazement, astonishment
áspero rough

aspirar to contend
asunto subject, topic; matter, affair
asustar to frighten
ataque attack
aterrado terrified
aterrorizar to terrorize
atestado full, crowded
atraer to attract
atrapado caught
atrapar to catch, to trap
atrás back, backward; behind
atrasar to delay
atraso backwardness
atreverse to dare
atuendo apparel, attire
auge apogee
aumentar to augment, to increase
aumento increase; raise
aunque although, even though
avance advance; progress
avanzado advanced
aventurar to venture
avisar to inform; to advise; to warn
ayer yesterday
ayuda help, aid
ayudar to help, to aid
ayuntamiento city hall
azar chance
azul blue

B

bacanal orgy, festival of Bacchus
baile dance
bajo low
balsa raft
baluarte bulwark, bastion
banca bank
barato cheap

barbaridad crass stupidity, outrage
barraca shack
barrio neighborhood
barro mud; clay
barroco baroque; elaborate, ornate
bastante enough, sufficient; sufficiently
bastar to be enough
beber to drink
belleza beauty
bello beautiful, fair, lovely
benefactor benefactor
beneficioso beneficial
blanco white
blando soft, tender
boda wedding
bonito pretty, beautiful
borrar to erase
borroso blurred
boscaje thicket
botella bottle
bovino bovine
brillar to shine
brindar to offer, to supply
brocado brocade
broma joke
bronceador suntan lotion
brutal brutal, cruel
bueno good
búlgaro Bulgarian
buscado looked for
buscar to look for

C

caballero gentleman; knight
cabello hair
caber to fit
cabezudo big-headed
cada each, every

cadena chain
caer to fall
caerse to fall down
cajón large box
calcificación calcification
calentar to warm, to heat up
calificar to classify; to consider
callar to quiet
callarse to be quiet
calle street, road
callejuela back street, alley
calma calm
cambiar to change
cambio change
caminar to walk
campamento military camp
campaña campaign
campera sport jacket
campesino peasant, country person
campo countryside; field; ground
canal waterway, canal; channel
canalizar to channel, direct
candado padlock
cansado tired
cantar to sing
cantar de gesta epic poem
cante singing
cantidad quantity
cantina canteen
canto song, epic poem
capa cape; layer; cover
capaz capable
capellán chaplain
capilla chapel
carácter character; personality
cárcel jail, prison
carecer to lack
carga load
cargo charge; position

carguero freight
caricaturizado caricatured
cariñoso loving, affectionate
carmesí crimson, red, scarlet
carraspeo hoarseness
carreta cart, wagon
carta letter
cartón cardboard
casadero marriageable
casarse to get married
cascarón thick shell, eggshell
casi almost, nearly
casilla lodge, cabin
castigar to punish
castillo castle
castro hillock, fort
cátedra professorship
catedral cathedral
causa cause
causar to cause
cavar to dig
caza hunting
cazar to hunt
ceder to yield
cegador blinding
celoso jealous
celtíbero Celtiberian
cementerio cemetery
ceniza ash
centenar one hundred
centinela sentry
centrifugación centrifugation
ceñido close-fitting
ceñir to girdle; to surround
ceño frown
cera wax
cerca near, nearby, close
cercano close, nearby
ceremonia ceremony

cernido sifting of flour
cerrado closed
cerrar to close
chaparro short, stubby person
cheurón chevron
chico boy; little, small
chileno Chilean
chino Chinese
chiquillo rowdy youngster
chivo goat
cicatriz scar
ciclo cycle
cierto certain
cifra number; cypher
cimiento foundation; root
cine cinema; movies; movie theater
circense related to the circus
cita quotation; date, appointment
ciudad city
ciudadano citizen
claridad clarity
claro clear
clavadista diver
clavado dive
clave key
cobrar to charge
cochino pig
codicia greed
codiciado desirable
código code
coger to seize; to take
cohete rocket
coincidir to coincide
cola tail; line
cólera anger, rage
colgar to hang
colocar to place
colonizador settler
colorado reddish

colorido colorful
comentar to comment
comenzar to begin
comer to eat
comercio commerce, trade
comienzo beginning
comodidad comfort
comparar to compare
compartir to share
complicación complication
componer to compose; to fix
comportamiento behavior
comprar to buy
comprender to include
comprobación verification
comprobar to confirm, to verify
comprometerse to pledge oneself
compromiso promise; commitment
compuesto compound
con with
con mucho gusto with pleasure
con prisa in a hurry
conde count (nobility title)
condecorado decorated with honors
condenado condemned
conducir to lead; to drive
confirmar to confirm
confundir to confuse
conjunto whole, entirety; set
conjurar to plot
conmemoración commemoration
conmigo with me
conmover to move (emotionally)
conocer to know, to meet
conocido known
conocimiento knowledge, familiarity
conquista conquest
conseguido attained
consejo advice

consistir en to be composed of
constar to consist of, to be composed of
constituir to constitute, to compose
construcción construction
construido built
consumir to consume
contador storyteller
contaminado polluted
contar to count; to tell, to relate
contemplar to contemplate
contener to contain
contenido content
contestar to answer, to respond
contienda fight, battle
contra against
contraer to contract
contrapunto counterpoint
contrato contract
contribuir to contribute
controlar to control
controversia controversy
convencer to convince
convencido convinced
convención agreement, contract
convertirse en to turn into
convincente convincing
convivio invitation; feast
convivir to cohabit
coquina a small shellfish
cordobés from Cordoba
corear to accompany with a chorus
cornada horn thrust, goring
corona crown
corregir to correct
correr to run
corrida bullfight
corriente current; trend
corromper to corrupt
cortada cut; choppy

cortejado escorted
cortijo farm
cosa thing
cosecha harvest
costar to cost
costumbre custom
cotidiano daily, everyday
crear to create
crecer to grow; to increase
creciente growing; increasing
crecimiento growth
creencia belief
creer to believe; to trust
cresta crest; peak
cría breeding; offspring
criado servant
criador breeder
criatura creature
crisol crucible
cristiano Christian
criticable censurable
crucero cruise
cruz cross
cruzar to cross
cuadrado square
cuadro painting; scene
cualidad quality
cualquier whichever; any
cuando when
cuanto as, as much as
cubierto covered
cubrir to cover
cuenta bead
cueva cave
cuidado care
cuidar to take care of, to care for
culminar to culminate
culpa blame
cultivar to cultivate; to develop

cultivo cultivation
cumpleaños birthday
cumplir to carry out; to fulfill
cúmulo heap
cupo quota
cursilería vulgarity
cuyo whose

D

danzón popular Cuban dance
dañar to damage
dañino harmful
dañosísimo extremely harmful
dar to give
datar to date
dato fact
debajo underneath, below
deber duty, obligation; should
debido due
debilidad weakness
decantación decanting
decantado settled
decena group of ten
decidir to decide
decir to say, to tell
declarar to declare
declinar to decline
dedicación dedication
deducir to deduce, to infer, to conclude
defensa defense
defensor defender
defraudar to disappoint
degenerar to degenerate
degradado demoted
dejar de to stop
dejar to leave; to let, to permit
delante de before, in front of
delicadeza fineness, daintiness

demás (los) the rest, the others
demasía excess, surplus
demasiado too, too much, excessively
demostrar to demonstrate
denigrante slanderous
dentro inside, within
denunciar to denounce, to accuse
deparar to furnish
deportista sportsperson
derecho right
derramar to spill
derretirse to melt, to thaw
desafiar to challenge
desafío challenge
desagradable unpleasant
desaparecer to disappear
desaparición disappearance
desarrollar to develop
desarrollo development
desastre disaster
desbordamiento overflowing
descendencia lineage
descender to descend
descifrar to decipher
descomponer to break down; to decompose
desconocido unknown
describir to describe
descubierto discovered
descubrimiento discovery
descubrir to discover
desde from; since
desde luego of course
desembocadura mouth of a river
desempeñar to fulfill, to carry out
desencaminado misdirected, misguided
desenlace conclusion, end
deseo desire
deseoso anxious

desequilibrio unbalanced

desertor deserter

desgarrar to tear

desgastado worn out

desgraciado unfortunate; wretched

deshacer to undo

desintegración disintegration; decay

desmayarse to faint

desmesura excess

desnutrición malnutrition

desolado desolate

desorden disorder

desperezo stretching

despertar awakening

despertarse to wake up

desplome collapse

despreciable despicable, abject

desprecio contempt, disdain

después later, afterwards

destacar to emphasize

destacarse to be outstanding

destemplado inmoderate, intemperate

destreza skill

destrozar to break to pieces, to destroy

destrucción destruction

destruir to destroy

desvelarse to keep awake

desventaja disadvantage

detalle detail

detención arrest, detention

detener to stop; to arrest

detentar to keep unlawfully

detractor slanderous

detrás behind

deuda debt

devastador devastating

devoción devotion

devolver to return (something)

devoto devout, pious; devotee

día day

diario newspaper; daily

dibujo drawing

diccionario dictionary

dicho saying

dictadura dictatorship

difícil difficult

difusión diffusion

digerir to digest

digno meritorious, deservings

diminuto small, little, minute

dinero money

dios god; idol

dirigido directed

disco disk, disc; record

discreción discretion

discurrir to roam, to ramble

diseñado designed

disfrutar to enjoy

disímil unlike, different

disminuir to reduce, to lessen

disonante discordant

disparar to shoot, to fire

disponible available

dispuesto ready, prepared

distinguir to distinguish

distinto different

distribuido distributed

disuelto dissolved

divertido amusing

divertirse to have fun, to amuse oneself

dividido divided

divulgar to make known, to reveal

docena dozen

doloroso painful

dominar to dominate

dorado golden

dormir to sleep

dormirse to fall asleep

dorso back

dotado gifted, endowed with

duda doubt

dulce sweet

durante during

durar to last

dureza hardness

duro difficult; hard

E

echar to throw

echarse a to start to

eco echo

edad age

edificar to construct, to build

edificio building

edil edile

editar to edit

editorial publishing

edredón eiderdown

educado well-mannered; educated

efectuado carried out

eficaz efficacious

egipcio Egyptian

ejemplar copy (of a book)

ejemplo example

ejercer to exercise

ejercicio exercise

elaboración elaboration

elaborado elaborate

elaborar to elaborate

elegir to elect

embarazada pregnant

embarcación ship

eminente outstanding, prominent

emisora broadcasting station

emocionar to move, to touch (emotionally)

empalmar to join

emparentado related by marriage

empezar to begin

emplazado summoned

empleado employee

empleo employment, job; use

emprender to undertake

enamorado lover

enamorarse to fall in love

encantador charming

encantamiento enchantment

encantar to enchant

encanto charm

encaramado lifted up

encarcelamiento imprisonment

encendido ignited

encontrar to find

encuadernado bound

encubierto hidden

encuesta survey

encuestado surveyed

enemigo enemy

enero January

enfermo sick

enfrentar to confront

enfrente in front

enfriar to chill

enfurruñado angry

enjambre swarm

enmarcado framed

enorme enormous

ensayar to rehearse

enseñar to teach; to show

entender to understand

entendido understood

enterarse to find out about

entero whole, entire, complete

enterrar to bury

entierro burial, funeral

entonces then, in that case
entrada entrance
entrañable very affectionate
entrar to enter
entre between, among
entrecejo frown
entregar to deliver; to hand in
entrenado trained
entretenerse to amuse oneself
entretenimiento amusement
entrevista interview
entrevistado interviewed
envejecer to age
envejecimiento aging
envenenar to poison
enviar to send, to mail
envidia envy
episodio episode
época epoch; era
equinoccio equinox
equipo team; equipment
equitativa equitable
equivaler to be equal
erigido erected
erizado spiky, spiny
esbozo sketch, outline
escapar to escape
escarlata scarlet
escarnio scoff
escenario stage, scenery; setting
esclavizar to enslave
esclavo slave
escoger to choose, to select
escogido choosen
esconder to hide
escrito written; writing, document
escritura writing
escuchar to listen to
esculpir to sculpt

escurrir to drain
esforzarse to strive to
esfuerzo effort
esmerarse to be meticulous
espantar to frighten
espectáculo spectacle, performance
esperar to wait for; to hope; to expect
espeso thick
espesura thickness
espícula spicule
espíritu spirit, soul
esplendor splendor
esponjado puffed up
espontaneidad spontaneity
esporádico sporadic
esposado handcuffed
esqueleto skeleton
esquema plan; outline; pattern
esquiar to ski
esquina corner (of a street)
estación station; season
estadio stadium
estadista statesman
estadounidense from the United States
estancia stay, sojourn
estantería bookcase
estar to be
estar de moda to be in fashion
estar listo to be ready
estar seguro to be sure
estatua statue
este East
estimular to stimulate
estrella star
estremecerse to shiver, to tremble
estrenar to inaugurate
estreno debut
estropear to spoil, to ruin
estruendo clamor, noise

estudio study; studio

estudios studies

estupendo stupendous, wonderful

etapa stage, step

euro European common unit of money

evitar to avoid

exilio exile

existencia existence, life

existir to exist

éxito sucess

explicado explained

explicar to explain

exponente exponent

exponer to expose, to exhibit, to show

exterminar to exterminate

extraer to extract

extranjero foreigner; foreign

extraño strange

exuberancia exuberance, abundance

F

fábrica factory

fabricante manufacturer

fabricar to manufacture

faceta side, aspect, facet

fácil easy

facilitar to facilitate

facultad ability; school in a university

fallas fire festival in Valencia

falsedad falsehood

falta lack of

familiarizado accustomed; familiarized

famoso famous

fantasma phantom, ghost

farol streetlamp

fascinar to fascinate

fecha date

feliz happy

fermentar to ferment

feroz fierce, ferocious

fertilidad fertility

festejo celebration

festividad festivity

fibra fiber

fiel faithful

fiesta party, holiday

figurar to figure; to appear

fijarse en to pay attention to

fijo fix

filólogo philologist

fin end; goal; purpose

finca ranch, farm

firma signature; company, firm

firmar to sign

florecer to flourish

florido full of flowers

fluir to flow

flujo flow

fogón kitchen range

forastero stranger, outsider

forjar to forge

formar parte to be part of

formidable tremendous, enormous

formulario form, application

fortalecer to fortify

fortaleza strength; fortress

fortificación fortification

fracasado unsuccessful

francés French

frasco bottle, flask

frenos brakes

frito fried

frontera frontier; border

fruncido shirred, gathered

fuego fire

fuente fountain; source

fuera outside

fuerza strength, power; force
función function
funcionar to function, to work
funcionario official, functionary
fundamento foundation, basis
fundar to found, to establish
fundido cast
fusilado executed by a firing squad

G

gallardo elegant, graceful
gama gamut
gana desire, wish
ganadero cattle breeder
ganado cattle
ganar to win; to earn
ganga bargain
gasto expense
gatuno catlike
gemelos twins
gemido groan, moan
generado generated
gente people
gerente manager
gesta exploit
gestionar to arrange
gigante giant
gobierno government
golpe blow, hit
golpear to hit, to bang
gozar to enjoy
gozo joy, delight, pleasure
grabar to engrave; to record (music)
gradas bleachers
graduarse to graduate
gramática grammar
grano grain
grasa fat, grease

grave serious, grave
griego Greek
gris gray
gruñir to growl
guardar to guard, to keep
guardería day-care center
guatemalteco Guatemalan
guayabera loose-fitting men's shirt
guerra war
guijarro small round pebble
guión screenplay; script
guisado casserole; stew
guisar to cook
gustar to like
gustoso tasty, savory

H

habitante inhabitant
habitar to inhabit
hablar to speak, to talk
hacer to do; to make
hacia toward
halado pulled
hallado found
hallar to find
hambre hunger
hasta until
hecho fact; deed; event
hembra female
hereje heretic
herida wound; injury
herido injured
hermosura beauty
hiena hyena
hierba grass; herb
hincar to prick
hispano Hispanic
hito milestone

hogar home
hoguera bonfire
hombre man
homenaje homage
horrorizado horrified
hosco gruff, bad-tempered
hoy today
hoy en día nowadays
hoya hole, pit
huelga strike
huesoso bony
huir to flee
húmedo humid, wet
humilde humble
humo smoke
hundimiento sinking
hundir to sink
huraño unsociable
hurgar to rummage

I

idioma language
idóneo suitable
iglesia church
igual equal; same, similar
iluminar to illuminate, to light up
ilustre distinguished, illustrious
imaginativo fanciful, visionary
impartir to impart
impasible impassive
impedir to impede, to hinder
imperio empire
implantar to introduce; to established
imponer to impose
imprescindible essential, indispensable
impreso printed
impulso impulse
impureza impurity

inaudito unheard of
incapacitado disabled
incendiado set on fire
incendio fire
incesante continual, unceasing
incluido included
incluir to include
incluso including; even
incómodo uncomfortable
incrementar to increase
indefinible undefinable
indicio indication, sign
inesperado unexpected
infanzón noble person
infeliz unhappy, unfortunate
inferir to infer
inflar to inflate
influir to influence
ingreso income; admission
iniciar to initiate
inicio beginning
inimaginable inconceivable
injusticia injustice
injusto unjust; unfair
inmensidad inmensity
inmisericorde merciless
innato innate
innominado unnamed
inolvidable unforgettable
inquietar to upset
inquietud uneasiness
inscripción engraving; enrollment
insecticida insecticide
inservible useless
instaurar to establish
intercambiar to exchange
interesante interesting
internarse to go into
intrincado intricate

inundar to flood
inventar to invent
invernar to hibernate
invertir to invest
investigador investigator, researcher
investigar to investigate
ir to go
ir de cacería to go hunting
irradiación radiation
isla island
isleño islander
izquierdo left

J

jamás never
jarana joke
jarocha native of Veracruz
jarrón vase
jerga slang
jitomate tomato
jubilarse to retire
jubiloso jubilant, joyful
judío Jew; Jewish
jugar to play
juicio judgement, opinion; sanity
julio July
junto together
justo just, fair

L

lacustre pertaining to lakes
lado side
lago lake
lágrima tear
lama slime, mud
lamentarse to lament
lamento moan, lament
lamer to lick

lamido very clean
lanza spear
lanzado ranking, inclined
lanzar to hurl, to throw
largo long
lata can, tin
latifundio large estate
lavar to wash
lavar en seco to dry clean
laxante laxative
lector reader
lectura reading
leer to read
legendario legendary
legitimación legitimation
lejano far, distant, remote
lejos far
lencería lingerie
lentitud slowness
lento slow
leña firewood
lesionar to injure
letra letter (of the alphabet)
levantarse to get up
levantino from the Levant region of Spain
leve light; trivial
ley law
liberado liberated
libre free
ligado tied, linked
ligero light
limo slime, mud
limosna charity
limpieza cleanliness
limpio clean
linajudo highborn
litoral coast, shore
litro liter

llama flame

llamar to call

llamar la atención to call attention to

llegada arrival

llegar to arrive; to reach

llenar to fill

llevar a cabo to carry out

llorar to cry

local local; place, site

localidad locality

localizar to locate

locomotora locomotive

lodo mud

lograr to achieve; to attain

lona canvas

longitud length

lucha fight, struggle

luchar to fight, to struggle

lucir to appear

luego then, later

lugar place

luminoso luminous

luna de miel honeymoon

luz light

M

macho male

maderera pertaining to lumber

madrugada dawn, daybreak

madrugar to get up early

maduración ripeness

madurar to ripen

madurez maturity

maduro mature; ripe

magia magic

mágico magic

magnicidio assassination

magnífico magnificent

maldad evil

maletilla an amateur bullfighter

malicioso malicious

mamá mom

mamífero mammal

mancha stain

manchado stained

mandar to order, to command, to send

mandato command, order

manejo use, operation

manía habit, whim

mantener to maintain, to support

manuscrito manuscript

mañana tomorrow; morning

maquillaje makeup

máquina machine

máquina de coser sewing machine

mar sea

maraña tangle

maravilla wonder

maravillar to amaze

maravilloso marvelous

marca mark

marcar to mark

marcha march; walk

más more

masas the crowd

matanza slaughter

matar to kill

materia matter

maternidad maternity

matrícula enrollment

matrimonio marriage

mayor older, oldest

mayoría majority

mecanografiar to type

medida measure, step

medio middle; means; half

medir to measure

mediterráneo Mediterranean

mejor better, best

mejorar to better, to improve
melodramático melodramatic
menor younger, youngest; minor; lesser
menos less, least; fewer
mensajero messenger
mentir to lie
mentira lie
menudo minute, small
mercancía merchandise
merecer to deserve
mes month
metáfora metaphor
meter to get into
meterse to enter
mezcla mixture
mezclar to mix
mezquita mosque
miedo fear
mientras while
miércoles Wednesday
mil one thousand
milagro miracle
milicia military service
milla mile
millón one million
minifalda miniskirt
mirar to look at, to watch
mismo same
mitad half
moda style, fashion
modo manner, way
molde mold
molestar to annoy, to bother
molino mill
monarca monarch
moneda coin
mono cute
monstruo monster
montar to ride
monte mountain

montero hunter
montón heap, pile
moño bun, chignon
mordacidad sarcasm
morder to bite
morenez darkness
morir to die
morisco Moor; Moorish
mosaico mosaic
mostrar to show
mover to move
muchedumbre crowd
muerte death
muerto dead
muestra sample
mujer woman
mundial worldwide
mundo world
munición ammunition
muñeco doll
museo museum
musgo moss

N

nácar mother of pearl
nacer to be born
nacimiento birth
nacionalidad nationality
nada nothing
nadar to swim
nadie nobody, no one
naturaleza nature; character
naturista natural healer
navegar to sail, to navigate
necesario necessary
necesidad necessity
necesitar to need
negado denied
negar to deny

negocio business

negro black; black person

neutro neuter

nieves sorbet, ice cream

nihilista nihilist

ninguno not any

ninguneada a nobody

niño child, boy

nivel level

nobiliario peerage; title (of nobility)

nobleza nobility

noche night

nocivo harmful

nombrar to name

nombre name; noun

noreste northeast

norte north

noticia news

novela novel

novia girlfriend, fiancée

noviembre November

nuestro our

nuevo new

número number

numeroso numerous

nunca never

O

obedecer to obey

oblicuo slanting

obligar to oblige, to obligate

obra work

obstáculo obstacle

obtener to obtain, to get

ocasionado caused

ocasionar to cause

ocupado occupied, busy

ocurrir to occur, to happen

oeste west

ofrecer to offer

oír to hear, to listen

ojeada glance, glimpse

óleo oil painting

oler to smell

olfato the sense of smell

olvidar to forget

olvido forgetfulness, oblivion

onda wave

óptimo excellent, best, optimal

orgullo pride

originarse to originate

orilla edge, border, shore

ortografía orthography, spelling

oscuridad darkness

oscuro oscuro

óseo pertaining to bone

ostentado displayed

ostentoso sumptuous

otorgar to grant, to award

otro other, another

P

paciencia patience

pagano pagan

pagar to pay

página page

país country

palabra word

palaciego pertaining to a palace

palacio palace

paladín knight

paleta small shovel; palette

pálido pale; colorless

palo stick

papel paper; role

paradoja paradox

paralizar to paralize

parar to stop

pardillo linnet
parecer to appear, to seem, to look like
parecido alike, similar
partícipe participant
partido game, match; political party
partir to depart
pasado past, former
pasado de moda old-fashioned
pasar to happen; to spend (time); to pass
pasear to walk, to stroll
pasión passion
paso step
pasta paste
pastar to graze
patinar to skate
patria homeland
paz peace
pedazo piece
pedir to ask for, to request; to order
pedrada blow with a stone
pegado stuck to; close to
peineta ornamental comb
pelaje fur coat
peldaño step of a staircase
pelear to fight
película film, movie
peligro danger
pena sorrow; pain
pensamiento thought
pensar to think
pensativo thoughtful
peor worse, the worst
pequeño little, small
percal percale
perder to lose
perderse to get lost
pérdida loss
perdido lost
perdonar to pardon; to forgive

perfil profile
perfumería perfumery
periodismo journalism
periodístico journalistic
perjudicial harmful
permanecer to remain
permanencia permanence
permiso permission
pero but
perruno canine
perseguir to pursue; to persecute
personaje personality; character
pertenecer to belong; to pertain
perturbado disturbed
pesadilla nightmare
pesar to weigh
peseta former monetary unit of Spain
pésimo very bad, terrible
peso monetary unit; weight
pesticida pesticide
piadoso merciful
picar to prick, to puncture
pico peak (of a mountain)
picota gibbet
pilar pillar
pintar to paint
pintoresco picturesque
pionero pioneer
pirata pirate
pisar to step
placentero pleasant
placer pleasure
plaga plague
plantar to plant
plantear to set forth
plasmar to form, to shape
plateresco plateresque
platillo small dish
playa beach

plaza town square

población population; town

poblado populated; town

pobre poor

pobreza poverty

poco little

poder to be able

poderoso powerful

polémico controversial, polemical

policíaco pertaining to the police

polinizador pollinizer

polvo dust

pólvora gunpowder

pomada ointment

pompa ostentation, pomp

poner to put, to place

poner en marcha to start (a car)

poner en orden to organize

populoso populous

por casualidad by chance

por correspondencia by mail

por el contrario on the contrary

por eso that is why

por lo general in general

por supuesto of course

por tanto therefore

por un lado on one side

porque because

portal arcade, portico, porch

portar to bear, to carry

poseer to possess, to own

practicar to practice

prado meadow

precio price

precoz advanced, precocious

predecir to predict

pregunta question

premio prize

prenda jewel

prensa press

preocupación worry, concern

preocuparse to worry

presentar to present

presión pressure

preso prisoner

pretender to aspire

previo previous

primero first

primordial fundamental

principal main

principio beginning; principle

prior parish priest

prisa hurry

privilegiado privileged

proceder to proceed

proclamar to proclaim

producir to produce

profecía prophecy

proferir to utter

profeta prophet

profundidad depth

profundo deep

prohibir to prohibit

promontorio headland, promontory

promovido promoted

pronóstico prediction; omen

pronto soon, quick

propagarse to propagate

propiciar to sponsor

propio own; itself; proper

proponer to propose

proseguir to continue

protagonista protagonist

proteger to protect

protegido protected

proveniente originating

provenir to originate, to come from

provocar to provoke, to cause

proyecto project
prueba test, exam; proof
publicar to publish
pueblo town, village; people
puente bridge
pues since, because
puesto stand, booth
pulgada inch
puntería aim
punto point, period, dot
punto de vista point of view
puré purée
pureza purity
purificación purification
purista purist

Q

quedar to remain, to stay; to be left
quedarse to remain
queja complaint
quejarse to complain
quema burning
quemado burnt
quemar to burn
querer to want, to desire; to love
quien who, whom
quieto calm, still
quijotesco quixotic
químico chemical
quiniela lottery
quitar to remove, to take away
quizá perhaps, maybe

R

rabia anger
radicar to take root
rapidez speed
rapiña pillage

raro rare, uncommon
rascar to scratch
rasgo trait
rastrear to track
rastro vestige, trace
rato while, short while
raza race
real royal
realizado accomplished
realizar to accomplish
rebelar to revolt, to rebel
rebuscar to glean
rechazar to reject
recibir to receive
reciente recent
recinto enclosure; space
recodo bend, angle
recoger to pick up
recogimiento meditation
recolección collection
reconocer to recognize
recopilado compiled
recopilar to compile
recordar to remember
recorrer to go through
recorrido journey
recuerdo memory
recuperación recovery
recurso resource
red net; network
redondo round
reducir to reduce
reflejado reflected
reflejar to reflect
refrescarse to refresh oneself
regalar to give (a present)
regalo gift
regañar to scold
registrar to check

regla rule

regresar to return, to come back

rehén hostage

rehuir to avoid

reinado reign

reino kingdom

reírse to laugh

rejuvenecimiento rejuvenation

relato story, narrative

reliquia relic

rematar to finish off

remediar to remedy

remembranza memory

remontarse to go back (to the past)

renacer to be born again

renacimiento rebirth

rendir to yield

renegar to deny

renegrida blackish

reparar en to pay attention to

repartir to distribute

repentino sudden

repercusión repercussion

replicar to reply

repugnancia repugnance

reputación reputation

requerir to require

residir to reside

resolver to resolve

respaldar to back up

respirar to breathe

responder to answer

responsable responsible

respuesta answer

restablecer to reinstate

restar to substract; to be left

restos remains

resultado result

retirar to retire; to remove

retraso delay

reunión gathering

reunir to bring together

revelación revelation

revelar to reveal

rey king

rezar to pray

ribazo mound, hillock

rico rich; tasty, delicious

ridiculizar to ridicule

riego irrigation

riesgo risk

rimero heap, pile, stack

rincón corner (inside)

riña quarrel

río river

riqueza wealth, richness

risa laughter

rito rite, ceremony

robar to steal

rodaje filming

rodar to film

rodear to surround

rogar to beg

rojo red

romper to break

rosado pink

rostro face

roto broken

ruedo bullring

rugir to roar

ruido noise

ruina ruin

rústica (en) paperbound

S

sábado Saturday

sabana savanna

saber to know

sabio wise person; scholar

sabor flavor

sabroso delicious, tasty

sacar to take out

saco bag

sacudimiento shaking

salario salary

salida exit; departure

salino saline

salir to go out, to leave

salpicado splotchy

saltar to jump

salvación salvation

salvar to save; to rescue

salvo safe, saved

sanar to heal

sangrante bloody

sanguíneo pertaining to blood

santo holy

santuario sanctuary

saqueo plundering, pillaging

sazonado spicy

secar to dry

seco dry

sede headquarters

sedentario sedentary

sedoso silken

seguido continuosly; consecutively

seguir to continue, to follow

según according to

segundo second

seguro secure; sure

sello stamp; seal

selva jungle

semana week

sembrar to cultivate; to plant

semejante similar

sensibilidad sensitivity

sentarse to sit down

sentido sense, meaning

sentimiento feeling

sentir to feel

señal signal, indication

señor sir, mister (Mr.); gentleman, man

señora lady; missus (Mrs.); woman

señorita miss, young lady

sepultado buried

sequía drought

ser to be

ser humano human being

servidor servant

servir to serve

sevillano from Seville

siempre always

sierra mountain range

siglo century

significado meaning

significar to mean

siguiente following, next

silbato whistle (instrument)

silbido whistle

silencioso silent, quiet

silueta silhouette; outline

silvestre wild

símbolo symbol

simpático pleasant, nice

simulacro mock representation, drill

simular to simulate

sin without

sin embargo however

sincero sincere

siniestro sinister

sino but (rather)

sitio place

sobre above, over; about, concerning

sobrevivir to survive

soler to be in the habit of

solicitar to apply for

solicitud application

solidificación solidification

solitario reclusive

sólo only

solsticio solstice

solucionar to solve

sombra shade, shadow

sonido sound

sonrisa smile

soñador dreamer

soñar to dream

soportar to sustain; to endure

sorprendente surprising

sorteo raffle

sostener to support; to hold

suave soft, smooth

súbdito subject, citizen

subir to rise, to go up, to climb

subsistir to subsist

subsuelo subsoil

subterráneo underground

suceder to happen

sucesivo successive

suceso event

sucio dirty

suculencia succulence

sueldo salary

suelo ground

suerte luck

suficiente sufficient, enough

sufrir to suffer

sugerir to suggest

sujetar to fasten

suma sum, amount

sumerio Sumerian

superar to exceed

superficie surface

suponer to suppose

sur south

surco furrow; groove

surgir to arise

suscitar to cause

suspendido interrupted

sustancia substance

sustituir to substitute

susto scare

T

tableta tablet

tablilla small board

tacaño stingy

taciturno reserved

tacón heel

tal such

talla size

tallar to carve

talle waist

taller shop

tamaño size

también also, too

tampoco neither

tanto so much

tapa lid, cover

tapia adobe wall

tapiz tapestry

tardar to take a long time

tarde late; afternoon

tarjeta card

teatro theater

tedioso tedious

tejido fabric

telefonear to telephone

temor fear

temprano early

tendencia tendency

tender to spread

tenebroso dark, gloomy

tenencia tenure, holding
tener to have
tercero third
terminar to finish, to end
término term, word; period
terrestre terrestrial, earthly
territorio territory, region
tesoro treasure
testigo witness
textil textile
tiempo time; weather
tiempo libre free time
tierra land
tipo type, kind; guy
tiranicidio tyrannicide
tirano tyrant
tirar to throw
tirarse to throw oneself
título title
tocar to touch; to play (an instrument)
todavía still, yet
todo all
tolerar to tolerate
tomar to take; to drink
tomatazo blow with a tomato
tómbola charity raffle
tonalidad tonality
tonelada ton
tonificar to invigorate
topo mole
torear to bullfight
tormentoso stormy
tornarse to become
torneo tournament
torrencial torrential
traba hindrance, obstacle
trabajar to work
trabajo work; job
traca strake; string of firecrackers
traducción translation

traducido translated
traducir to translate
traer to bring
tragedia tragedy
transcurrir to pass
transeúnte transient
tránsito transit; traffic
transparente transparent
tras after
trasladar to move, to transfer
trastornado perturbed
trastorno disorder; complication
tratamiento treatment
tratar to treat; to try
trato deal, agreement; treatment
trebejo tool; utensil, implement
triste sad
tristeza sadness
triturar to grind
triunfar to triumph
trompearse to come to blows
tropas troops
tropezar to stumble
trovador troubadour, minstrel
trozo chunk
turco Turk
tutelar guardian

U

ubicado located
ubicar to locate
último last
ungüento ointment
único only, sole; unique
untar to cover with
usar to use
usted you (formal)
útil useful
utilizar utilize

V

vacío empty

vacuno bovine

vagabundo vagabond

vaina sheath

valenciano Valencian

valer to be worth; to cost

válido valid

valle valley

valor worth, value; courage

vara rod

vareo collecting fruit with a rod

variante variant

variedad variety

varilla rod

varios various, several

vasco Basque

vasija vessel, receptacle

vasto vast

vecinal adjacent

vecindad neigborhood

vecino neighbor

vega fertile lowland

vehículo vehicle

velludo hairy

veloz swift

vencedor victor, winner

vender to sell

vendido sold

veneno poison

venerar to venerate

venezolano Venezuelan

ventaja advantage

ventanilla window (in a vehicle)

ver to see, to look at

veracruzano from Verarcruz

verdad truth

verdadero true, real

verde green

verdoso greenish

versificación versification

vestimenta garments

vestirse to get dressed

vez time, occasion

viajar to travel

viajero traveler

vibración vibration

vida life

vidriero glassworker

vidrio glass

viernes Friday

viga beam

vinculación link

viscoso sticky

visigodo Visigoth

vistoso colorful, attractive

vitalidad vitality

vivo alive, living; lively

vocación vocation

volador flying

volante flounce

volar to fly

volumen volume

voluntad will

voluntario volunteer

volver to return; to come back

votar to vote

voz voice

vuelta turn

Y

ya already

Z

zahones leather overalls

zumbar to buzz

zumbido buzzing

Two CDs are included with this book. They include audio content that will help you prepare for the actual AP Spanish Language Exam. The table below has a brief explanation of what the CDs contain.

CD 1		
Track Number	*Type*	*Used In*
Track 1	Dialogue	Part II: Dialogues and Narratives
Track 2	Short Narrative	
Track 3	Longer Narrative	
Track 4	Dialogue	
Track 5	Short Narrative	
Track 6	Longer Narrative	
Track 7	Picture Sequence Directions	Part II: Picture Sequences
Track 8	Directed Response	Part II: Directed Response
Track 9	Directed Response	
Track 10	Dialogue	Diagnostic Test
Track 11	Short Narrative	
Track 12	Longer Narrative	
Track 13	Picture Sequence Directions + Oral Directions	
Track 14	Directed Response	
Track 15	Dialogue 1	Practice Test 1
Track 16	Dialogue 2	
Track 17	Dialogue 3	
Track 18	Short Narrative 1	
Track 19	Short Narrative 2	
Track 20	Longer Narrative 1	
Track 21	Longer Narrative 2	

Track Number	Type	Used In
CD 2		
Track 1	Picture Sequence Directions + Oral Directions	Practice Test 1
Track 2	Directed Response	
Track 3	Dialogue 1	
Track 4	Dialogue 2	
Track 5	Dialogue 3	
Track 6	Short Narrative 1	
Track 7	Short Narrative 2	Practice Test 2
Track 8	Longer Narrative 1	
Track 9	Longer Narrative 2	
Track 10	Picture Sequence Directions + Oral Directions	
Track 11	Directed Response	
Track 12	Dialogue 1	
Track 13	Dialogue 2	
Track 14	Dialogue 3	
Track 15	Short Narrative 1	
Track 16	Short Narrative 2	Practice Test 3
Track 17	Longer Narrative 1	
Track 18	Longer Narrative 2	
Track 19	Picture Sequence Directions + Oral Directions	
Track 20	Directed Response	

A complete transcript of the CD is on the Web at www.cliffsnotes.com/extras